INTERNATIONAL POLITICAL ECONOMY SERIES

General Editor: Timothy M. Shaw, Professor of Political Science and International Development Studies, and Director of the Centre for Foreign Policy Studies, Dalhousie University, Nova Scotia, Canada

Recent titles include:

Pradeep Agrawal, Subir V. Gokarn, Veena Mishra, Kirit S. Parikh and Kunal Sen
ECONOMIC RESTRUCTURING IN EAST ASIA AND INDIA: Perspectives on Policy Reform

Solon L. Barraclough and Krishna B. Ghimire
FORESTS AND LIVELIHOODS: The Social Dynamics of Deforestation in Developing Countries

Jerker Carlsson, Gunnar Köhlin and Anders Ekbom
THE POLITICAL ECONOMY OF EVALUATION: International Aid Agenicies and the Effectiveness of Aid

Steve Chan (*editor*)
FOREIGN DIRECT INVESTMENT IN A CHANGING GLOBAL POLITICAL ECONOMY

Edward A. Comor (*editor*)
THE GLOBAL POLITICAL ECONOMY OF COMMUNICATION

Paul Cook and Frederick Nixson (*editors*)
THE MOVE TO THE MARKET? Trade and Industry Policy Reform in Transitional Economies

O. P. Dwivedi
DEVELOPMENT ADMINISTRATION: From Underdevelopment to Sustainable Development

John Healey and William Tordoff (*editors*)
VOTES AND BUDGETS: Comparative Studies in Accountable Governance in the South

Noeleen Heyzer, James V. Riker and Antonio B. Quizon (*editors*)
GOVERNMENT–NGO RELATIONS IN ASIA: Prospects and Challenges for People-Centered Development

George Kent
CHILDREN IN THE INTERNATIONAL POLITICAL ECONOMY

Gary McMahon (*editor*)
LESSONS IN ECONOMIC POLICY FOR EASTERN EUROPE FROM LATIN AMERICA

David B. Moore and Gerald J. Schmitz (*editors*)
DEBATING DEVELOPMENT DISCOURSE: Institutional and Popular Perspectives

Juan Antonio Morales and Gary McMahon (*editors*)
ECONOMIC POLICY AND THE TRANSITION TO DEMOCRACY: The Latin American Experience

Archibald R. M. Ritter and John M. Kirk (*editors*)
CUBA IN THE INTERNATIONAL SYSTEM: Normalization and Integration

Ann Seidman and Robert B. Seidman
STATE AND LAW IN THE DEVELOPMENT PROCESS: Problem-Solving and Institutional Change in the Third World

Tor Skålnes
THE POLITICS OF ECONOMIC REFORM IN ZIMBABWE: Continuity and Change in Development

John Sorenson (*editor*)
DISASTER AND DEVELOPMENT IN THE HORN OF AFRICA

Howard Stein (*editor*)
ASIAN INDUSTRIALIZATION AND AFRICA: Studies in Policy Alternatives to Structural Adjustment

Deborah Stienstra
WOMEN'S MOVEMENTS AND INTERNATIONAL ORGANIZATIONS

Larry A. Swatuk and Timothy M. Shaw (*editors*)
THE SOUTH AT THE END OF THE TWENTIETH CENTURY: Rethinking the Political Economy of Foreign Policy in Africa, Asia, the Caribbean and Latin America

Sandra Whitworth
FEMINISM AND INTERNATIONAL RELATIONS

The World Bank and Non-Governmental Organizations

The Limits of Apolitical Development

Paul J. Nelson
Associate Director for Development Policy
Church World Service and Lutheran World Relief
Washington, DC

First published in Great Britain 1995 by
MACMILLAN PRESS LTD
Houndmills, Basingstoke, Hampshire RG21 6XS
and London
Companies and representatives
throughout the world

A catalogue record for this book is available
from the British Library.

ISBN 0-333-64577-4

 First published in the United States of America 1995 by
ST. MARTIN'S PRESS, INC.,
Scholarly and Reference Division,
175 Fifth Avenue,
New York, N.Y. 10010

ISBN 0-312-12620-4

Library of Congress Cataloging-in-Publication Data
Nelson, Paul J, 1956–
The World Bank and non-governmental organizations : the limits of apolitical development / Paul J. Nelson.
p. cm.
Includes bibliographical references and index.
ISBN 0-312-12620-4
1. World Bank.   2. Non-governmental organizations.   I. Title.
II. Series.
HG3881.5.W57N45   1995
332.1'532—dc20   95-7825
                                                                      CIP

© Paul J. Nelson 1995

All rights reserved. No reproduction, copy or transmission of
this publication may be made without written permission.

No paragraph of this publication may be reproduced, copied or
transmitted save with written permission or in accordance with
the provisions of the Copyright, Designs and Patents Act 1988,
or under the terms of any licence permitting limited copying
issued by the Copyright Licensing Agency, 90 Tottenham Court
Road, London W1P 9HE.

Any person who does any unauthorised act in relation to this
publication may be liable to criminal prosecution and civil
claims for damages.

10   9   8   7   6   5   4   3   2   1
04   03 02 01 00 99 98 97 96 95

Printed and bound in Great Britain by
Antony Rowe Ltd, Chippenham, Wiltshire

Contents

List of Tables and Figures	vi
Preface	vii
Acknowledgements	ix
Acronyms and Abbreviations	xi
1 Introduction and Overview	1
2 The World Bank Takes Center Stage	13
3 'Accountable to Whom?' And Other Issues for NGOs	36
4 World Bank-NGO Project Cooperation: Less than Meets the Eye?	67
5 Moving Money: Organizational Aspects of a Development Model	87
6 The World Bank and Apolitical Development	112
7 Organizational Culture and Participation in Development	142
8 Conclusions	176
Appendix 1 Key to Interviews Cited in Text	198
Appendix 2 Methodological Note	199
Notes	200
Bibliography	202
Index	221

List of Tables and Figures

Tables

2.1	Top Five Voting Powers, IBRD, 1945, 1971 and 1993	14
2.2	World Bank Lending by Sector, 1961–65, 1975–79, and 1989–93	16
4.1	NGO Participation in World Bank-Financed Projects 1973–90, by Type of Involvement	72
4.2	Breakdown of NGO Roles in Project Design, for World Bank-Financed Projects Reported to Involve NGO Design, 1989–90 and 1991–92	78
4.3	Major Involvement in World Bank-Financed Projects, Community-Based Organizations Alone and Community-Based Organizations and Intermediary NGOs Together	80
4.4	NGO Involvement in Major Roles in World Bank-Financed Projects, by Involvement of International NGOs, National NGOs, and Both	82
4.5	Professional and Interest-Based NGOs, and Major Roles in World Bank-Financed Projects	83
4.6	NGO Involvement in World Bank-Financed Projects, by Region and Year of Approval, 1973–90	83
4.7	World Bank-Financed Projects with NGO Involvement, 1973–90, by Region and Major and Minor Roles	84

Figures

4.1	World Bank-Financed Projects with NGO Involvement, by Year of Approval	75

Preface

The fiftieth anniversary year of the Bretton Woods organizations has been a turbulent one for the World Bank. 1995 has already been marked by a political shift in the Congress of its largest financial contributor, a major financial crisis in Mexico, the resignation of the late Lewis Preston and the nomination and appointment of James D. Wolfensohn to become its new President in June of 1995.

It is difficult to predict the significance of any of these events and changes for the Bank. Internal and external reformers, including NGOs, have pressed for reforms in environmental policy, changes in policy and practice with respect to structural adjustment and popular participation, freer access to information and channels for complaints about Bank-financed projects. Reforming efforts found some support at the top during Preston's presidency. A new, somewhat less secretive information disclosure policy was enacted and an independent inspection panel created to hear complaints. Preston emphasized poverty reduction and the environment in speeches and policy documents throughout his tenure.

The incoming President has announced his intention to reshape the Bank. Wolfensohn's long-time interest in environmental and social development issues has raised hopes and expectations among many observers. But he takes over a large and conservative bureaucracy whose entrenched interests, myths and organizational dynamics have resisted and reshaped changes promulgated by previous leaders.

How the new President's agenda will take shape, and how it will intersect and interact with NGO and social movements' agendas and with the changing politics of multilateral cooperation, remain to be seen. The research on Bank-NGO relations reported here, together with a review of policy changes in the 1970s and 1980s, points to some of the organizational features that have resisted change. These same features – including a relatively rigid project cycles, the protective organizational myth of apolitical development, and a hierarchical and insular information management system – should be among the targets for determined leadership within the Bank. They also suggest indicators by which reformers and observers can assess the response.

NGOs and social movements that have targeted the Bank appear prepared to continue pressing for changes in policy and practice at the

Bank. The present political turn in Washington threatens to reduce drastically US participation in most multilateral and international cooperation, and has slowed the momentum of critique and reform momentarily. But interaction between the Bank and nongovernmental bodies, both cooperative and conflictive, continues to grow. And as networks of NGOs seek influence over the Bank, NGOs themselves are inevitably reshaped by their relations with World Bank programs and practice.

PAUL J. NELSON

Acknowledgements

The research and writing of this book has spanned seven years, beginning as a Ph.D dissertation and ending as a focus of four years of activist research in Washington, DC. I hope that I have recognized specific intellectual debts clearly along the way, but there are a few people to whom I wish to give particular thanks.

At the University of Wisconsin-Madison, Russ Middleton, Bill Thiesenhusen, David Stark, David Trubek and Joanne Csete offered instruction and encouragement. Doug Hellinger and his colleagues at the Development GAP were generous with advice and office hospitality during research in Washington, as was Bill Rau. The Mennonite Central Committee program in the Philippines gave much-needed hospitality and guidance during a visit there.

Many NGO colleagues have made the work enjoyable and rewarding. Marcos Arruda, Steve Commins, Nancy Alexander, Marijke Torfs, Chad Dobson, Rajesh Tandon, Paul Spray, Lisa McGowan, Ross Hammond, Veena Siddharth, Jo Marie Griesgraber and Alex Rondos have inspired through their energy and selfless work, and reminded by example that even serious work should be fun.

Church World Service and Lutheran World Relief, and my colleagues in their Office on Development Policy, have supported continued engagement with the World Bank, and this writing owes much to my experience as a part of that advocacy effort. The research and writing, however, have been done in my individual capacity, and the book and the views expressed are neither a project of nor attributable to any agency.

James Riker and Kathryn Sikkink offered valuable advice in a research working group, and I have benefitted from conversations with Gerald Schmitz, David Williams and David Gillies. The dissertation research was funded by the John D. And Catherine T. MacArthur Foundation, which has also supported continuing conversation among researchers on international conflict and cooperation. Thanks to Series Editor Tim Shaw for probing comments on the manuscript, and for his commitment to exchange among participants in and scholars of international affairs, across boundaries of the university, government and NGO.

Many staff and consultants at the World Bank have helped clarify issues, pointed the way to documents or individual sources, and given their time for interviews. Most of these will remain unnamed, but among those who helped in official capacities are David Beckmann, John Clark, Chris Hennin, Carmen Malena, Kris Martin and Aubrey Williams. None of these colleagues from NGOs, universities or the Bank bears any responsibility for the books's remaining shortcomings.

Thanks to friends and family who have provided companionship and hospitality along the way: Wayne Sigelko and Nancy Didion, the La Samaritaine Community in Madison, Joanne Csete, Brian Best and Jane Lincoln, Carol Bradford and Robert Laslett, Craig and Edith Eder, Margaret and Paul McNamara, Wally and Demaris Nelson and Tony and Lill Scommegna.

Paola Scommegna, my partner in the home economy, knows the impositions of this project better than anyone. Thanks to her for editorial advice and untold other forms of support, and to Renata and Ted for interrupting my work as often, delightfully and imaginatively as possible.

Mount Rainier, Maryland   PAUL J. NELSON

Acronyms and Abbreviations

ADF	African Development Foundation
AKF	Aga Khan Foundation
APRODEV	Association of Protestant Development Organizations in Europe
BRAC	Bangladesh Rural Advancement Committee
CARE	Cooperative for American Relief Everywhere
CBO	Community-based organization
CCIC	Canadian Council for International Cooperation
CGAPP	Consultative Group to Assist the Poorest of the Poor
CGIAR	Consultative Group on International Agricultural Research
CIDA	Canadian International Development Agency
CIDSE	Cooperation Internationale pour le Developpement et la Solidarité
CLUSA	Cooperative League of the USA
CRS	Catholic Relief Services
Development GAP	Development Group for Alternative Policies
ED	Executive Director
EDI	Economic Development Institute, a World Bank-managed institute for training government officials of borrowing countries.
EIA	Environmental Impact Assessment
EMENA	The World Bank's Europe, Middle East and North Africa Region. The EMENA grouping was eliminated in a recent reconfiguration of the regional Vice Presidencies, but is retained here for regional comparisons.
EXTIE	The International Economics Relations unit of the External Relations department, responsible for NGO relations. SPRIE was moved to External Relations early in 1990, and renamed EXTIE. In 1992 it was shifted to Operations Division and renamed OPRIE.
FDC	Fundacion del Centavo, Guatemala
FY	Fiscal Year

Acronyms and Abbreviations

GEF	Global Environmental Facility
IAF	Inter-American Foundation
IBRD	International Bank for Reconstruction and Development, the World Bank's main lending window
ICVA	International Council of Voluntary Agencies
IDA	International Development Association, the concessional lending arm of the World Bank
IDA-10	The tenth three-year replenishment by donor countries ('Part I Members') of IDA's lending funds
IFAD	International Fund for Agricultural Development
IFC	International Finance Corporation, affiliate of the World Bank, part of the World Bank Group.
IMF	International Monetary Fund
INGI	International NGO Forum on Indonesia
LAC	The World Bank's Latin America and Caribbean region
MIGA	Multilateral Investment Guarantee Agency
NAM	Non-Aligned Movement
NGO	Non-governmental organization
NIC	Newly industrialized country
NRECA	National Rural Electrification Association
OD	Operational Directive. Formal written guidance for World Bank staff on operations and procedures. Formerly called Operational Manual Statements (OMS).
OECD	Organization for Economic Co-operation and Development
OED	Operations Evaluation Department of the World Bank
OMS	Operational Manual Statement. See OD.
OPRIE	The International Economic Relations unit within the Bank's Operations complex. Responsibility for NGO policy has rested in Operations since 1992.
ORT	Organization for Rehabilitation through Training
PCR	Project Completion Report, done for each project at the end of disbursements from the Bank
PRIA	Society for Participatory Research in Asia
PVO	Private voluntary organization
SAL	Structural adjustment loan
SAP	Structural adjustment plan
SDA	Social Dimensions of Adjustment

Acronyms and Abbreviations

SECAL	Sectoral adjustment loan
SPR	The World Bank's Strategic Planning and Review unit
SPRIE	The International Economic Relations unit within Strategic Planning and Review. SPRIE's personnel and function were moved in 1990 to External Affairs, then in 1992 to Operations Division.
TFAP	Tropical Forest Action Plan
UN	United Nations
UNCED	United Nations Conference on Environment and Development, held in Rio de Janeiro in 1992
UNDP	United Nations Development Program
UNICEF	United Nations Children's Fund
USAID	United States Agency for International Development
WDR	*World Development Report*, published annually by the World Bank

1 Introduction and Overview

The World Bank's 1990 *Annual Report* (World Bank, 1990a, pp. 95–6) includes two pages of text and charts detailing its operational relations with non-governmental organizations (NGOs). The new, high-profile presentation (a format followed in subsequent Annual Reports) highlights a growing number of World Bank-financed projects in which NGOs have a role and reports a 'deepening' of these operational relationships: NGOs are involved more frequently, it is reported, in the design of projects and in programs to 'mitigate the adverse social costs of structural adjustment.' Finally, an expanded policy dialogue with NGOs is reported, 'on important development policy issues of common concern.'

The World Bank has climbed onto the NGO bandwagon in a big way. The Bank's public reports note expanded collaboration with private agencies and grassroots groups in projects, a growing policy dialogue with NGOs, and an important role for NGOs in 'mitigating the adverse costs of structural adjustment' (World Bank 1990a, p. 96).

This study reports on several years of observation of, and participation in, the relationship between the World Bank and NGOs, interpreting them in light of evidence from other cases of policy change at the Bank. Its primary purpose is to understand the World Bank better by:

1. evaluating its claims and performance in relating to NGOs;
2. analyzing its implementation of poverty- and NGO-related policies, through the lens of its organizational dynamics and culture;
3. assessing the potential for more systematic and responsive interaction with NGOs, and for policy change in line with a broadly shared NGO agenda; and
4. assessing the significance of the engagement for the Bank and for NGOs.

In addition, the study reports on the varied postures of NGOs toward the Bank and on the effectiveness of various NGO strategies to date, and suggests guidelines for planning and assessing future interaction.

The issue has important implications for pressing policy issues, and for theoretical debates that underlie them. What are we to make of the World Bank's commitments to refocus on poverty and environmental protection? How do its mandate, organizational form and financial and intellectual resources dispose it to address the changing world of globalized production and capital, weakened national governments and degraded natural resources? Is the policy conditionality associated with structural reform a suitable basis for global development that is economically, environmentally and ethically 'sustainable'? How does NGO engagement with the Bank affect NGOs' role in developing articulate and representative institutions in civil society?

The Bank's record on issues related to NGOs' concerns does not offer much basis for optimism. Rather, it suggests that:

1. Deeply-rooted organizational characteristics reflect the Bank's mandate and the interests of its powerful members and of financial markets.
2. These organizational traits – structural, intellectual, cultural – limit change and promote stability at the Bank. They are key factors to watch for indications of fundamental change.
3. While the Bank's relations with NGOs put pressure on several of these organizational traits – its imperative to 'move money,' its myth of apolitical development, and the insular information system of its organizational culture – there has been little change at these key pressure points.
4. NGO agendas, strategies and impact have been inconsistent and uneven. They have won policy concessions, but often lack the political and institutional clout to secure their implementation. Further progress will require expanded and coordinated efforts.

At the same time, the Bank's engagement with NGOs has broken some new ground for international agencies. The Bank's approach is pragmatic, informal and often *ad hoc*. While its formal governance bodies are less open to NGOs than those of many UN bodies, it is also less caught up in the formalities of NGOs' legal relations to its operations, and has been quite willing to allow experiments and minor innovations to facilitate operational engagement. If the World Bank has been less accessible than the Inter-American or Asian Development Banks to NGOs in those regions, it has none the less not stifled a small but energetic internal effort to encourage greater access.

THE NGO PHENOMENON AT THE WORLD BANK: CLAIMS AND PERCEPTIONS

The World Bank's relationship to NGOs is intrinsically important for project performance and for the impact it can have on the development of national civil societies. The Bank's considerable intellectual and financial influence with borrowing governments means that its approach to NGOs can also shape their evolving views of NGOs in their own societies. The intrinsic importance is heightened by the public relations campaign the Bank has built around it, advertizing the engagement of NGOs in World Bank-financed projects while seeking to minimize the damage from NGO criticism.

Since 1988 a series of Annual Reports, a World Bank-published book (Paul and Israel, 1991), articles in the World Bank/IMF journal *Finance and Development*, and speeches by various Bank executives have all highlighted the Bank's 'NGO work.' This ongoing promotion reached a fever pitch in the materials prepared for the 50th Anniversary of the Bretton Woods agreements. The widely-distributed press packet includes the expected pamphlets ('Making a Difference in People's Lives,' 'What Others Say About Us'), plus an entire 29-page booklet featuring work with NGOs (World Bank, 1994c). From a nearly unmentioned liaison ten years ago, the Bank-NGO connection has grown to take a place on the Bank's official 50-year timeline of its history. The establishment of the Bank-NGO Committee appears there along with McNamara's presidency, the creation of the International Development Association (IDA), the first structural adjustment loan and the creation of the Multilateral Investment Guarantee Agency (MIGA) (*World Bank News* 13, p. 29, 21 July 1994).

The perception that the Bank is deeply engaged with NGOs has also made its way into recent outside commentaries. The 'NGO work' wins positive comments from mass-circulation magazines (*US News and World Report*), global policy journals (*National Journal*), research foundations (the Esquel Group Foundation, 1993, p. 18) and donor governments. A *US News and World Report* article (1989, p. 47) closes a stinging critique of some notorious Bank-financed projects by noting that the Bank 'is moving to address the problems' by 'sharply increasing the involvement of native community groups... and farmers' clubs.' And the *National Journal*, widely read among US government policy makers, reported at the end of 1988 that the World Bank had been 'dragged' by NGOs into 'participatory-public-interest politics and may never be the same' (Stokes, 1988, p. 3250).

These and other references, along with World Bank policy statements, give the impression that the Bank, once tied exclusively to governments and official donors, is now opening itself to a systematic and open-ended collaboration with grassroots, national and international non-governmental agencies.

WORLD BANK POLICY AND NGOs

The World Bank and NGOs may be thought of as opposite poles of a continuum of organizations involved in development assistance. Their operations differ in many ways that present formidable challenges to collaboration. Differences in size, access to resources, location, constituencies, charters, and operating styles are seen by some as obstacles, by others as the complementary strengths that argue for cooperation. Some at the Bank, and a few NGOs, have tried to collaborate operationally in the face of these differences, with varied results. The record of such collaborations is now extensive enough that some preliminary conclusions can be drawn about its nature and significance. Chapter 4 of this study reviews the record.

But I have not focused primarily on these obstacles to or arguments for cooperation. Beyond the logistical and managerial difficulties lies a more fundamental question: Are NGOs becoming tools of a development paradigm most do not support? Or can NGOs shift the World Bank's practice and performance in the areas of environmental impact, popular participation and structural adjustment? What aspects of NGO strategy and NGO and government policy are the most important in achieving such changes in policy and performance?

This study's findings are not optimistic: political-economic commitments and interests and deep-seated organizational characteristics affect the World Bank's capacity to cooperate systematically and responsively with NGOs, notwithstanding the intentions of individuals. NGOs' tendencies to process-oriented programming, emphasis on participation, and partisanship in support of poor people – the very virtues that are said to argue for cooperation – contradict the interests and organizational characteristics of the Bank so directly that systematic, collaborative relations are extremely difficult. Policymakers, NGOs and supportive World Bank staff need to understand the potential and limitations clearly, or they will find themselves engaged in a process that undercuts the potential significance of NGOs without fundamentally altering the Bank's impact.

Introduction and Overview

The World Bank's record of collaboration with NGOs is best interpreted in the context of the broader policy and direction of the Bank itself. The 1980s was a period of expanded activity for the Bank, as it initiated policy-based, non-project lending. Attaching policy conditions to loans opened a larger role for the Bank in managing and shaping countries' participation in the global economy.

NGOs, on the other hand, are associated with a constellation of issues that, with the exception of the environment, had a lower profile at the Bank in the 1980s: poverty alleviation, popular participation, small-farmer agriculture, environmentally sustainable development. Issues related to poverty alleviation and income distribution were given much less frequent mention by the World Bank than they received under the presidency of Robert McNamara (1968–81). Their return to a higher profile in Bank publications was signalled by the 1990 *World Development Report* (WDR), focused, as was the 1980 WDR, on poverty.

The World Bank's environmental policies and the environmental impact of some Bank-financed projects were sharply criticized by international environmental NGOs in the 1980s. Its response to this environmental criticism and its engagement with NGOs have led some to hope for a 'greening' of the World Bank (Holden, 1987). A new emphasis on the environment, human resources and poverty in former President Barber Conable's public addresses and the 1990 WDR reinforced this hope, as did President Lewis Preston's re-emphasis of poverty alleviation as 'the overarching goal' of all lending. But the Bank remains the leading proponent of orthodox, export-oriented adjustment and debt-management policies; its internal review of lending performance shows a strong tendency to retreat to financial appraisal as the central indicator of programmatic 'success;' and many critics and NGOs are skeptical of its commitment to the 'softer' environmental and social issues.

One measure of the World Bank's orientation will be how it handles the dialogue and collaboration with NGOs. How open and responsive the Bank is in its relationship with NGOs and what organizational and policy changes it makes in response to its dialogue with them are indicators of its willingness and ability to listen and respond to new constituencies and interests.

CONTRASTING VISIONS OF 'DEVELOPMENT'

The dialogue and working relations between the Bank and NGOs are the setting for an important debate over the shape and direction of 'development.' The contrasting visions of development are manifest in their styles of operation. The World Bank raises capital from member governments and major financial markets. Its projects and loans are planned, negotiated, supervised and evaluated by Washington-based staff together with national governments and consultants. The key criteria by which success is measured are production and productivity gains and financial returns on the investment. In the course of lending to support projects and policies in a country, Bank staff are likely to develop working relationships with high- and mid-level government officials in the relevant ministries. Through macro-economic policy conditionality it has gained influence and direct financial leverage over major national economic policies.

NGOs – or a widely held image of NGOs – challenge this model by example. NGOs that are organized 'above' the local, grassroots level generally collect funds from non-government constituencies and often from government aid programs, and they are said to operate effectively because of the small scale of the development initiatives they support. Staff often work out of a regional city or a town or village, and plan projects in the field in consultation with local leaders and groups. The NGO's evaluation of a program is more likely than the World Bank's to depend in part on assessment by intended beneficiaries and on direct indicators of people's welfare. NGO staff are likely to develop working relationships with leaders of cooperatives, farmers' and women's associations, religious and civic groups.

The 'NGO model' (generalizing and idealizing) differs from that of the World Bank by being partisan, process-oriented, and participatory. NGOs' partisan character derives from overtly taking the side of poor people and communities. 'Process-oriented' refers to a willingness to have project activities evolve in response to changing conditions or perceptions of local people. And many NGOs are 'participatory' in that they take active participation by local communities to be a virtue in itself, as well as a means to successful project implementation.

The two styles do represent, in part, two approaches with distinct 'comparative advantages' in supporting economic change. But they suggest a more important distinction as well. The World Bank's operations suggest that 'development' is fundamentally about amassing capital through investment, borrowing and savings, creating the right incentives, adopting the right policies, introducing the right technologies and building the right institutions and infrastructure, where 'right' is defined by agreement between the national government and World Bank experts. The image of NGO operations outlined here suggests

Introduction and Overview

that 'development' is fundamentally about people's articulation of needs, priorities and wishes, and about organizing and marshalling resources to facilitate their fulfillment.

The World Bank's version of 'development' is the domain of governments; it follows from plans, and benefits the population at large, although groups may be 'targeted.' NGOs' 'development' emerges, in some measure at least, from a process of discussion and planning by the people affected by the project. Projects are often specifically planned to respond to the needs of poor groups in an area, whose interests may be in conflict with those of others.

The World Bank, chartered and owned by its member governments, has historically had rather little contact with NGOs. The vast differences in scale and in the resources they offer to support programs and projects sometimes leads to the assumption of a disjuncture between the 'kinds' of development they promote. The World Bank mobilizes resources and expertise for national-level economic programs, while NGOs organize local self-help efforts, meet acute emergency needs, and are sometimes a proving ground for innovative approaches that may be adapted and expanded by governments and international agencies.

But some NGOs insist that this is a false dichotomy. Large-scale investments and programs, they argue, can and should take advantage of the same sources of local and community organization and energy as do smaller programs, and should be subject to mechanisms of popular control and accountability. The wide variety of non-state and non-corporate social groupings referred to as NGOs are proposed as the vehicle for connecting the planning and implementation of World Bank investments with the dynamics of popular participation.

This proposal implicitly offers accountability via various organs of civil society (NGOs) to affected populations as an addition to the World Bank's formal accountability to governments. It has implications for the role of NGOs in the politics of economic and social change in the poor countries, and implies that the institutions of a kind of global civil society have some standing in shaping World Bank policy. And, if its implications for accountability were fully accepted, it would challenge the foundations of the World Bank's operations.

OVERVIEW

Development economist Hans Singer (1989) poses two questions about World Bank policy toward NGOs in his review of the Bank's 1987

Annual Report. What is the nature and intensity of the reported cooperation with NGOs in Bank-financed projects? And is the World Bank establishing an internal capacity for 'genuine two-way collaboration'? These two questions remain central seven years later, and form the kernel of this inquiry.

Chapters 2 and 3, devoted to the World Bank and to NGOs, respectively, set the stage by outlining the key issues facing the Bank and NGOs, and reviewing the history of the dialogue between them. Chapter 4 begins the review of World Bank-NGO experience by examining 304 projects reported to have involved NGOs. The project review focuses on three sets of questions:

1. How are NGOs involved? At what stage, with how much input?
2. What kinds of NGOs are involved? Are local, national or international groups most frequently involved? Professional 'development NGOs' or interest-based associations? Are different sorts of NGOs equally likely to be influential in shaping World Bank projects?
3. How have these patterns changed over time, especially since 1988, which the Bank calls a turning point in its interaction with NGOs?

NGO implementation of a component of a government- and World Bank-planned scheme is the dominant mode of project collaboration. In most projects reported to involve an NGO, the NGO is an implementing agent mobilizing people to carry out pre-designed changes.

While implementation is the dominant NGO role, there is good reason to focus on the minority (one quarter) of World Bank-NGO projects in which NGO roles have gone beyond implementation. In these cases – involving NGO participation in project design, direct funding of NGO activities, or significant conflict with project authorities – the potential and limitations for collaboration can be seen most clearly.

Such 'major' roles have occurred most often when grassroots, national and international NGOs are all involved. The quality of NGO involvement has varied by region: Africa dominates the roster of projects numerically, but major NGO roles have been relatively rare in Africa. Reported gains in NGO involvement in project design in the late 1980s and early 1990s appear to rest largely on zealous reporting and generous standards for what constitutes 'design,' and on increased NGO involvement in social service programs to cushion the effects of structural adjustment.

The remaining chapters present evidence from documents, interviews, more detailed reviews of some projects, and from NGOs, to assess the

Introduction and Overview

potential and the limitations of an institutionalized 'genuine two-way collaboration.' Each chapter focuses on a contradiction inherent in the Bank's efforts and claims.

Chapter 5 argues that the imperatives of organizational survival and of lending large amounts of capital quickly limit the World Bank's capacity for concerted collaboration with NGOs. This 'disbursement imperative' dominates policy at the organizational level and pervades individual incentive and motivation. It is driven by external political pressures to manage Third World debt and promote global integration, and although Bank management has become sensitive to the problem, it remains enshrined in an organizational structure that promotes the kind of planning and disbursement required for capital-driven, growth-oriented lending. These structures and procedures are ill-suited to collaboration with NGOs. Indeed, the Bank tends to protect its standard operating procedures against the kind of uncertainty and spontaneity that NGOs promote.

'Sovereignty' and 'development' are introduced in Chapter 6 as two 'myths' that underpin and justify the World Bank's operations. These myths not only define the World Bank's mission and establish formal ground rules for its relations with borrowing countries, they also shape thinking about development in many circles. Both myths rest on the notion that the Bank and its work are apolitical, an image it carefully maintains. Paradoxically, the myths enable the Bank to exert influence over highly political issues through methods including aid coordination, policy-based lending, and training. Their influence is observed in the self-evaluation and perpetuation of structural adjustment programs and lending, and in the limits placed on NGO roles.

The World Bank's organizational culture (Chapter 7) is hierarchical and assigns great value to specialization, technical expertise and control of Bank-supported operations. This culture, I argue, is incompatible with the participatory, flexible operation that many NGOs require. As with any organizational culture, it systematically selects and processes information to maintain a consistent view of the world and of its role in that world. This 'information bias' is examined in the processing of information from 'rural development' lending in the 1970s, in the genesis and internal evaluation of structural adjustment policies, in policy dialogues with NGOs in the 1980s, and in the financing of energy and major dam projects in India, including the controversial Sardar Sarovar project. Selectivity in handling information lends stability to the World Bank's view of the world and, together with other features, limits its ability to learn as an organization.

The concluding chapter reviews the findings and outlines policy issues and recommendations for NGOs; touches on implications for more general debates about democratization, multilateralism, and possible directions of the economic 'world order;' and raises questions for further monitoring and study.

STUDYING THE WORLD BANK: ORGANIZATIONAL THEORY AND METHODOLOGY

The three organizational contradictions that shape the Bank's relations with NGOs are examined through interviews of World Bank staff, readings of internal and public documents, review of selected experiences of project collaboration, and analysis of the course of other policy changes at the Bank in recent years.

Combining sociological theories of complex organizations and political economy offers a valuable perspective, different from that of either approach taken alone. The political economy perspective has stressed the interests to which the Bank responds (industrialized country governments, foreign and local capital) in promoting national development strategies that open economies to international investment on virtually any terms.

When organizational considerations – structural, procedural, ideological and professional dynamics – are systematically added to the analysis, a fuller picture emerges of the factors that drive policy and practice in the Bank, and that reinforce and constrain its influence. Five principles from organizational theories are the basis for understanding how these factors shape relations with NGOs and performance on related issues:

1. *The World Bank is an entity with imperatives, priorities, and strategies of its own, not merely a creation and servant of states and financial institutions.* Like other organizations, it protects its standard operations – the essential processes for production – from sources of uncertainty in its working environment.
2. *The World Bank conforms to and shapes social myths that establish expectations and standards for evaluating its work.* In any field of work, and especially fields where standards of 'success' are not widely agreed, organizations strive to conform to and shape the expectations that add up to a standard for evaluation. The myths, important sources of stability for the organization, are usually carefully upheld and protected.

Introduction and Overview 11

3. *Organizational cultures systematically select and screen the information to be considered in organizational decision making.* The World Bank's highly hierarchical culture fosters organizational stability but inhibits organizational learning by defining the kinds of information that are considered relevant for decision making, and filtering data to match these standards.
4. *Organizational learning, which entails consideration of basic premises in light of new experience, is almost impossible in such a culture.*
5. *These organizational features are not bureaucratic foibles or maladaptive managerial strategies.* They interact with, reinforce and institutionalize the interests, pressures and influences that shape World Bank policy and priorities.[1]

This perspective guides the strategy and methodology of the study. The structural, ideological and social-psychological variables suggest both points of resistance to policy change, and indicators to distinguish important changes from cosmetic reforms. The choice to rely on such indicators, rather than primarily on official statements, budgetary trends, or the views of organizational leaders, calls for a methodology focused on the standard operations used in planning, policy-making and lending, on beliefs and assumptions that underpin these standard operations, and on the management of information and learning.

The study focuses on a minority of projects and staff that are in the forefront of interaction with NGOs. It is fairly easy to show that significant NGO involvement in Bank-financed projects is the exception, and that many staff are uninterested in NGOs. What is more revealing is what can be learned from activities with the most substantial NGO involvement: participation in design, receipt of funds from a World Bank-financed fund, NGO-Bank conflict over the course of a project, or broader policy dialogue. By examining Bank staff's most advanced efforts, I identify the extent of the collaboration to date and the factors that limit it now and in the future.

To avoid the excessively narrow focus that strategy might promote, I have also paid attention to a range of issues closely associated with NGOs but not strictly tied to the World Bank's interaction with them. The 'NGO issue' in the Bank is part of a complex of issues including poverty reduction, gender equity, popular participation in projects, aboriginal peoples' rights and the protection and management of the environment. Each of these has ties to the Bank-NGO interaction, but has broader significance for the Bank and its borrowers as well. Evidence from discussions of participation, environmental policy and anti-poverty lending illustrate the tendencies and characteristics of the Bank that affect its relations with NGOs.

Research conducted at the World Bank during 1989 and 1990 was carried out with the understanding that documents and interviews would not be cited in a way that would compromise relations with a member government, or reflect personally on any staff member. Under this agreement no limitations were placed on my interviews. To ensure the anonymity of some staff interviewed who asked not to be quoted by name, all staff interviews are cited by their department or regional position. I have participated extensively in subsequent discussions with Bank officials, as an NGO representative. Statements made in these meetings, for which there is a public record, are attributed by name. A list of interviews is included in Appendix 1, and further details on the study's methodology are outlined in Appendix 2.

2 The World Bank Takes Center Stage

The debt crisis and the World Bank's entry into policy-based structural adjustment lending boosted its global profile and influence in the 1980s, and the collapse of the Soviet bloc and new membership of more than a dozen governments in 1991 and 1992 made the Bank a truly global financial institution. At the same time, an array of issues and pressures for change are creating apparent opportunities for NGO influence at the World Bank. Dissatisfaction with government implementation of donor-funded projects, commitment to structural adjustment and to minimizing the reforms' social and political costs, pressure from environmental advocates, desire for greater cost recovery in irrigation and social service programs, pressure on human rights issues – all these create an environment in which NGOs are an increasingly relevant actor for the Bank.

This chapter discusses some of these issues and trends. The perspective developed here – of an institution closely tied to industrial country and major bank economic interests, committed to global integration and bound to a economic adjustment strategy that has become indefensible in the low-income countries – will be the foundation for an organizational analysis in later chapters.

THE WORLD BANK: STRUCTURE, FINANCE AND OPERATIONS

Created in 1945 by the Bretton Woods Agreements, the World Bank is owned by its 178 member governments. The International Bank for Reconstruction and Development (IBRD) makes loans at commercial rates, with 5 or 10 year grace periods on repayment of principal, to finance projects and programs of member governments. The International Development Association (IDA), established in 1959, lends with only a 0.75 per cent service charge to governments of some 70 countries with per capita income less than $765. The IBRD and IDA share a common staff, and IDA credits and IBRD loans are here referred to collectively as loans, unless otherwise specified.

Table 2.1 Top Five Voting Powers, IBRD, 1947, 1971 and 1993

1947	%	1971	%	1993	%
US	35.07	US	23.82	US	17.18
UK	14.52	UK	9.81	Japan	6.64
China	6.85	West Germany	5.19	Germany	5.13
France	6.03	France	4.02	UK	4.92
India	4.66	Japan	3.92	France	4.92

Sources: (1947, 1971) Mason and Asher 1973, pp. 800–2.
(1993) World Bank, *Annual Report* 1993, pp. 199–202.

A third member of the World Bank Group, the International Finance Corporation (IFC), was established in 1956 to finance and insure corporate investment in poor countries. In 1988 a Multilateral Investment Guarantee Agency (MIGA) was created to promote foreign investment in poor countries by 'mitigating non-commercial risk' to investors through insurance and policy dialogue with member governments (World Bank, *Annual Report*, 1989, p. 3).

IBRD and IDA are governed by a shared Board of Governors and Board of Executive Directors. Governors, one per member country, meet annually to handle certain aspects of World Bank governance, but oversight of day-to-day operations is delegated to the Executive Directors (EDs). Member countries are assigned voting power in the governing bodies proportional to their payments (capital subscriptions) under a formula that slightly over-represents small subscribers. The United States is the largest voting power, although US dominance has diminished since the original capital subscriptions in 1947, as Table 2.1 shows.

The concentration of voting power has fallen somewhat: the top five members held more than two-thirds of all votes in 1947, fewer than 40 per cent in 1992. Each of the five largest subscribers is represented by an ED; others are represented in groups (e.g. the Scandinavian countries have a single ED). (For more detail on formal governance, see Osieke (1984), Lister (1984), and Gerster (1993)).

IBRD lending is financed primarily through sale of bonds on international financial markets. Member governments' financial support to the IBRD is primarily in callable capital, backing for IBRD loans, available but not appropriated. Ten per cent of government subscriptions to the IBRD are actually paid up.

In 1993 the IBRD borrowed $12.67 billion on international markets (*Annual Report*, 1993, p. 69), and had a net income of $1.13 billion. IBRD profits are divided among the IDA, the Consultative Group on International Agricultural Research (CGIAR) institutions, and reinvestment. The IDA is financed in part by IBRD profits, but some 90 per cent of IDA capital is provided in triennial replenishments by its member governments.

Lending for Global Integration

In fiscal year 1993 loans totalled $23.7 billion: $16.9 billion in IBRD loans, and $6.7 billion in IDA credits (*Annual Report.* 1993, p. 11). Cumulative lending since 1948 (IBRD) and 1961 (IDA) amounts to $312.9 billion, of which concessional IDA lending makes up $77.8 billion (World Bank, *Annual Report*, 1993, pp. 168-9).

Loans are either to governments or guaranteed by governments, and lending has been dominated by a relatively small group of major borrowers. After early reconstruction loans to Europe and Japan, lending shifted almost exclusively to Third World countries. The concentration of lending among its top 20 borrowers increased from 66.5 per cent to 76.5 per cent between 1971 and 1993 (Mason and Asher, 1973, pp. 830-1; World Bank *Annual Report*, 1993, pp. 166-7). The sectoral makeup of loans has also changed over the years, as Table 2.2 shows.

Regardless of sectoral emphases, the World Bank has pursued the integrative role in the world economy that its Articles of Agreement prescribe. Promoting foreign capital investment in member countries is emphasized in three of the IBRD's five statements of purpose (Article I, p. 1), and has remained central through its 45 years. The annual *World Development Report* (WDR), for example, highlights the importance of integration into the world economy every year, from the 1980 WDR on basic needs and poverty, to the 1987 Report, perhaps the World Bank's strongest manifesto on economic integration and adjustment (World Bank, WDR 1980, chs 2 and 3; World Bank, WDR, 1987, ch. 5). The integration of borrowing members' economies into global markets is reinforced and assisted by the IFC, which finances corporate investment and provides advisory, risk management, and technical assistance services to international investors and to its member governments.

In agriculture, the world food crisis of 1972-74 stimulated a surge of investment by the World Bank in rural infrastructure, credit, livestock production and research and extension on high-yielding seed

Table 2.2 World Bank Lending by Sector, 1961–65, 1975–79, and 1989–93 (amounts in millions of US dollars)

Sector	1961–65 amount	%	1975–79 amount	%	1989–93 amount	%
Agriculture	466.6	9.0	12 542	29.6	10 014	15.8
Education	65.9	1.3	1 835	4.3	8 592	7.6
Energy/Power	1 622.6	31.5	5 986	14.1	21 489	18.9
Industry	566.7	10.9	7 589	17.9	6 610	5.8
Non-Project	219.7	4.3	1 963	4.6	15 340	13.4
Pop., Health, Nut.*	0	0	302	0.7	5 824	5.2
Technical Asstc.	0	0	120	0.3	1 266	1.1
Tourism	0	0	371	0.9	0	0
Transp/Comm.[†]	2115.6	41.1	8 155	19.2	13 183	11.6
Urban	n.a.	n.a.	1 123	2.7	6 800.8	5.9
Water/Sewerage	93.4	1.8	2 349	5.5	5 013.7	4.4
Dev. Fin. Corps.	n.a.		n.a.		7 637.3	6.8
Pub. Sect. Mgmt.[§]	n.a.		n.a.		2 877.6	2.5
Sm-Scale Ents.[¶]	n.a.		n.a.		1 103.5	1.0
Total	5 150.5	99.9	42 435	99.8	105 750	100.0

* Population, Health and Nutrition
[†] Transportation and Communication
  Development Finance Corporations
[§] Public Sector Management
[¶] Small Scale Enterprises

Percentages do not total 100 due to rounding

Sources: 1961–65: Mason and Asher, 1973, pp. 833–43.
1975–79: Sanford, 1980.
1989–93: *Annual Report*, 1993 pp. 106, 114, 120, 126, 134, 140, 165.

varieties and farming input packages. James Cypher credits the Bank with leading 'the latest phase of capitalist expansion, in which the resource-rich Third World is fully incorporated into the capitalist world economy' (Cypher, 1989a).

The emphasis on economic integration through investment and trade extends to local and national economies as well. World Bank staffer Robert Ayres (1983) describes rural anti-poverty lending as based on the premise that participation in national markets is the road to prosperity for poor farmers. Whether this integrative role is progressive or exploitative is a central issue in the literature on the Bank.

Coordinating the Aid Regime

The World Bank's financial role is supported by leadership in publishing, training and an expanding coordinating role among donors that has led Bonné (1989) and Gibbon (1992) to describe a new 'aid regime.' Its research, economic forecasting and modeling work is disseminated widely through the *World Debt Tables*, *The World Bank Economic Review* and *The World Bank Research Observer*, the journal *Finance and Development*, and series of Staff Working Papers and other informal papers. Staff economists develop and publish models and projections of international markets, prospects for growth and other indicators, projections that are often a basis for planning by national policy makers (Cole, 1987).

Training through the Economic Development Institute (EDI) also promotes the Bank's perspective on development. Between 1985 and 1989 the EDI averaged 167 training 'activities' per year for middle- and senior-level policy makers from borrowing countries (De Lusignan, 1986, p. 31). In 1993 a total of 152 were held, continuing the EDI 'strategic objective' of mobilizing 'knowledge and experience accumulated in the World Bank' to improve member governments' 'development decisionmaking' (*Annual Report*, 1993, p. 87). EDI's director observes that a newly trained team from a government ministry can be '... a dynamic cadre capable of reinforcing each other in the application – and further propagation – of their new skills' (De Lusignan, 1986, p. 29).

The Bank also convenes and chairs coordinating meetings of donors on specific countries and regions (17 in fiscal 1993) (*Annual Report*, 1993, p. 20). It also promotes coordination with commercial banks and international and bilateral donor agencies by co-financing projects. In fiscal 1993 more than half (118) of new World Bank-financed projects involved co-financing, the Bank providing $11.1 billion of their $35.5 billion total value (*Annual Report*, 1993, p. 71).

The World Bank's 6800 professional staff have undergone several reorganizations since the mid-1980s, including a major shake-up in 1987. Most recently, President Lewis Preston located three influential Managing Directors in the Executive Office. Under the Executive Office, the bulk of Bank staff are organized under sixteen vice presidencies. Six of these have responsibility for regional lending and policy, three for Bank finance and accounting functions, three deal with cross-cutting policy areas, and four others are responsible for economic policy direction, co-financing, personnel and evaluation.

The regional units (formerly grouped in an Operations complex), along with the Vice President for Development Economics and the three new Vice Presidencies for Human Resources Development, Private Sector Development and Environmentally Sustainable Development, have the greatest role in formulating lending policy and in identifying, designing and implementing projects. The centralization of staff has been a constant through the Bank's reorganizations: more than 95 per cent of professional staff work in the Washington, DC headquarters.

POVERTY, ADJUSTMENT AND POLITICS

A plethora of articles, pamphlets and books by NGO activists have attacked the World Bank over the last decade on topics ranging from environmental impact, forced resettlement to public information policy, structural adjustment and debt management (among many others, see Abugre, 1992; Bello, Kinley and Elinson, 1982; Clark, 1990; NGO Working Group on the World Bank, 1989; Woodward, 1992; Rau, 1991; Rich, 1990; Bello, 1992; Rich, 1994; George and Sabelli, 1994; Danaher, ed., 1994).

As this storm of criticism suggests, the World Bank is at the center of several pivotal issues for NGOs. Among them are income distribution, structural adjustment and debt management, issues where the Bank's role has been largely inegalitarian, defined by its own organizational interests and closely identified with the interests of the major industrial countries and banks.

The Ebb and Flow of 'Poverty Lending'

The World Bank's official position on the relationship between growth and poverty reduction, and on the appropriate strategies for pursuing both, has varied considerably since the beginning of the McNamara presidency. Comments such as those of a past External Relations Vice President ('... there isn't a project that doesn't help the poor [in poor West African countries]. Are these people rich?') (in Ayres, 1983) are the exception to a pattern of carefully phrased statements that aim to balance and render compatible the needs for economic growth and attention to the particular needs of the poor.

The McNamara presidency (1969–82) placed strong rhetorical emphasis on poverty alleviation, stressing the 'large areas of complementarity between the two objectives of growth and poverty alleviation' (World Bank, 1982, p. 2). The 1982 task force on poverty summarized the Bank's approach: 'A balanced strategy of growth combined with poverty alleviation provides the best general framework for development in the 1980s.... This policy ... conforms to the stated priorities of many lenders, of most borrowers, and of the United Nations system' (World Bank, 1982, p. 22). The 'balanced strategy' is rearticulated in the 1990 WDR, after a decade of relative quiet on poverty issues. The WDR (1990, p. 56) advocates 'the adoption of appropriate economy-wide and sectoral policies and of measures to help the poor grasp new income-earning opportunities.'

In agriculture, for example, the WDR (1990, p. 59) argues that better infrastructure 'can lead to increased productivity, technical change, and strengthened market linkages.' New higher yielding varieties of food crops benefit landowners the most in absolute terms, but 'income gains from infrastructure can be widely dispersed.' Studies of rural Bangladesh are cited to show that all households, 'including the poor and landless,' enjoyed some income gains from infrastructure investments. The evidence cited focuses exclusively on average incomes in a community, and the writers seem satisfied with any income gain for those in lower deciles, regardless of the change in their relative status and ability to command food and other commodities in the market, or of gains and losses within households.

For Ayres (1983, p. 106), the 1970s New Directions campaign in the Bank succeeded in isolating the greater part of its lending program from the poverty debate. The split allows the Bank to measure its commitment and performance in poverty reduction by the amount of its targeted 'poverty lending.' Such 'poverty lending' has been modest: the 184 rural development projects funded in the 1970s cost roughly as much as the Bank's investment in one Brazilian steel mill ($2.1 billion) during the period (Ayres, p. 106).

The comparison puts the poverty-lending campaign in context, but it also illustrates the prevalent acceptance of the Bank's historic segmentation of 'kinds' of development and of development lending. The steel mill's relation to poverty is not carefully probed, and such industrial and infrastructure lending has a kind of happy, unproblematic relation to anti-poverty lending. The alternative – analyzing the new steel mill's impact on the poor and the measures needed (labor rights, environmental protection, destination of profits, etc.) for a positive benefit to the poor – is avoided by the segmentation that the World Bank offers and Ayres (and others) accept.

The World Bank now distinguishes a 'core poverty program' of agricultural and social sector lending that aims specifically to benefit the poor. Even loans that are not part of the core poverty program, however, are beneficial to the poor (World Bank, *Annual Report*, 1990, p. 57). For fiscal years 1990 and 1991 combined, the Bank lent $3.8 billion for 'operations whose primary objective is to reduce poverty.' These 44 loans made up 15 per cent of total lending. In fiscal 1992 the figure remained at 14 per cent (World Bank, 'Implementing the World Bank's Strategy to Reduce Poverty,' 1993), rising to 21 per cent in 1993 (World Bank, 1994d).

Much of the discussion of the World Bank's role in poverty alleviation accepts statements of policy at face value, as indicative of priorities and commitments shared bank-wide. But John Clark, then at Oxfam-UK (1988) suggests that the Bank's publications on poverty be read in context. In reviewing policy papers from the late 1980s, he asks which is the 'real World Bank': the few specialists who produce insightful analyses of poverty, gender and other issues for a small audience, or the apparent majority of the institution whose programming seemingly continues to be based strictly on orthodox economic theories of growth, adjustment and fiscal discipline.

Managing Debt and Adjustment: The Bank Takes Center Stage

At the Bank's 1979 annual meetings McNamara announced a new kind of lending for 'structural adjustment.' Adjustment loans are offered in exchange for commitments to change certain macro-economic policies (Structural Adjustment, SAL) or policy at the sectoral level (Sectoral Adjustment, SECAL), rather than to finance specific development projects. Between 1979 and 1991, 258 adjustment loans were made to 75 countries, totaling $41.5 billion. Adjustment lending made up 16 per cent of commitments in FY 1993, down from the 25 per cent mark in 1991. The percentage has been consistently higher for lending to middle-income highly indebted countries of Latin America and the Caribbean (39 per cent of lending) and to low-income Sub-Saharan Africa (45 per cent of lending) (Country Economics Department, 1988, p. 10).

The World Bank sees institutional and policy changes that remove non-market restraints from economies as the essential complement to external funding for adjustment to economic crisis. Improving policies means removing 'sources of inefficiency' in public spending and employment, agricultural policy, the state role in markets, fiscal and monetary policy including currency valuation, and tariff reductions and export promotion (Country Economics Department, 1988, p. 12; Nicholas, 1988, p. xi).

Adjustment lending allowed the Bank to pursue two objectives at once: lend to cover debt servicing costs, and remove policies that obstructed progress toward its vision of growth through integration with the global economy. Non-project lending was superior to projects for these purposes, in that it allows loans to match the broad nature of the economic issues, facilitates cutting back on new projects and new government spending, and allows quick disbursement (Nicholas, 1988, p. 12). The loans are to help in designing national adjustment programs, underwrite some of the changes required, and encourage further lending from donors and commercial banks.

The World Bank's entry into policy-based lending raised its profile and stimulated debate about its role in the world economy. Much of the debate involving NGOs has addressed the 'social dimensions' of adjustment, but some NGO participants are increasingly aware that broader economic issues need to be addressed, in order to prevent the debate from focusing solely on social sector spending and compensatory safety net programs. In addition to poverty and income distribution issues, adjustment lending has largely failed by its own macro-economic standards in the low-income countries; it has failed to elicit the anticipated flow of external and domestic investment; it directs countries into already over-supplied 'niches' in the global economy; it takes decisions about basic development strategies largely out of the hands of affected citizens; and it lacks a fair and coherent policy toward debt burdens and imbalances in the global economy.

The following sections summarize some major lines of criticism, and trace the evolving World Bank response.

Poverty and income distribution

The United Nations Children's Fund's (UNICEF) call for 'adjustment with a human face,' (Jolly, 1985; Cornia *et al.*, 1987; UNICEF, 1986) argues that the short-term impact of adjustment on the poor must be addressed for humanitarian reasons. UNICEF's 'human-face' campaign calls for compensatory measures to soften the effects of adjustment on the poor – notably unemployment among fired state and parastatal employees, rising food prices for net consumers among the poor, and reduced social services as government spending is cut. Protection of certain social expenditures, fair-price shops for urban consumers, job-creation schemes and similar measures are advocated as necessary and neglected components of adjustment. The UNICEF concerns have been reiterated recently (*State of the World's Children*, 1989 and 1992; Cornia, van der Hoeven and Mkandawire (eds), 1992). The 'human face' campaign began a remarkably unsuccessful decade-long campaign to challenge the legitimacy of the Bank's adjustment program. NGOs, UN agencies and scholars documented and decried the aggravation of poverty by adjustment programs in Latin America, Africa and parts of Asia. Studies in Nigeria (Bangura, 1987), Ivory Coast (Bassett, 1988), Senegal and Ghana (Hodges, 1988), Ghana (Hagan, 1992), The Philippines (Cruz and Repetto, 1992), Jamaica, Pakistan, Ghana and Côte d'Ivoire (Mayatech Corporation, 1991); Mexico (Heredia and Purcell, 1994) have also documented adverse effects on nutrition, infant mortality, employment and health indicators.

The Bank's response to the human-face critique

The Bank has sometimes downplayed the effects on the poor, or argued for their necessity, while selectively adopting the social safety net measures proposed by UNICEF. The most consistent theme in Bank-published papers on the social effects of adjustment is that regardless of the transitional costs, adjustment is a prerequisite to alleviating poverty (Development Committee, 1987, p. 6; Development Committee, 1990, p. 31). Consistent with its position on project lending, the Bank argues that the two objectives are compatible, but that growth, which is expected to follow adjustment, is the fundamental element.

The World Bank advances a variety of other arguments in defense of adjustment programs' impact on the poor. One theme is essentially counterfactual: models and projections are introduced to show that the poor would have suffered as much or more in the absence of adjustment, because of deteriorating economic conditions under pre-reform economic policies. (See, for example, Glewwe (1988) on Peru; *Protecting the Poor during Periods of Adjustment* (Development Committee, 1987; Country Economics Department, 1992, in general.)

An important variant on this counterfactual argument appears in the Bank's ten-year assessment of adjustment lending (Country Economics Department, 1988). The impact of global recession and national economic difficulties is hard to distinguish from the impact of adjustment measures implemented to facilitate recovery. In the absence of conceptual and empirical tools to separate the effects of the two, social dislocations are often blamed on adjustment (p. 30; also Development Committee, 1987, pp. 4–8).

Despite this caveat, World Bank publications accept that adjustment policies have harmed the poor in many situations. This is said to have surprised many staff, who expected adjustment to restore growth and benefit the poor quickly (Nicholas, 1988, p. 36; Zuckerman, 1989, p. 2; Country Economics Department, 1988, p. 10). Early adjustment lending 'focused almost exclusively' on efforts to increase the efficiency of resource allocations, assuming that the poor would quickly benefit from such measures. The World Bank's Elaine Zuckerman (1989, p. 2) says that neglect of social considerations continued 'until recently.' (The Bank's treatment of the differential impact of adjustment on women is discussed in Chapter 7).

In the wake of UNICEF's 'human face' campaign, the World Bank-IMF Development Committee endorsed the analysis of Protecting the Poor as Bank policy in 1987. This document argues that effects on the poor can be softened by three kinds of measures. First, proper design and implementation, including early and orderly adjustment, staged reforms, and generous external finance can reduce social costs. The difficulty of obtaining finance in the face of its declining availability to most countries is noted but not addressed.

Second, government social services can be redirected and refocused more directly on the poor. New fee schedules for social services, for example, allow reduced social services to be focused on the poor, recovering costs by collecting fees from those better able to pay (Nicholas, 1988, p. 37). Whatever the merits of the emphasis on cost-recovery measures in social services, it is, as Singer (1989) notes, hardly a rallying cry in a campaign to address the needs of the poor.

Third, compensatory services may be provided directly to the poor. The Bank argues that targeted public works employment, local fair-price food shops, and other measures by governments, donor agencies and NGOs have shown in countries such as Chile and Costa Rica that adjustment need not devastate the poor (Zuckerman, 1989; Nicholas, 1988).

Finally, in some quarters there is discussion of the need and opportunity to design adjustment measures that not only protect the poor, but work to increase their access to productive assets. This use of policy conditionality, unfortunately, has never been substantially implemented. The reporting on poverty-related adjustment conditionality in the Bank's annual reports on poverty alleviation reveals how limited the employment of such conditionality has been.

The Bank's 1993 Report on implementing anti-poverty strategies notes that 18 of 32 adjustment loans made in 1992 'contained an explicit poverty focus' (p. 19). The 1994 update notes that the proportion for

1993 was down to six of 17 (World Bank, 1994d, p. 8). But in most cases the 'poverty focus' was either monitoring the effects of adjustment on the poor, or targeting social service spending or supporting compensatory programs.

The 1993 report cites one example of a condition that shifts productive assets to the poor: the transfer of land rights in Mozambique from state farms to private enterprises and smallholders (p. 20). Other 'poverty-related objectives' in 1992 adjustment loans include changes in Zimbabwe's Labor Act 'to provide employers with authority to retrench workers . . .' (p. 54), and deregulation of the labor market in Côte d'Ivoire, to allow formal sector wages to drop (p. 53). These measures to free labor markets are said to 'remove distortions that especially disadvantage the poor' (p. 21), and they may be a route to eventual job growth in the formal sector. But it is difficult to see such restrictions as disadvantaging primarily the poor; it seems likely that employers were most interested in the reforms. It requires a good deal of confidence in unregulated labor markets – more than the experience with market reforms inspires in Africa – to take these seriously as anti-poverty measures.

Recent reviews of adjustment lending

The 1992 (third) review of adjustment lending is the Bank's most spirited defense. The collective findings of the Bank's research are summarized in a highly positive tone, asserting that consumption increases documented in adjustment countries in the late 1980s 'reduced the incidence of poverty in the intensive adjustment lending countries.' Further, 'the distributional effects of well-designed policies often favor the poor' (Country Economics Department, 1992, pp. 19–20).

But having announced these findings, the 1992 review begins to hedge. 'Many of the poor are vulnerable in the transition, especially where recession and declining labor demand are unavoidable. . . .' The overall positive effects depend on the 'structure of the economy and of poverty.' In Costa Rica, where smallholder agriculture is a major employment of the poor, effects were positive. The improvements indicated by overall consumption increases may not really mean that poverty was diminished, because populations grew. And while 'well-designed' macro and sectoral reforms benefit the poor, 'intergroup shifts that favor the poor are not always consistent with political realities, . . . and a balance often has to be struck to make a program feasible' (Country Economics Department, 1992, pp. 20–1).

The World Bank's slowness in recognizing the human and social costs to adjustment mirrors the slow entry of poverty considerations into project lending some twenty years before. As with project lending, the rising tide of growth was at first said to be sufficient to lift all boats. But as the 1980s wore on, the effects of new economic policies and government funding reductions became increasingly difficult to ignore.

Macro-economic performance in low-income countries

World Bank documents have invoked a variety of external and internal factors, particularly for low-income and Sub-Saharan African countries, to explain the weak growth response to a decade and more of fiscal discipline and economic restructuring.

The ten-year evaluation (Country Economics Department, 1988) concludes that the external economic environment in general 'turned out to be substantially worse than was assumed at the start of the 1980s,' and 'made adjustment slower and more difficult than initially expected' (see also Ribe, Carvalho, Liebenthal, Nicholas and Zuckerman, 1990). The 1992 review shifts attention to internal factors. Adjustment measures in Africa have been 'swimming against the tide' of institutional and infrastructure decline. The particular obstacles to successful adjustment read like a catalogue of the woes of low-income countries: '... a weaker human resource base, inadequate and sometimes declining economic infrastructure, less diversified economic structures, and poorly functioning institutions' (Country Economics Department, 1992, p. 25). Were it not for these weaknesses, the review implies, adjustment could have achieved growth rates comparable to the middle-income countries'.

Self-exoneration by pointing to disappointing developments in the global economy – or internal institutional weakness – is hardly a satisfactory response to the severe and extended social dislocations in most low-income SAL countries. Adjustment programs are negotiated with governments on the basis of results the Bank predicts will flow from the changed policies, results drawn from models that specify or predict performance of the variables the Bank later calls exogenous and unpredictable. Global economic performance is, of course, not under the World Bank's control. But models and projections are the basis for SAL negotiations, so the Bank's package should be considered to include not only the loan and conditions, but also its forecasts of conditions essential to adjustment policies' success.

When the obstacles are internal institutions and resources, as in the 1992 review, the argument is even more curious. How could a reform program that requires certain kinds of markets, infrastructure, information, and skills in the workforce be prescribed so regularly for countries that lack these prerequisites?

In Africa, where the experience was again evaluated in a 1993 report, adjustment plans have often been incompletely or even intermittently implemented. This leaves the Bank essentially comparing relatively fully-implemented plans with plans that, for a variety of reasons, are not. The most that can be said is that in the few cases where Bank-style adjustment was relatively fully implemented, it worked somewhat better than in the many cases where it was not. *The Economist*, noting this fact, observes that the Bank's confidence about adjustment in Africa 'veers towards complacency' (5 March 1994, p. 22). A corporation would fire a financial advisor whose services ignored prevailing economic and institutional conditions. But most borrowing governments have no alternative to the Bretton Woods institutions as their financial directors.

Simultaneous adjustment and competition

The broad dissemination of export-oriented adjustment strategies adds a further dimension to the Bank's role, as governments are urged essentially to compete for investment and shares of the global productive process by holding the costs of labor and relevant primary commodities lower than their neighbors.

Economists Robin Broad (1988) and Broad and John Cavanagh (1988) show how the changing structure of international production and the World Bank's role in promoting non-traditional export strategies have limited the options for would-be NICs (newly industrialized countries). During the 1970s, as transnational corporate and banking activity expanded and production of apparel, electronics, and other light manufactures was fragmented and globalized, labor-intensive stages of production began to move from the Asian NICs to a second tier of would-be NICs. The character of investment and the division of labor changed: no longer was substantial capital investment or the growth of a lasting industrial base assured.

Broad and Cavanagh argue that the East Asian NIC strategy is not generalizable, and trace the World Bank's role in shaping and promoting the strategy. At least 16 would-be NICs had been encouraged (by 1988) to adopt non-traditional export policies through SALs and SECALs.

Many within the Bank who promote the strategy know that the NIC 'niche' in the global economy is overcrowded, and promote the strategy with unduly optimistic models and forecasts. In so doing the Bank assumes a pivotal role in reorganizing the international division of labor.

Questions about economic projections used to sell the SAL packages to governments reinforce this critique. Economist Sam Cole (1987, p. 369, 383) shows that projections of global growth and investment rates are 'biased high' by several percentage points throughout the 1970s and 1980s. He attributes the systematic bias to a variety of factors: flawed methods and models, a volatile global economy, peer group reinforcement and critique among modelers, and the World Bank's need for optimistic projections to leverage national policy changes. The Bank's ten-year review of adjustment loans acknowledges that 'projections of outcomes during the adjustment phase were optimistic. . . . The persistence of negative external shocks [and] lags in implementation and supply response were underestimated' (Country Economics Department, 1988, p. 53).

Adjustment and debt management. Adjustment loans and the World Bank's role in debt-for-equity swaps and other debt buy-out schemes suggest that the Bank manages a creditors' cartel. Eaton and Gersovitz (1981, pp. 35-6) argue that even as World Bank and IMF lending made up a declining portion of total international capital flows in the 1970s, the agencies' importance in international finance grew with their debt management role. They gather and disseminate information for lenders, organize to penalize defaulters, exert political influence in some borrower countries, and protect private loans through austerity and adjustment regimes.

Two contrasting interpretations of the World Bank's debt management role are possible. In Robert Pastor's (1989) view, the Bank (but primarily the IMF) stabilizes and maintains the economic order by restraining creditors from acting alone against debtors. If creditors acted independently to maximize individual utility, the crisis created would shake the international economy. The Bank and IMF facilitate collective action that sustains the status quo. Former World Bank economist Art Van de Laar (1980) sees the Bank as managing the debtor countries' strategies. He argues that for most debtors the strongest strategy would be to negotiate deals individually with creditor institutions and countries. By persuading debtors to negotiate with a central authority rather than employing their strongest strategy, the Bank acts in creditors' favor. Adjustment loans establish and maintain an element of self-enforcement for debt repayment by conditioning further loans or tranches on continued debt servicing. The arrangement serves the Bank's interests nicely, as it maintains its status as a privileged creditor, assured of continuing service payments by all but those few countries who drop of the international finance system altogether.

Whether by influencing creditors' or debtors' strategies, or both, the debt management approach the Bank and IMF have guided has maintained a strong and relatively stable debt management regime (Lehman, 1993). Despite growing calls for more decisive action to relieve the burden of servicing debt owed to the IBRD and IMF, the Bank's management remains determined not to write down obligations to it. Whatever its other effects, Mosley, Harrigan and Toye call Bank adjustment lending an effective safety net under the international financial system. The regime has entailed net capital outflows from the poor countries, debilitating debt burdens on many economies, and a pattern of adjustment whose burden rests almost entirely on debtors.

Adjustment plans have promoted non-traditional export strategies and opening economies to foreign investment on almost any terms, promote investment and reinvestment by foreign capital that ties would-be NICs to a newly structured division of labor in which their sole comparative advantage is the ability to maintain low wages, tax and tariff holidays, and a docile workforce.

Adjustment, politics and governance This strategy has potent implications for national politics in borrowing countries. World Bank-promoted economic strategies have often been associated with a tendency to authoritarianism in government. John Loxley (1986) argues that 'orthodox models of growth' have 'a very tenuous domestic political base' in many developing countries. 'Without repression it is unlikely that the distributional implications of demand restraint and of correcting the 'bias' in relative prices – the keys to most adjustment programs – could have been constrained politically' (p. 38). (See also Pion-Berlin, 1983; McCormack, 1978, on South Korea; Hamilton, 1983, on the Asian NICs; O'Donnell, 1981, on South America.)

But while Bank-style adjustment has often been associated with political repression, it has also been carried out by more open, pluralistic governments. Recent studies find that neither the degree of government repression nor of political instability is closely associated with the character of adjustment programs. (Bratton and van de Walle, 1992; Mosley, Harrington and Toye, 1991; Lafay and Lacaillon, 1993).

A subtler, still pervasive influence – the erosion of domestic political authority over economic policy making – may have more serious and lasting implications in many societies. The effect of an external agency neutralizing powerful interest groups is often considered salutary, as in shifting education or health expenditures away from urban elites, reducing high effective subsidies on energy consumption, or loosening the tight hold of political elites over parastatals, regulatory and licensing agencies, or other government-held bodies.

But this external role puts the Bank's economic program in tension with its growing interest in 'good governance,' especially transparency and broad participation in public life (see *Governance and Development*, World Bank, 1992a). This tension emerged in the 1980s as it became clear that the Bank's structural reform agenda extended beyond fiscal austerity and monetary policy into the redesign of national production, marketing and trade strategies. The tension between structural adjustment and political liberalization has been widely noted (Joan Nelson, 1989a; Healey and Robinson, 1992; Callaghy, 1993). The issue for the Bank and NGOs is explored more fully in Chapter 6. For the present, it is enough to take note of three elements of the politics of World Bank conditionality.

First, under World Bank leadership a single economic strategy has become the program of a united front of donors and financial institutions. 'Donor coordination' has been effective in preventing recalcitrant governments from playing one donor's strategy off against another's. But in the process national policy makers lose a menu of options from which to choose, confronting instead 'a stifling monolithic orthodoxy that bars skeptical questioning . . .' (Levinson, 1992, p. 47). The issue is not whether it makes sense for the Bank to encourage and even insist upon fiscal discipline and adherence to consistent economic plans. It is whether propagation of a single strategy is healthy economically or politically.

Second, the Bank and other donors have generally not sought out and encouraged locally initiated reform movements. Donors' support for domestic political initiatives could be an effective route to economic reform and political accountability. But reform packages have generally been crafted by Bank planners and a small group of likeminded economists and planners in Finance or Planning ministries. Some in the Bank have recognized this: New procedures in the Southern Africa department recognize the need for governments to initiate policy packages, and spell out an alternative approach for the department's nine countries ('Managing Quality', 1994; Denning, 1994).

Third, adjustment plans have been highly selective in their choice of economic 'distortions' to reform, de-emphasizing problems such as ineffective or regressive tax systems, capital flight, maldistribution of land or host countries' difficulties retaining revenues from many varieties of investment. A global reform effort that presented a broader menu of such reforms – a variety of routes by which adjustment could be achieved – would preserve an element of political choice, and make broad social and political commitment to reform plans more feasible.

But the technical requirements of orthodox economic adjustment have overridden domestic political opinion, producing an artificial conformity and uniformity, with the principal variation among countries resulting from the variety of ways governments find to undercut, delay or distort the intentions of external reformers.

The World Bank and the United States: Use and Limits of Power

Many see the World Bank as essentially a tool of US foreign policy. These critics go beyond the view that the Bank promotes 'political stability through defensive modernization' (Ayres, 1983, p. 226), to portray it as part of a 'dovish containment strategy' (Pratt. 1983, p. 57), acting out US foreign policy interests throughout the Cold War era in the Philippines (Bello, Kinley and Elinson, 1982), Vietnam (Kolko, 1975), and elsewhere in the South (Payer, 1982; Bello, 1994). That World Bank lending has risen and fallen where US policy interests have called for it is a matter of record in the Philippines and Vietnam.

A 1982 US Treasury Department report intended to shore up congressional support for the multilateral development banks argued that '...we are capable and willing to pursue important policy objectives in the banks by exercising the... leverage at our disposal (US Department of Treasury, 1982, p. 47). A close, informal relationship between US government officials and the Bank gives the US influence over lending, especially early in the project preparation process (Schoultz, 1982, p. 543; Hellinger *et al.*, p. 150). The US capacity to influence Bank policy, and enlarge its own leverage over borrowers' economic policies, is a theme that the US executive branch re-emphasized throughout the 1980s, when the need arose to convince the Congress that funds for the Bank or IMF were in the US interest.

But World Bank policy on many important issues cannot be read from the wishes of the US administration; there appears to be substantial autonomy in many policy areas. The sheer volume of loans to be approved taxes the Board of Executive Directors' oversight capacity.

Further, the staff's high level of training and professional status, and their own perception that they are more sophisticated and less politically compromised than staff of national agencies (Thomas, 1980, p. 110; Pratt, 1983, p. 57; Bello, Kinley and Elinson, 1982, p. 205) make them disinclined to submit to pressure from national agencies in operational decisions. Financially the World Bank is less beholden to its members than are other United Nations bodies. Members' capital payments are a relatively small portion of its holdings. And, according to some on the Bank's Board of Executive Directors, frequent US initiatives for changes in environmental policies and for freedom of information policies have weakened support from other donors for US proposals on the Board.

The Bank has been able to balance its obligations to subscribers, commercial banks, borrowers and the development profession, and in so doing has carved out a range of discretion and relative autonomy. It benefits from widely accepted norms of national 'sovereignty' and an apolitical image of 'correct' development policy – discussed in Chapter 6 – in maintaining this degree of freedom and exerting its influence on borrowers' economic policy and institutions.

The significance of the end of the Cold War, and resultant shifts in US foreign policy priorities, remains to be seen. Some Bank staff argue that in the absence of a Soviet threat to contain, US policy toward the Bank will become less intrusive – or at least more benign, focused for example on the environment. But arguably the most important US influence in the Bank in the 1980s has not been over strategic lending priorities but the promotion of a debt management and adjustment strategy. Neither the end of the Cold War nor the change in US administrations with the 1992 elections has substantially changed the US position on these issues at the Bank. It remains to be seen whether the new Republican majority in the US Congress, generally hostile to multilateral programs and initiatives, will significantly change the US posture in the Bank.

PRESSURE ON THE WORLD BANK: ENVIRONMENT, IMPLEMENTATION PERFORMANCE AND HUMAN RIGHTS

The new membership and acute capital needs of the Eastern European and former Soviet countries expand the World Bank's scope and the demands on staff and capital. While global capital requirements stretch its resources, external and internal pressures are straining its capacity to satisfy various constituencies. Responding to government and NGO pressure on environmental issues, the Bank has positioned itself to coordinate and manage several global initiatives for environmental protection. Growing pressure for consideration of human rights issues has gained the attention of some in its legal department. Concerns about the effectiveness and sustainable impact of Bank-financed projects also threaten to put pressure on business as usual.

No area of World Bank policy received public attention in the last decade comparable to that focused on its impact on the environment. Environmental organizations have used case studies, print and electronic media coverage and legislative pressure to mount a highly visible challenge to the Bank's conduct of lending and policy making.

The pressure – often with support from the US Executive Director and resistance by many borrowing governments – has led to the creation of a new environmental division in the Bank, operational divisions within each regional vice presidency, and the elaboration of an environmental impact assessment process now required for many loans. The World Bank has seized the opportunity by seeking to assert leadership in efforts to address global environmental issues. Its coordination of the Global Environment Fund (GEF), role in the Tropical Forest Action Plan (TFAP), and the unsuccessful call for a 5 billion dollar 'earth increment' to its IDA-10 replenishment all illustrate the effort to take a leading role in the emerging global environmental protection regime, a role viewed with skepticism by many NGOs (see Chapter 3).

Human rights advocates have long pressed donor governments and international organizations to use their leverage to secure adherence to internationally adopted standards of political and civil rights. The World Bank and the IMF have historically been the least responsive, but the Bank's own attention to governance issues, focusing largely on government performance in implementing adjustment plans, has given human rights advocates a new lever. The World Bank's handling of governance and human rights, and their impact on its myth of 'apolitical' development, are discussed in Chapter 6.

Internal questions about the effectiveness and implementation of Bank-financed projects gained a new high profile under the presidency of Lewis Preston. Issues have been raised about the lasting impact of investments by the Bank's Operations and Evaluation Division (OED) for some years. For OED, the issue is the economic sustainability of the investments: did loans create changes that outlasted the life of the project?

A 1992 study by retired Bank Vice President Willi Wapenhans raises the question more urgently and publicly, and raises the pressure on management for change to a new level. The Report points to weaknesses in implementation of Bank-financed projects, to country portfolios full of poorly performing projects and to a staff overly concerned with the quantity of lending and ill-equipped to handle important issues that affect the quality of investments. It finds that the Bank has tolerated 'poor performance' in many investments, and that 39 per cent of borrowing countries have 'poorly performing portfolios.' Faced with pressure from the Board over the handling of the Sardar Sarovar project, and needing to inspire confidence to push through the IDA-10 replenishment, Preston signalled in 1992 that the issues would be taken seriously (*Early Warning*, 1992).

But the report itself, as well as management's proposed 'next steps,' consolidate the Bank's definition of 'success' in terms of rates of return on investments and adherence to schedules and legal covenants, rather than social and human indicators of development impact. The Bank's use of this power to define its own 'success' is the subject of Chapter 6.

Competing New Initiatives

In the wake of Wapenhans, several new initiatives have emerged from two of the Bank's three 'central' vice presidencies. Among them are a renewed 'participation fund,' now in place, to encourage participatory initiatives in the Bank's regional divisions by making matching funds available (see Chapter 7); and consultations with operational NGOs on issues in Bank-NGO contracting and collaboration (see Chapter 3). The Operations complex under Vice President Armeane Choksi initiated a Fund for Innovative Social and Human Development, within the Bank. The fund is now to be phased out over three years, as internal budget cuts put pressure on such innovative initiatives.

But one proposal from Vice President Ismail Serageldin, for a microfinance facility and consultative group, has gained a good deal of attention. Serageldin's proposal would establish a donor consultative group for advancing learning, practice and finance of micro-finance assistance. The Bank proposes to supply as much as $30 million to an initial fund of up to $100 million, and to house the secretariat at the Bank. The Bank has convened discussions among major donors, and its board will take up the proposal if sufficient interest emerges from donor discussions.

Some NGO critics of the Bank regard the proposal, which the Bank calls a response to the 1993 conference on Reducing Global Hunger, as a high-profile attempt to address hunger and poverty concerns without responding to the conference's concerns regarding adjustment and participation. The Bank, whose experience in micro-enterprise lending is slender, would benefit in the public eye by associating itself with this popular and highly-regarded form of anti-poverty lending.

But most NGOs involved in the discussions have agreed that the fund would be useful both as a source of finance (although questions of additionality and substitution arise with respect to the bilateral donors' funding), and, potentially, as a forum for discussion of donors' financial sector policies. The draft memorandum does open this possibility, placing discussion of finance sector policy within the consultative group's purview ('Draft Proposal for Establishing a Consultative Group to Assist the Poorest of the Poor (CGAPP)' 1994). Should the proposal be approved and funded, its success in forcing critical reflection on national-level financial policies would be a key measure of its success.

Despite the substantial public relations content in these proposals for the Bank (see the following section), they also do respond to pressure and to new opportunities associated with the Bank's increased contact with NGOs. All but the Participation Fund, however, share a common characteristic: they basically propose to add new initiatives to existing operations and program, rather than to change or transform some aspect of that program.

Many of the Bank's NGO interlocutors accept that change, even eventual transformation, will likely come slowly and in small discrete steps. Some have observed that it may be possible to take advantage of internal dynamics, such as the curious competition between two Vice Presidencies for association with the Bank's NGO agenda, to accelerate the rate of change. But whether individual changes are large-scale or small, the Bank and its governmental and NGO observers should give priority to those that change mechanisms, incentives, priorities and participation for the Bank's existing activities. Chapters 5 through 7 of this study treat past and present changes at the Bank in this light.

Polishing the Image

The Bank's response to internal and external pressures does include substantive policy reviews and changes, but it has also featured a high-level and aggressive public relations effort to improve its image. The minutes of a Vice Presidents' meeting in 1993 signal the high level of concern. Preston notes the Bank's 'increasingly negative external image' and calls for a 'proactive approach' to its image, rather than defending itself 'against criticism from well-organized environmental and human rights groups' (Office Memorandum 23 February 1993).

Upcoming United Nations conferences and the Bretton Woods 50th anniversary are noted as events for a public relations campaign; other strategies are urged, including information dissemination and 'reaching out to under-exploited constituencies in developed countries such as private sector industrialists or major academic centers. . . .' The eighteen months since this meeting have seen the hiring of a top-flight public relations firm and, separately, of a new external affairs director; the production of materials, including an extensive press packet, for the 50th anniversary celebrations; a Bank-sponsored conference on combatting World Hunger; and other events and publications. In all of these, the Bank's liaison with NGOs is an important part of the message.

CONCLUSIONS

The World Bank plays an important role in articulating and coordinating patterns of economic integration in the global economy. Structural adjustment lending has raised this role to new heights, and highlights the World Bank's responsiveness to the interests of commercial banks and the industrialized countries in matters of debt and international finance. In guiding and maintaining a new international division of labor, the Bank smooths relations among the parties to economic change: international investors, host states, and local capital. Its influence rests on its capital and financial leverage, its expertise and intellectual leadership, its apolitical image, its ability to mobilize other donors, and its role in certifying governments' creditworthiness.

But the Bank's critics are less clear on the limitations of these powers, and on the extent of its responsiveness to international capital and the major industrial powers. These limitations, and the Bank's ability to define its own tasks and resist criticism and external influence are better understood by adding to political economy the perspective of organizational analysis.

Such an analysis may be especially enlightening at the present juncture, as the Bank faces pressure for change on issues ranging from the expanding needs of new middle-income members and the economic performance of its investments to environmental policy and human rights. NGOs are important actors on several fronts in shaping this agenda.

3 'Accountable to Whom?' And Other Issues for NGOs

Non-governmental organizations (NGOs) are attracting increased attention and recognition among practitioners and scholars of development and development assistance. Whether because of frustration with frequent government corruption and repression, the failure of major donors' projects substantially to alleviate poverty, or the attraction of smaller scale efforts, NGOs are often touted as a solution to many of the problems that bedevil official development aid. Networks of voluntary associations are seen as a valuable resource for building strong civil societies and accountable governments. This chapter explores some issues in these discussions that have special relevance to the NGOs' engagement with the World Bank.

Much has been written about NGOs in the past decade. They are hailed for their proximity to remote communities and to the poor (Wasserstrom, 1985), their efficiency and the low cost of their operations (USAID, 1986), their promotion of 'sustainable' development (Durning, 1989a), and their potential role as organizing and representative bodies in civil societies (Brown and Korten, 1989). Focusing on issues that confront NGOs in relating to governments and international aid donors, this chapter identifies some of the most fruitful analytic approaches.

The four analytic approaches to NGOs all contribute to the construction of criteria for distinguishing the sorts of NGOs involved in projects collaboration and in policy discussions with the World Bank. One's evaluation of the character of Bank's collaboration depends in part on how one views NGOs, and on what distinctions among them are taken to be most important. In Chapter 4 these distinctions will be employed in weighing the quality and nature of collaboration in the World Bank-financed projects reported to involve NGOs.

Some issues facing NGOs in their contacts with major donors such as the World Bank are reviewed in the latter part of the chapter, as are NGO approaches to the World Bank and several issues particular to US-based NGOs active in lobbying the Bank.

DEFINITION AND DESCRIPTION

'Non-governmental' is an exceedingly broad and imprecise category of social organizations, a residual category generally understood to include organizations that are neither governments nor for-profit firms (Nerfin, 1986). The category includes a vast and varied array of organizations that has defied adequate definition, concise description, and accurate enumeration (Cernea, 1988, p. 9).

The World Bank's working definition is inclusive, specifying only that organizations be:

1. largely or entirely independent of governments;
2. working for humanitarian or cooperative rather than commercial ends, and to relieve suffering, promote the interests of the poor, protect the environment, provide basic social services, or undertake community development (World Bank, Operational Directive 14.70, 1989, p. 1).

The definition (accepted for present purposes) encompasses a wide range of organizations. NGOs include private organizations of international scale whose stated mission is to support development or protect the environment such as CARE, Save the Children Federation, OXFAM, or the National Wildlife Federation. Some 1702 such NGOs are officially registered with the aid agencies of the OECD countries, and perhaps 4000 participate in donor supported activities (OECD, 1988).

National-scale NGOs abound as well in the South; examples include Solidarios of the Dominican Republic, the Bangladesh Rural Advancement Committee (BRAC), Rural Reconstruction Movements of the Philippines and other countries, the Kenyan National Council of Women and Sri Lanka's Sarvodaya Shramadana movement.

But the current enthusiasm for NGOs extends beyond these formal, professional, national-level organizations to local, community-based groups involved in self-help, organizing, collective assistance and advocacy for economic advancement, social change and environmental protection. Worldwatch's Alan Durning calls 'cooperatives, mothers clubs, suburban groundwater committees, peasant farming unions, religious study groups, neighborhood action federations, collective aid societies, tribal nations, and innumerable others ... an expanding latticework covering the globe' (Durning, 1989a, p. 6). Lester Salamon refers to a 'global associational revolution' that 'may prove as significant as the rise of the nation-state' (1994, p. 109,114).

The broad use of 'NGO' adopted for this study sacrifices precision for inclusiveness. Recent treatments have made some valuable distinctions, and created a welter of new acronyms, for some of the subsets of organizations (Carroll, 1992; Bebbington and Farrington, 1993). Some of these analytic distinctions are treated in this chapter, but I have retained the general and inclusive term 'NGO.'

The enormous variety and number of local organizations makes a brief history of the development of NGOs impossible. Northern-based development NGOs emerged mostly after World War II, and several of the largest were founded during or immediately after the war to provide relief in Europe (OECD, 1988, p. 16). NGOs in the South are much more varied. Some are forms of long-standing local institutions that survived colonialism and the economic transformations that accompanied and followed it (Durning, 1989a, p. 8). Many formed or re-formed since the 1950s, and particularly in the last two decades, responding to frustration with ineffective state action, growing political space for organizing, and increasing impoverishment and natural resource degradation. Some, also, are the efforts of middle class university graduates in Latin America (Macdonald); new career options for professionals denied public employment by government spending cuts (Stiefel and Wolfe, 1994, p. 206); or efforts by young entrepreneurs, with or without commitments to a social program, who create NGOs in order to pursue government and donor funds.

The current fashion for NGOs in the development industry has its basis in important growth and changes among local organizations in the South, and in the national and international networks that increasingly connect and support them. Development and environmental NGOs are increasingly connected by organizational networks, newsletters, and electronic communication. Events even in remote areas cannot be expected to remain isolated and unknown.

But the enthusiasm for NGOs in official circles also has some of the elements of previous 'development decades,' passing emphases such as the decade of children, of women, and emphases on community development, basic needs, or integrated rural development. Each of these has risen to a height of fashion only to disappoint those with high expectations and recede into a modest role in development business as usual (Holdcroft, 1978; Ruttan, 1984).

The new emphasis on NGOs creates the danger that they will be called upon to do more than they in fact can to promote development in the poor countries. Moreover, it fosters myths about NGOs that obscure important problems and distinctions. NGOs' reputed virtues – low cost, ability to benefit the poor, access to local knowledge and awareness of local needs and capacities, flexibility and participatory style, freedom from corruption – are generally believed but largely untested and unproven (Tendler, 1982; Dichter, 1988; Rahmena, 1985; Overseas Development Institute, 1988; Esquel Group Foundation, 1993; for efforts to test these claims see Esman and Uphoff, 1984; USAID, 1986). Robert Shaw of the Aga Khan Foundation stresses the need for NGOs to demonstrate and document their effectiveness, in dialogue with the World Bank and in general (personal correspondence, 14 May 1990).

One contribution the World Bank is offering is the relatively rigorous and critical reviews it has commissioned for its forthcoming sourcebook on participation. A draft chapter by Schmidt and Carroll, which challenges and tests assumptions about intermediary NGOs' promotion of participation, is an unusually probing and critical survey of NGO performance and practice.

Some NGO critics, participants, scholars and aid agencies have made efforts to distinguish NGOs from other sectors of society and draw analytical distinctions among NGOs. The following two sections discuss important distinctions among their diverse operating styles; and explore the proposition that NGOs play an important democratizing role in strengthening civil societies. Distinctions developed in these sections will be an important foundation for analyzing Bank-NGO relations.

SOME ANALYTIC APPROACHES AND CATEGORIES

Some widely-used typologies of NGOs are created for administrative convenience (USAID; World Bank Operational Directive 14.70). But four more analytic approaches offer bases for classifying NGOs in more cohesive sub-groups, and making distinctions relevant to their relations with the World Bank.

1. Pyramidal Networks

The obvious distinction between international, national and local NGOs offer one basis for analysis. NGOs may be seen roughly as a pyramid, with a great number of grassroots or people's organizations at the bottom, a large number of intermediate organizations above them, and fewer international NGOs, acting as coordinators, donors, partners and advisors, at the top. These levels of activity are the distinguishing feature used in analyses of development NGOs by Peruvian scholar Mario Padrón (1987).

Padrón shows that tensions among the three levels must be faced and overcome to maximize the abilities of each to support social change. National level NGOs exist and operate by establishing relations with popular sector organizations and carrying out projects for and with them. Many of these NGOs (and global international development cooperations institutions) do not distinguish themselves clearly from grassroots organizations, as Padrón argues they must. Those that do, seek to work as partners to grassroots groups in development cooperation. Padrón stresses the pivotal role of national NGOs in promoting two-way exchanges that promote development, learning and change in the societies of aid donors and recipient alike.

International NGOs have confronted these tensions in the last decade. Like mission organizations that preceded them in the colonial South, most Northern-based NGOs administered relief and development programs directly through expatriate staff. As counterpart organizations in the South grew in size and sophistication, calls for new relationships between international and national/local NGOs became stronger. Many Southern NGOs and a growing number of those based in the North call for international NGOs to reduce their direct program role and take on supporting roles as mobilizers of funds for Southern partners, and as advocates and educators in their own countries and with donor institutions (UN Economic and Social Council, 1994, p. 7). The Dutch NGO NOVIB, OXFAM-UK and OXFAM-America, Canadian Council for International Cooperation (CCIC), and other European NGOs are among those leading the way in building a new supportive role.

Tim Brodhead (formerly of CCIC) refers to the 'twilight of the Northern NGO era' in this regard (Hellinger, Hellinger and O'Regan, 1988, pp. 102–3), and Sjef Theunis (1988) (formerly of NOVIB) argues for steps to integrate an international non-governmental community of advocacy, education and assistance to sustainable development. Rajesh Tandon of the Society for Participatory Research in Asia (PRIA) argues that such networks, if they strengthen the links among civil societies, could become important to the growth of an 'international civil society' (1991, p. 11). International civil society institutions will be needed to respond to the increasingly internationalized institutions of governance, finance and production.

Not all Northern NGOs have embraced these new roles, nor are they moving at the same pace. Many, including the largest US-based NGOs, continue to fund and administer many of their development and relief programs directly, and are likely to do so in the foreseeable future. But while the new division of labor is not pervasive, the model Padrón advances describes new roles being taken on by a growing number of NGOs.

2. Shared Values, Shared Interests

NGOs may be distinguished from government and commerce by the energy that motivates them, or alternatively, the way they mobilize social energy. The distinctive feature of NGOs, for activist-researchers David Brown and David Korten (1989), is their reliance on shared values as the primary source of 'social energy' that mobilizes action. States and firms, whose distinctive sources of energy are coercion and markets, have advantages in carrying out some kinds of tasks. But shared values and voluntarism contribute to NGOs' ability to promote 'social diversity' and 'democratic pluralism' and to experiment and behave flexibly. NGOs are, in Nerfin's words, 'neither prince nor merchant [but] citizen.'

Brown and Korten place a premium on NGOs' political roles in society. In a paper written for the World Bank, they argue that donor agencies too often see NGOs solely through an economic lens, as providers of certain public goods, correctives in case of market failure, or means of consumer control and efficiency. The more important roles in civil society – as watchdog on the state, training ground for democratic governance, models of accountability and proving ground for new ideas and approaches – are too seldom appreciated. That these capacities may be idealized in NGOs has been noted above. The potential political roles for NGOs is seen here as an important contrast to the vision of NGOs as service deliverers.

The 'shared values' perspective, however, under-emphasizes NGOs' identification with interest groups. Ties to women's associations, peasant movements, trade unions or cooperatives make some NGOs not only values-based partisans of an alternative development, but representatives of concrete interests, and sometimes agendas, of marginalized groups. This distinguishes NGO engagement with the World Bank from, for example, some advocacy on human rights or on biodiversity by values-based NGOs. (See Sikkink, 1993 for a discussion of campaigns by values-based 'issue networks.')

The importance of these values- or interest-based representative roles underlines the political importance of how and when donors enlist NGOs in project cooperation. When donors do involve NGOs, the civil roles should also affect how the NGOs' performance and the success of the collaboration is assessed. If NGOs are not simply contractors for donors' projects, then their services should be engaged and evaluated not on usual contract terms (deadlines, quantitative benchmarks, etc.) but in ways that emphasize the 'distinctive competence' they offer.

In particular, donors should ask: Will the arrangement help the NGO uphold voluntarism and its mission and values? Does the arrangement promote 'balanced pluralism and mutual influence' in society (Brown and Korten, 1989, p. 23)? By ignoring this distinctive competence and treating NGOs as contractors, donors lose an essential asset that some NGOs offer in project cooperation. This selective and non-political appreciation and use of NGOs – with potentially profound implications for NGOs' roles in civil society – is a characteristic of World Bank-NGO interaction. Its practice at the Bank is discussed in Chapters 5 and 6.

The emphasis on values suggests a division between NGOs whose work builds on shared values (development catalyst NGOs) and those that operate simply as non-profit service providers. This distinction does not imply that only development catalyst NGOs perform important functions. But the distinction does provide a useful perspective on the World Bank's record: is the Bank simply employing the services of cheap, efficient service deliverers, or opening projects to the input of groups with a claim to speak for affected people?

3. Visions of the Task: Generations and Environments

Korten's (1987) discussion of three 'generations' of NGOs defines three different understandings of the kind of service development NGOs have provided. The three 'generations', relief and welfare, small-scale self-reliant local development, and sustainable systems development, have emerged more or less chronologically. The generations do not necessarily replace each other, and the early generations are not expected to die out. Indeed, some NGOs represent all three generations in different activities.

The first NGO generation delivers services and goods to meet poor people's acute needs, addressing symptoms, not causes of underdevelopment. A second generation of local level community-development style projects aims to build self-reliance and yield benefits that outlast the NGO's programs. Its effects are limited to villages, neighborhoods, or groups of beneficiaries.

A third generation of NGO action, Korten argues, grows out of awareness that local projects will always have restricted impact, and that even these initiatives will endure 'only to the extent that local public and private organizations are linked together into a supportive national development system (p. 149).' The third generation strategy addresses policy and institutional issues at local, sectoral, or national levels. The emphasis for an NGO shifts from delivering services to catalytic roles, promoting learning and change in the sectors in which it works and often engaging in critique of and cooperation with government and international agencies.

Working strategically to change larger institutions by demonstration effect, active cooperation, advocacy or other methods, requires different skills from relief and development projects. Along with new kinds of technical and strategic competence, third-generation work requires patience and a long-term commitment to address systemic issues for years or decades in order to bring about change.

A NGO practitioner in Zimbabwe, Martin DeGraaf (1987) refocuses the issue on how well NGOs recognize and help beneficiaries address the social, cultural, economic and political environment in which they live. Organizations vary in the extent of their cognizance of and interaction with such environments; NGOs have often treated issues such as land distribution, war, and government corruption as 'environmental' issues no more subject to their influence than is the weather. The more an NGO interacts with these environments, the more likely it is to come into contact with state and other institutions, and assume third generation roles as catalyst or advocate for change. NGOs may aim to appreciate the impact of the environment, influence it, or (rarely) control an element of the environment.

4. Blueprint, Broker and Process

Sociologist David Gow's (1979) tripartite division, applicable mainly to intermediate-level groups, is based on NGOs' styles in assisting community-based groups. For Gow, NGOs approach their supportive role in one of three styles: blueprint, broker, or process. The blueprint, adaptable to local conditions, offers an outline of technical or social changes – an irrigation system, latrines, etc. – that the NGO facilitates.

The broker NGO serves as intermediary between a community and regional or national government or an aid donor. It helps the community develop plans or strategies to secure services or resources the community wants. The broker NGO is less service provider, more catalyst, although the plan for change in the community may still originate largely with the NGO.

A process style focuses initially not on providing services or brokering relationships, but on facilitating a community's agreeing to goals and objectives, and to strategies for achieving them. As the label implies, a process-oriented NGO values the growth of community institutions and democratic action in planning as highly as the material results of any project. A process-oriented NGO is likely to develop partnerships with local groups and to devote long periods of time to working in a community. Gow recognizes a fourth category, process-broker, acknowledging that the process approach often leads the NGO to support strategies the community develops to press for policy changes or improved government services.

5. Functional Roles

World Bank staffers Larry Salmen's and Paige Eaves' (1989) study places NGOs on two continua representing their 'function... in development work. They categorize NGOs by whether they serve public (common good) versus private (market-oriented) purposes;' and by 'the degree to which the NGO is directed towards the interests of its own membership versus oriented to a constituency beyond itself' (p. 17). A second continuum, from self-interest to service-to-others, produces a two-dimensional field in which, for example, cooperatives are private good/self-interest institutions; while an international relief and development NGO would likely be a public good/service to others institution.

The schema puts aside the usual World Bank classification by sector, irrelevant to many NGOs. The two-dimensional field sometimes conveys more insight about an organization than does a single set of categories. But Salmen and Eaves obscure the political dimension of NGOs' importance in civil society. Political and economic roles are reduced to the economic by reducing all five roles to kinds of economic goods, public or private. This may obscure an NGO's representative role by perceiving its action on behalf of a group's interest to be simply pursuit of a private or public good.

Their schema does not consider the extent of an NGO's connection to local groups or its accountability to those it purports to serve (except in categorizing advocacy NGOs). Salmen's and Eaves' approach is more useful for categorizing the roles of NGOs in particular projects than as a theoretical basis for categorizing NGOs more broadly.

NGOS, CIVIL SOCIETY AND DEMOCRATIZATION

One of the most important claims widely made for NGOs is their capacity to function within a civil society as institutions of democratization or pluralism. Considering the importance of the claim, it is somewhat surprising that it is made so widely with such imprecision. Neither the concept of civil society nor the actual performance of NGOs within civil societies is clearly delineated or tested in much of the discussion of NGOs. Only recently has the claim of NGO enthusiasts begun to attract more systematic attention.

Attention has been drawn to the concept of civil society itself by the economic and political conditions that have beset many states and societies in the 1980s, and a confluence of ideological perspectives on them. In Latin America, civil institutions' role in organizing and energizing the emergence from authoritarian rule has drawn attention from those interested in democratization. The great diversity of NGOs' own political programs makes it possible to see them either as agents of gradual political change, or even of forestalling major structural changes; or as vehicles for seeking 'transformations in the relation of social forces favoring the poor majority' (Macdonald, 1992, p. 16).

In Africa, where administrative collapse and the rigors of internationally-imposed austerity and reform programs have exposed the weakness of many national governments, the importance of networks of non-state institutions has again surfaced. NGOs, as institutional centers within the (re)-emerging civil society, have been treated as 'democratizing development' (Clark, 1991), or, perhaps more accurately, as promoting pluralism in evolving political and social systems (Bebbington and Farrington, 1993; Fowler, 1991).

In both regions, as in some of east and southeast Asia, organized groups of the poor and NGOs have been called on to take another role: cushioning the social shock of economic adjustment programs by delivering services and promoting and supporting coping mechanisms. What the India-based Society for Participatory Research in Asia (PRIA) calls the 'seduction of NGOs' has been observed globally (Steifel and Wolfe, 1994). Stiefel and Wolfe summarize their study of participation in development institutions with a sobering assessment: organized initiatives in the context of adjustment and of other state-sponsored initiatives sometimes secure influence for excluded groups on policies that affect their livelihood, but 'for the most part organized efforts by peasants represent self-defence against development more than participation in development.'

Given NGOs' diversity and the political and economic challenges to which they must respond, what contribution can they be said to offer to poor people's effective influence in their societies? Bebbington and Farrington, skeptical of some general claims on behalf of NGOs, review the record and conclude that NGOs do bring a capacity for methodological innovation; varieties of institutional organization; a superior capacity for implementation of development activities; and a general discontent, variously articulated, with existing distribution of resources and power (1993, pp. 206–7).

Rajesh Tandon (1991) of PRIA outlines the potential NGO roles in strengthening civil society's 'material, institutional and ideological bases.' NGOs could ('and sometimes do') support local communities' claims to land and other resources; encourage and inform an 'active citizenry;' build the capacity to critique 'the existing development paradigm' and construct alternatives; facilitate citizen participation in public policy issues; and, in a variety of ways, 'challeng[e] the continuous attempts to control the minds of people ...' (p. 11).

How effectively these assets and strategies are in fact deployed to strengthen civil societies depends in good part on how NGOs assess and manage their relations to government agencies and donors. NGOs have also been widely recruited to distribute social services and manage local self-help programs in the context of economic adjustment. Stiefel and Wolfe predict that this trend will continue, and optimistically foresee that both states and NGOs will 'win' in the process. NGOs will gain access to resources for expanded programs; the State will be increasingly challenged by NGO performance and critique to improve its own administration, and in the process will regain some of its authority and legitimacy at the grassroots (pp. 210–11).

Bebbington and Farrington wisely strike a more cautious note. They find within the NGO relation to government and donor a fundamental contradiction: NGOs want expanded influence, and need contact with official institutions to gain it. But the contact or engagement is being offered largely on unattractive terms: implementing government schemes without guarantees of influence, underwriting economic reform policies about which the NGOs have reservations. The task for NGOs is to find the 'room for manoeuvre' in this impasse (p. 215), space which is available but may be surrendered grudgingly.

The search and struggle for this room to manoeuvre is, at best, the story of NGO relations with official agencies. It is also an important portion of the story of NGO engagement with the World Bank. Good judgment and 'a high degree of political insight,' as Stiefel and Wolfe note, will be required of NGOs to ensure that they define their political and public service roles in ways that open up a greater range of choices to the 'excluded' people they aim to serve. The following section outlines some distinctions among NGOs and their organizational and operating approaches to donor agencies that are relevant to understanding their engagement with the World Bank.

NGOs AND AID DONORS

The 1970s and 1980s saw a rapid increase in NGO involvement in official donors' projects. (For a history of donor-NGO relations, see OECD, 1988.) Such engagement presents somewhat different issues for Southern NGOs than it does for international NGOs, some of which (CARE, Catholic Relief Services (CRS), Cooperative League of the USA (CLUSA), National Rural Electrification Association (NRECA), Organization for Rehabilitation through Training (ORT), for example) make project cooperation with official donors a major part of their programs. But for all NGOs, some common issues emerge in maintaining a distinct identity as NGO when cooperating with state or official donors.

Studies of NGOs in development, whether commissioned by major donors (Esman and Uphoff, 1984; USAID, 1986; Brown and Korten, 1989; Salmen and Eaves, 1989) or done by NGO participants, raise issues that confront NGOs in collaborating with government or donor programs. NGOs contemplating cooperative work with the World Bank face an organization with vast staff and financial resources, close relations with governments, a rigid project cycle and calendar, and expectations about the scale of activities to be financed. Most issues are matters of size, independence, accountability, organizational and management style, and strategy as a development promoter. These factors are discussed in turn.

The Question of Scale

The small scale of most NGO projects is an important part of the NGO ethos. Some donors such as USAID, the Canadian International Development Agency (CIDA), the US Inter-American Foundation (IAF) and African Development Foundation (ADF), and the International Fund for Agricultural Development (IFAD) have accommodated the size difference by establishing special windows or offices to fund small-scale

NGO or community development initiatives. But small-scale projects are not a part of other donors' repertoire. IBRD and IDA loans averaged $99.1 million in 1990 (World Bank, *Annual Report*, 1991). The World Bank, like most donors, presumes that if NGOs are to be involved in its projects, they must be able to 'scale up' or handle project activities in more than a local setting (Strategic Planning and Review, 1989, p. 19; see also Donnelly-Roark, 1991).

There is not unanimity about the relation between the size and effectiveness of NGO projects. Tendler (1982) argues for small-scale, more or less single-focus NGO activities, while Esman and Uphoff (1984) suggest that larger-scale integrated NGO activities can be equally effective. Esman's and Uphoff's review of size as a factor in local group's effectiveness produces mixed results. They stress that none of the largest groups reviewed fall into the ranks of least effective on their scale of performance. But without a history of each group, one cannot assume that larger groups fail less often. It is just as likely that only successful groups of any size survive long enough to become large enough and diversified by Esman's and Uphoff's standards.

Whatever the empirical relation, it is widely believed among NGOs that the rapid expansion often required by international donor projects is a threat to the NGO. Brown and Korten (1989, p. 18–19) offer three ways to scale up NGO programs that avoid simply enlarging the populations or geographic areas served. Size and impact can be increased by emphasizing the demonstration effect of NGO projects and promoting adoption of project methods by government; by intensive networking among voluntary and peoples' organizations and by promoting national policies that further enable self-help action. The authors in a collection edited by Edwards and Hulme (1992) outline similar alternatives, and document several NGO efforts. But these constructive suggestions do not change the fact that donor projects often call for capacity to implement a project or component on a scale larger than that of most NGO projects.

Accountability to Whom?

Challenges to NGOs' identity and accountability are often (but not necessarily) related to issues of scale. Most major donor projects involving NGOs enlist them to do community organizing or service delivery as part of an effort to extend benefits into poor or remote rural areas, or into urban or periurban areas where a government has little presence or credibility. But participating in a large-scale donor project can lead to a shift in an NGO's emphasis from community-based to donor-initiated activities, or reinforce that organizational style in an NGO already operating as broker.

NGOs in Guatemala, for example, were offered funding in the late 1980s by USAID for land purchases as part of a market-based land distribution scheme for landless and land-poor peasants. One NGO, Fundación del Centavo (FDC), developed a large land-purchase program, funded almost entirely by USAID, that came to dominate FDC's programming. Already a large-scale, blueprint-oriented NGO, FDC has not been changed fundamentally by the arrangement.

But other Guatemalan NGOs expressed concern about the potential for unwanted transformation of their programs and priorities, and sought assurances that their participation in land-purchase schemes could be on their terms, and in response to initiatives in communities where they work (author's interviews, 1988). In the end, FDC remained the lone Guatemalan NGO carrying out USAID-funded land purchases.

Along with questions of organizational identity come a cluster of issues relating to the degree of independence, accountability and 'privateness.' The challenge to NGO 'independence' is discussed by NGO activists such as Peggy Antrobus (1987, p. 99), and Hendrik van der Heijden (1987, pp. 107, 110). Ernesto Garilao emphasizes the danger of not developing independent financial bases (1987, p. 118). Esman's and Uphoff's (1984, pp. 163-5, 179-82) review concludes that locally-initiated activities are more effective than government- or outside-initiated programs, suggesting that the 'independence' issue has impact even in the most program-oriented evaluation. The International Council of Voluntary Agencies' (ICVA) 1985 guidelines for accepting government funding place the challenge of 'independence' at the top of its list of concerns.

But the issue of 'independence' is better thought of as one of shifting NGO accountability. If NGOs are viewed not as autonomous charitable organizations but as linked and responsive to local people's organizations, then diminished accountability to local partners weakens the NGO's very core. For international NGOs, whose links to local groups in the Third World are inherently difficult, forming close program associations with national and international donors can create tensions between donors' demands and those of Southern partner groups (Dichter, 1988, p. 185). Where competing demands come from the NGO's principal funding source and from the grassroots base it seeks to serve, the links to the community may become, as Brett puts it, 'attenuated' (Brett, 1993, p. 293).

Larry Minear (1987) outlines the extent of government funding for programs of large US-based NGOs (CARE, Catholic Relief Services), and warns that 'P' in PVO could soon be taken to mean not 'private' but 'public' or 'parastatal.' NGOs' responsiveness to increasingly frequent cooperative initiatives by major donors may threaten NGOs' reliance on local input in identifying projects, and compromise their ability to speak openly about problems in development assistance or foreign policy (Hellinger, 1987, p. 137). Even when donors do not intend to manipulate NGOs' agendas or programs, planning and reporting requirements and the scale of donor programs compel a small NGO's operations to become centered around bureaucratic and official procedures, rather than the dynamics of grassroots initiative and critique (LeComte, 1986; Edwards and Hulme, 1992; Bebbington and Farrington, 1993, pp. 207–8).

Alan Fowler's review of NGO-government relations in Eastern and Southern Africa urges donors in the region to take special pains to avoid 'steering' local initiatives by the presence of their project funding. Donor funds, which tend to steer NGOs toward modernization-style development also make organizations vulnerable to governments' withdrawal of permission for the funding, decrease the diversity of NGOs and increase the prevalence of NGOs substituting for government services, rather than providing a distinctive presence in society (p. 70–2).

Risks and Benefits: Choosing to Deal with Donors

These concerns about accountability, independence and organizational style should not be taken to imply a romantic view that NGOs represent and emanate from 'the people' and are subject to corruption by state and donor. A more realistic perspective acknowledges that NGOs already balance the interests of several constituencies (private donors, governments, official donors, partner organizations and intended beneficiaries). From this perspective, an NGO's relation to donors (or, for local NGOs and social movements, their relation to international NGOs), is a critical factor in the NGO's role and orientation in civil society (see Macdonald, 1992). Cooperation with donors does carry risks; but the risk is not an all-or-nothing loss of independence. Rather it is a reordering and distorting of existing relationships and accountabilities.

The potential costs of engagement with the World Bank are balanced, for some, by the opportunity for influence on behalf of populations whose interests they wish to serve. Studies of NGO influence on national and international policy environments have focused primarily on national government policies. BRAC's (1986) efforts to 'unravel webs of corruption' in Bangladesh and Bratton's (1989) exploration of the policy influence of three NGOs in Eastern and Southern Africa show the potential and limits of NGO influence on national government bodies and their policies and programs.

NGO policy engagement with the World Bank sometimes represents a strategic decision to take advocacy outside of national borders. International actors such as the Bank may be more susceptible to criticism on environmental or human rights issues than are some governments, or such actors may be seen as external influences to be swayed or neutralized in struggles over national policy (Rich, 1985; Hellinger, 1987).

Political scientist Jim Riker (1993) shows how Indonesian NGOs used this outward looking strategy as part of a carefully conceived strategy to increase their political space and influence national development priorities. Faced with an authoritarian state that limited political activity, NGOs used discourse on the acceptable area of environmentally sustainable development as a foothold from which to build a critique of state development policy generally. Coalitions with international NGOs and annual meetings of the International NGO Forum on Indonesia (INGI) beginning in 1985, became an integral part of that strategy. The international meetings, which rankled the government, none the less provided both legitimacy and another source of leverage for a campaign to influence politics and economics, social and natural resource policy in Indonesia.

NGO VOICES AND THE WORLD BANK

The greatest part of this study focuses on the World Bank, with little attention to details of NGO activities themselves. This section provides a skeleton outline of NGOs' various approaches to the Bank. Some NGOs have launched concerted campaigns to force policy changes, but the great majority have no dealings with the Bank. Many of the NGOs involved in project collaboration adopt strategies that lie between these two. They accept opportunities to collaborate, seeing participation as a valuable source of funds and as an opportunity for expanded program impact. A few cultivate collaboration deliberately to demonstrate and disseminate methods they have found effective.

NGOs that enter into sustained contact with the World Bank, through project-related interaction or advocacy on some policy issue, are a minority of the vast number of NGOs involved in development. In most parts of Africa, Asia, Latin America and the Caribbean, they are primarily local organizations that make contact with the Bank either because they are recruited to play a role in a project – as is the case with water users' associations as implementers and maintainers of tertiary irrigation schemes – or they actively object to some environmental or economic impact of a policy supported by the Bank. The project-level contact is discussed in Chapter 4. This section profiles some of the policy-level NGO efforts.

For NGOs based in North and South alike, engaging the Bank on policy matters requires an ongoing commitment, including staffing and other resources. For environmental organizations based in the North, and a handful of research or advocacy NGOs with human rights, trade or other development agendas, the strategic choice to address World Bank policy follows from a larger mandate. For Southern NGOs, contact sometimes flows from commitment to work on a policy area. Many of the organizations of the Philippine Freedom from Debt Coalition, for example, see the World Bank and IMF as principal agents behind Philippine government policies toward debt servicing, investment and trade.

The Coalition's 'Unity Statement' of June 1994 attacks government policies such as the Value Added Tax, budgetary priority to debt servicing and funding cuts in national environmental protection programs. But it focuses on the IMF and World Bank, charging that they have exceeded their original authorities. The statement proposes a number of specific steps to render ineffective conditions attached to several loans, and demands greater transparency from the Bank and IMF, reduced debt service obligations on debt owed to them, and that institutional alternatives to them be explored (Freedom from Debt Coalition, 1994).

Organizations and movements of India's vast 'NGO sector' include caste- and class-based organizations, local and national associations concerned with displacement and impoverishment of people resettled during large-scale infrastructure projects; and associations committed to self-reliant, environmentally sustainable development policies. Their engagement with the Bank has ranged from one-time cooperation in implementing a sericulture project, to multi-year organizing to prevent or redress the loss of farmland due to major Bank-financed dam projects. The government's assent to an IMF- and World Bank-supported adjustment program in 1992 has inspired a new surge of anti-Bank and

-IMF sentiment, reminiscent of anti-colonial struggles in the 1940s both in spirit and in language ('World Bank: Quit India!').

'Development' vs 'Environment': Agendas, Constituencies, Styles

Among NGOs based in the industrial countries, the division between 'development' and 'environment' NGOs remains relevant. Despite some successful coalition efforts, the gap between poverty-focused and conservation-focused constituencies, agendas and agencies has not been fully bridged. Their patterns of involvement with the World Bank reflect this disjuncture.

Deliberate project collaboration

Development NGOs have addressed the Bank in a variety of ways, systematic and episodic. The Aga Khan Foundation (AKF), which first invited the World Bank to evaluate its Rural Support Programme in Pakistan in 1986, has continued discussions with the Bank that included a second evaluation. The Bank published its favorable review, and AKF General Manager Robert Shaw believes that the cooperative professional relationships that have developed have 'had a certain influence on the ways in which the Bank does business' (personal letter, 14 May 1990). The contact has also led to further discussions of the participatory approaches used in AKF-sponsored projects, and possibly to further collaborative work in health, education, and agriculture in Pakistan and India. Shaw remains critical of some World Bank programming, but finds many staff now 'willing to learn and to consider the lessons of alternative experiences' (letter, 1990).

The Development Group for Alternative Policies (Development GAP), a Washington-based NGO primarily involved in advocacy on international economic and trade policy, worked with World Bank urban development staff in the early 1980s in an effort to demonstrate the feasibility and effectiveness of working through popularly based NGOs such as federations of credit unions. Managing director Doug Hellinger found Urban Sector staff willing to consider institutional arrangements that facilitated more effective project operation. But he expresses frustration at the apparent lack of integration of the lessons learned into regular urban project programming (interview, 1989). US-based CARE has been involved in reforestation projects that have influenced World Bank-financed projects in Asia and Africa.

Monitoring and country dialogue

NGOs in the northwestern Brazilian state of Rondônia are currently engaged in an exercise of critical collaboration, the World Bank-financed Planofloro project. Planofloro is the successor to the notorious and highly controversial Polonoroeste project, and locally based trade unions, producers' organizations and other associations, together with several regional and national NGOs, are meeting regularly with Bank and government officials and consulting closely in the design, implementation and (it is expected) adjustment and partial redesign of the project. With support from international NGOs, particularly Oxfam UK/Ireland, the Rondônia NGOs are offering both criticism and field collaboration in a project whose initial participatory design gave rise to high hopes. Although highly critical of some national agencies' performance, the NGOs remain engaged in unusually close and frequent exchanges with Bank supervision teams (Patricia Feeney (Oxfam UK/Ireland), 1994).

The Rondônia effort is one of several monitoring efforts, recent or ongoing, of Bank-financed projects by development NGOs. Perhaps inspired by the environmental NGOs' effective project-specific critique, development NGOs have established efforts to monitor specific projects or promote focused national dialogue with the Bank through the NGO Working Group on the World Bank (Sri Lanka, Senegal, Mexico), a steering group following up the Bank's World Hunger Conference (Mali, Nicaragua, Philippines), and under the aegis of the Institute for Development Research (Mexico and India) and through Oxfam UK/Ireland (Bangladesh, Brazil).

Ongoing policy dialogues

Other Northern NGOs have more ongoing discussions with Bank staff, donor governments and their representatives to the World Bank. Several US-based overseas aid agencies have staff or offices that focus on policy advocacy, and whose agendas have included reform or critique of World Bank policy. CARE, World Vision International, Church World Service and Lutheran World Relief are among them. Other advocacy-focused agencies such as Bread for the World, the Friends Committee on National Legislation and RESULTS have also put the World Bank on the agendas of their staffs and membership networks.

In Europe, a variety of agencies and networks have engaged the Bank in advocacy, including Oxfam in the UK and Belgium, Christian Aid, NOVIB, the Coalition of Swiss Development Organizations and the Bern Declaration, and Protestant and Catholic coalitions APRODEV and CIDSE.

Recently, solidarity organizations such as the US-Nicaragua Friendship Network, Religious Task Force on Central America, and Witness for Peace have encouraged their citizen memberships, long involved in advocacy for peace in Central America, to focus on the World Bank and IMF roles in the region. Their apparent success may signal the entry of an important new voice in the debate in the United States.

Environmentalist strategies

Environment-focused organizations, however, have been much more systematic and arguably more successful in their efforts. In 1983 environmental advocacy organizations in the US began to coordinate and expand scattered efforts to highlight environmental effects of World Bank-financed projects through direct lobbying of the Bank, lobbying and hearings in the US Congress, and public education and media campaigns. The campaign, outlined by Bruce Rich (1985) and Rich and Pat Aufderheide (1989), has focused on projects with dramatic environmental impacts and capitalized on the extensive constituency in the US and Europe for environmental conservation issues. Much of the activity has been carried out by the Audobon Society, Environmental Defense Fund, Friends of the Earth, International Rivers Network, Natural Resources Defense Council, and the National Wildlife Federation, involving national affiliates in countries such as the Philippines, Brazil, and Ghana, and independent organizations with whom the US-based groups have formed partnerships.

Their efforts have helped bring the international dimensions of global environmental issues to public attention in the US, and have introduced, however imperfectly, new considerations into the World Bank's rhetoric, organizational structure and loan portfolio. Focusing variously on Bank water policy, energy policy, forestry and infrastructure projects in countries including Brazil, Ecuador, India, the Philippines, Indonesia, Nepal, Zaire, Rwanda and Argentina, environmental NGOs have published popular critiques, produced documentaries, lobbied legislatures and Executive Directors, raised legal challenges and worked with Bank staff in an effort to devise and institutionalize policy changes.

Some development NGOs say they have learned from environmentalists' tactics (Stokes, 1988). Some environmental NGOs' efforts are cited in the chapters that follow, but the review of projects and of dialogue focuses primarily on the efforts of 'development NGOs.'

WORLD BANK-NGO DIALOGUE

Most of the efforts of development and environment NGOs are ongoing, focused on project-, country- or sector-specific issues. Internationally, the most visible episodes of the Bank-NGO dialogue are global gatherings of various kinds. Some of these have become focal points for Bank-NGO interaction, with issues that have surfaced in ongoing country or sectoral discussions gaining international exposure. In all of the fora for interaction the Bank has heard criticism and protest of its economic and environmental policies and programs presented with varying degrees of civility and collegiality.

The NGO-World Bank Committee

The NGO-World Bank Committee, established in 1984, brings representatives of 26 NGOs and several Bank staff together for semi-annual discussions. Agenda items have ranged from proposals for a World Bank fund for NGO projects, policy on disclosure of information to non-government groups, adjustment policies, and participatory development strategies. The NGO members rely increasingly on case studies on participation and adjustment as bases for discussions with Bank country and regional staff. Although sharp criticism is often raised, the discussions are collegial in tone and setting, and meetings are largely funded by the World Bank.

The evolution of discussions in the NGO-World Bank Committee reflects the structural limitations and some of the progress in the dialogue. Three features that limit dialogue in the committee may be in part results of deliberate action by participants, but are largely functions of the diverse nature of NGOs and of the World Bank's structure and culture.

1. *NGO diversity versus World Bank unity*: NGOs on the committee come from five continents and bring to the discussions a variety of agendas and priorities. World Bank representatives appreciate and encourage this diversity. Committee co-chair Alexander Shakow encouraged NGO members not to seek consensus or a unified position in the 1989 committee discussions, stressing that the Bank valued their varied positions.

The Bank's participants, however, come to the meetings with a clear, unified agenda: promote operational collaboration with NGOs, advance the participation learning process and minimize damage from public criticism. The Terms of Reference for representatives to the committee, as well as many informal documents and discussions single out operational collaboration as the Bank's primary interest in the discussions (Terms of Reference, 1981; SPRIE Progress Reports various years). A set of hastily typed memos circulated among the Bank delegation prior to the 1989 discussions orchestrated the response to NGO criticism, assigning themes and counter-points to the various participants.

Diversity inherently undercuts the strength of the NGO voice. When some NGOs are silent on subjects such as adjustment and information policy, World Bank representatives are able to report that agitation on these subjects is led by a vocal, policy-oriented minority. The NGOs' persistence in raising policy issues, however, has drawn criticism from Bank participants. Such 'stratospheric' issues, argues the Bank's current co-chair, are not the kind of input the Bank is now seeking from NGOs. What the Bank needs, he asserts, is a focused, pragmatic dialogue on operational issues including popular participation and implementation of the information dissemination policy. NGO members need to facilitate NGOs' operational engagement with the Bank.

2. *Ambiguity in the roles and constituencies of both parties give the dialogue an uncertain footing.* The NGO members have restructured their number over time to assure that two-thirds are from countries of the South. In so doing they strengthen their implicit claim to speak for popular organizations and for people affected by government and World Bank-supported development plans, as well as from their own experience. But as in the wider World Bank-NGO interchange, their legitimacy as a voice for 'the poor' is far from conclusive. The fact that new members are elected by already seated members further weakens the claim to speak for NGOs as a whole, but NGO members' attempts in 1989 to design a more representative form of selection did not succeed.

World Bank participants represent their institution to NGOs, as well as promoting NGO collaboration within the Bank. They frequently articulate this stance, asking for NGO members' patience and understanding, portraying themselves as allies and pleading their limited powers to effect change. They speak sometimes as the official voice of the agency and at other times as beleaguered internal sympathizers.

Recent Committee meetings have seen an improved, more focused agenda and greater exchange with staff from the World Bank's operational offices. The 1992 meetings in Washington, for example, saw discussions of adjustment in Mexico with the Director of the Latin America and Caribbean office; of Indonesian government policy toward

NGOs with the country officer for that country; and of the Sardar Sarovar project with the Country Director for India.

Committee members initiated a national India World Bank-NGO Consultation Committee, with representatives of 23 Indian NGOs and several staff of the World Bank's India Country Department, which met three times a year from late 1988 into 1992. The Indian Committee agreed to consultations between each Bank appraisal mission and 'grassroots NGOs,' and to meetings between World Bank specialists on mission from headquarters and 'NGO representatives concerned with that specialist' (World Bank-NGO Consultation Committee (India) – A Short Report – 1990). Staffing changes in the Bank's resident mission have left the operation of the committee on uncertain footing.

The NGO-World Bank Committee has also sponsored various national and sectoral meetings, bringing together World Bank, government and NGO representatives to discuss sectoral or regional issues. These have included a Regional Workshop on Cooperation for Education and Training in Eastern and Southern Africa (May 1986), a Southern Cone of South America Meeting (December 1989), Urban Sector Meetings in 1981, and national meetings in Honduras (1991) and Indonesia (1989).

Once the Bank's principal site for talks with NGOs, after a decade of NGO-World Bank contacts the Committee is no longer the almost exclusive forum it once was. Both the Bank and some NGOs have become critical of the forum and its NGO participants. Some participants from the Bank now say they need less dialogue on policy issues, more concrete work at facilitating collaboration with NGOs and adoption of participatory methods within the Bank (James Adams, NGO-World Bank Committee Meeting, Geneva, May 1994). The Bank's recent NGO Strategy Paper stresses similar priorities, in at least some of its 11 drafts (Draft 9, pp. 14, 20). Some NGOs, especially in the United States, are critical of the Committee for its failure to support more radical reform proposals and its weak and unsystematic accountability to the larger NGO community.

The NGO participants took a step toward improving this accountability by scheduling a round of regional consultations in Africa, Asia and Latin America and the Caribbean for 1995. Like other NGO networks, the Working Group has noted that neither single-country dialogue with the Bank nor networks built solely on a North-South axis are fully effective. The Working Group is now striving to strengthen continental and subcontinent-wide networks. Another, more advanced initiative in Latin America and the Caribbean has created a regional network with similar goals, with the Instituto del Tercer Mundo in

Uruguay and the US-based Bank Information Center providing staffing and coordination (Kay Treakle, 1994).

Other Settings for NGO-World Bank Dialogue

The Bank recently succeeded in assembling the kind of North American NGO forum, focused on operational collaboration, that its NGO liaison group now emphasizes. A July 1994 'Interaction with NGOs on the Bank's Project Cycle' was initiated by the Bank's Operations Department and planned in cooperation with several Washington-based NGO representatives. In two days' discussions, participants from North American-based NGOs and the Bank's operational offices probed the operational difficulties for NGOs who wish to participate in Bank-financed operations: procurement regulations, delays in advancing currency, resistance from government functionaries, contracting arrangements and the like.

The Bank's Operations Director, James Adams, expressed uncharacteristic enthusiasm for the meetings, saying that the Bank had finally found the kind of dialogue it was looking for with NGOs on operational issues. Similar meetings are being planned for at least two sites in Africa and Asia.

NGO gatherings coinciding with recent World Bank/IMF Annual Meetings have been another, generally more acrimonious, site for Bank-NGO exchanges. At the meetings in Berlin (1988), in Washington, DC (1989, 1990 and 1992), and in Bangkok (1991), NGOs assembled for parallel conferences, public protests of World Bank and IMF policies, and for meetings and discussions with Bank staff and executive directors.

The Berlin meetings were marked by conflicts over the admission of NGO observers, as NGOs from India, the Sudan, Malaysia, Indonesia were rejected when their own governments refused to accept their accreditation (Wirth, letter to World Bank President Conable and IMF Managing Director Camdessus, 4 November 1988). The 1989 meetings saw a more open accreditation process, and featured the publication of 'A Critical Look at World Bank and IMF Policies' by NGO observers. NGOs also produced materials critical of the Bank at the 1990 meetings, including a daily newspaper *Bank Check* (now published as a periodical), which featured criticism of Bank policies and insider stories of dissension and dissatisfaction among staff.

Another NGO forum, focused on responses to World Bank and IMF structural adjustment lending, was held in Washington at the time of the 1992 Annual Meetings. NGOs from 45 countries met to compare experiences in dealing with Bank-supported adjustment programs. Strategy sessions produced coordinated programs of information sharing, national activities, and plans for internationally coordinated activities to coincide with the fiftieth anniversary of the Bretton Woods organizations in 1994.

The Madrid meetings themselves drew broad NGO participation in a People's Forum, policy debates, press conferences and other events. The meetings, which also featured demonstrations and acts of civil disobedience by some NGO representatives, provoked angry reactions from some Bank staff. Some threatened that the Bank would segregate NGOs into two groups – those the Bank can work with, and those against which it must simply defend itself.

The United Nations Conference on Environment and Development (UNCED) in 1992 is the best known of the venues where the Bank and NGOs have faced off. Sometimes touted as the international event at which NGOs sharply expanded their international roles and legitimacy (Kakabadse and Burns, 1994), UNCED featured an active, high-profile NGO presence that took on industrial country policies as well as World Bank and IMF lending.

NGOs and the Tenth Replenishment of IDA (IDA-10)

The triennial 'replenishments' of the World Bank's soft loan window are a regular occasion for action by donor governments, NGOs and others who hope to influence Bank policies. As donor governments negotiate the terms and amounts for a new replenishment, NGOs that hope to influence them stake out positions on IDA performance in various sectors or policy areas. Several groups of NGOs, with overlapping membership but only loose coordination, sought to influence the funding process in 1991–92. The three strands of work show the diversity of NGO voices, and some strengths and weaknesses of NGO advocacy with the World Bank.

A coordinated effort, by Washington-based environment and development groups, to develop a set of policy recommendations for IDA-10 and advocate them with US Treasury officials involved in World Bank policy, is one strand. Beginning late in 1991, some 10 NGO staff began to meet to develop a critical paper with concrete policy recommendations for IDA. Agreeing to defer funding questions and focus on a policy agenda, the group produced a paper calling for changes in information policy, poverty and structural adjustment lending, and energy and water sector policies, and secured signatures of more than 40 US agency representatives.

The paper, which took no position on US funding for IDA, received a mixed response in discussions with US Treasury representatives. Generally supportive of at least the spirit of the water and energy sector demands and some changes in information policy, Treasury was unenthusiastic about proposals for further anti-poverty measures and for limiting structural adjustment lending. The negotiations over IDA continued, with a US government position reflecting some of the sectoral policy concerns adapted from the NGO document. NGO participants in the effort monitored the negotiations and waited for a next stage of advocacy, when the US contribution to IDA-10 came before Congress for consideration.

But others were engaged in another, simultaneous effort: the critique of the World Bank's involvement in the notorious Sardar Sarovar dam project in the Narmada river basin of western India. Years of advocacy to reform the project or end its funding, capped by an unprecedented independent review authorized by the World Bank in 1991, prepared many NGOs to make World Bank performance in the project the basis for opposing funding, or calling for reduced allocations, to IDA-10.

NGO involvement in the project centered around treatment of people to be displaced by flooding and irrigation schemes in the river basin. (These issues are reviewed thoroughly in *Sardar Sarovar*, 1992.) The project, and the World Bank's determination to continue funding despite problems, objections, and finally the recommendations of the independent review, became emblematic to some NGOs of its failure to learn and to reform itself, and the failure of years of critique and reform to make a decisive impact. Working with Indian organizations, some US and other NGOs placed a full-page advertisement in *The Financial Times* to announce their conclusion that the Bank was beyond reform and their opposition to funding for IDA-10. US NGOs, including the Environmental Defense Fund, International Rivers Network and Bank Information Center, sought to mobilize support for their position among European NGOs, in hopes of securing a commitment to smaller contributions to IDA-10 and scuttling the World Bank's appeal for an additional $5 billion 'Earth Increment.'

The World Bank, some of whose staff objected to the critique embodied in the US NGO position paper, set in motion a third process of NGO consultation, even as the movement opposing IDA funding was developing. Stimulated by the US NGO critique, World Bank Managing Director Ernest Stern invited six Southern NGO representatives, including four members of the NGO-World Bank Committee, to discuss issues around the IDA replenishment with IDA's governing board (the IDA Deputies).

The six – including an outspoken Indian critic of the Sardar Sarovar project and of the World Bank – were flown to Washington in September 1992. After separate conversations with Bank staff and some Washington-based NGOs, met for several hours with the IDA Deputies on 16 September. The written record reflects a strong critique of Bank policies, couched in an acknowledgement that IDA funding is essential for many governments, and a call for replenishment at least continuing the previous three-year fund, in real terms.

The NGO Working Group on the World Bank followed the lead of the Southern NGO group at their October meetings. The Working Group members voiced their support for continued IDA funding in an open letter to Bank President Lewis Preston, and while they expressed their continued concerns about social, economic and environmental impacts of Bank lending, they reinforced the message of the meeting with IDA deputies on the 'bottom line.'

These episodes in the debate over IDA-10 offer some insights into the NGO voices that address the World Bank. First, the Bank worries and reacts when the NGO community, or a segment thereof, expresses views that threaten its funding. NGOs in the US are considered an important constituency for IDA in a political context where multilateral aid has found few strong supporters. The personal reactions of some World Bank staff and the unprecedented discussions with the IDA deputies demonstrate that the NGO constituency is important to the Bank.

That constituency is also highly varied in its views and priorities. Among Northern NGOs alone, there is an important divide between most environmental NGOs and most development and poverty-focused organizations. Many US development NGOs articulate at least a general critique of World Bank lending and structural adjustment policies. But almost all have none the less supported IDA funding, leaving them, some argue, without serious leverage in trying to shift World Bank performance. Even where the flaws in IDA lending are believed to be serious and the development model destructive, most organizations have not seen fit to urge reduced funding.

The diversity of approaches is partly a function of the nature of US NGOs' associations with Southern NGOs. Environmental NGOs have developed partnerships with organizations threatened by or opposed to particular World Bank-supported projects. Other organizations in IDA borrowing countries, including some development NGOs, church bodies, and research or training institutes, see IDA funding through a different lens. Even some of those who oppose the development strategies the Bank promotes in their countries see reduced IDA concessional funding as disastrous, and their views influence the positions and perhaps reinforce the predispositions of many US NGOs.

US-based NGOs involved in policy advocacy increasingly cite their relations with Southern counterparts as a major source of their authority and credibility. This relationship has come into play in the IDA-10 debate, and some in the World Bank clearly understand that the relationship underlies the Northern groups' advocacy credibility. The Bank's inivitation to the NGO representatives to meet with the IDA deputies was made knowing that, while the deputies were likely to hear a stinging critique of some IDA policies, they would also hear expressions of support for continued funding from Southern NGOs. And such an endorsement from prominent Southern NGO leaders could be a highly effective counterbalance to Northern criticism or opposition.

The 'Problem' of Washington-based NGOs

By the fact of location, Washington-based NGOs have a privileged access to staff and management of the World Bank. Their access to the US Congress makes them doubly worrisome to the Bank, which has never found it easy to win full US funding for its IDA replenishments. (On NGO lobbying of the Congress see Rich, 1994). Because the Washington-based NGOs, especially environmental groups, have also pressed the critique of the Bank the farthest, the Bank and some of its defenders have questioned their standing and challenged their legitimacy in speaking for NGOs more broadly.

There are at least three dimensions to the 'problem' of US-based NGOs: they are said to be un-representative; they drown out more 'legitimate' NGO voices and in so doing alienate borrowing governments of the Bank; and they are too closely tied to the US government in pressing their demands.

The issue of representativeness is the most serious, and is increasingly remarked in a variety of policy circles (Kakabadse and Burns, 1994; Stiefel and Wolfe, 1994; Berg and Sherk, 1994). The Bank's representatives often distinguish between, for example, making information about a Bank investment available to Southern NGOs and to Washington-based NGOs who, they argue, have no particular 'right to know.' It is true that while NGO advocacy agendas are often developed in an effort to represent the concerns of Southern partners, they involve selectivity as to which 'partners' to consider, and are influenced by domestic considerations such as the interests of private supporters and donors and the personal interests of activist staffs.

The charge that the Washington-based NGOs dominate the debate and drown out diverse Southern voices has some basis in fact. It is not unusual for a meeting called by a Bank office director or Vice President with a dozen Washington NGOs to be the extent of the airing that an issue receives. The problem is inherent in the Bank's centralized Washington-based staffing, and if the Bank wants to hear the views of the NGO community more broadly, it will have to work harder at it. NGOs based in the industrial countries, which have staff resources to devote to monitoring the Bank that Southern counterparts lack, need to press themselves and the Bank to do so.

The alienating effects of US-based advocacy on borrowing governments is another element of the Washington NGO 'problem.' Pressure for environmental standards, information disclosure requirements and transparency, galling enough from some governments when they come from official donors, are even more upsetting when the critics are foreign-based NGOs. NGOs' implicit claim that they represent some poor Indians' interests better than the New Delhi government, for example, rankles the Indian government.

Many of the best known 'NGO issues' – resettlement, information disclosure, required environmental impact assessments and poverty assessments – have the effect of strengthening the Bank with respect to its borrowers. Many borrowers would surely be more sanguine about proposals that expand their options and strengthen their bargaining position with the Bank on important issues.

NGOs have missed some opportunities to improve this relationship. There are substantial areas of concern to NGOs where their interests are largely aligned with at least factions in many borrowing governments, and would be perceived as strengthening government positions in relation to the Bank. Debt relief, for example, could unite NGOs and debtor governments. But debt relief has not risen high on the list of priority NGO issues. A strategic approach to structural adjustment that urged more flexibility or room for variation could also provide some common ground with some governments, but adjustment has not been pressed vigorously by most Washington NGOs.[1]

This unbalanced agenda relates to the final 'problem' with Washington NGOs: the portions of their agenda that the US government supports ultimately rise to the highest levels of consideration in the Bank. Environmental Impact Assessments, proposals for an ombudsman, and information disclosure are not the only, or even the dominant subjects of interest to the range of Washington-based NGOs. They have attracted the support of the US government, while concerns about adjustment, the poverty impact of IDA lending, and debt relief have not. The close association of US government representatives with some NGO-favored proposals identifies the proposals with wealthy industrial interests and compromises the NGOs' identity.

One result: even a determined advocate for major changes in the Bank, the Executive Director to the Bank for the Netherlands and a number of Southern and Eastern European countries, Evelyn Herfkens, asserts that while she shares the criticism of the Bank, 'within the institution the US nongovernmental organizations are taken too seriously' (*National Journal* 18, September 1993).

CONCLUSIONS

This survey of NGOs raises important issues for understanding and distinguishing among them, evaluating their role in cooperating with major donors, and for understanding the World Bank's record in collaboration with NGOs. Among the most important:

1. Are the NGOs with which the World Bank collaborates connected to networks of international, national and local NGOs? Such networks have the potential to combine the strengths of grassroots groups with close relations to poor people in the affected area, and of national or international-level groups that can coordinate activities, broker relationships and provide resources.

   Working either with local organizations unconnected to any network, or with national level or international groups not closely tied to local people's organizations, is different in important ways from collaborating with a network of organizations determined to involve community-based groups in decision making, and prepared to use organizational, technical, and political resources on a large scale to support local groups' positions.

2. The reshaped partnership being proposed between Northern and Southern NGOs implies supportive, coordinating and advocacy roles for Northern NGOs. The review of some 300 World Bank-financed projects involving NGOs offers an opportunity to observe how these relationships are operating, and whether the nature of NGO involvement and influence is affected by the dynamics of North-South partnerships among participating NGOs.

3. Is NGO participation in projects structured so as to permit NGOs to act as organs for political participation, representation and

accountability, as well as testing grounds for innovation and local initiative? Few major NGOs are now acting out this role, nor are major donors fully prepared to appreciate and nurture NGOs in this role. One important question about the 300 projects is the extent to which NGOs participate on terms that allow this role to be played and developed.

These issues, and questions suggested by the organizational analysis of the World Bank – questions about the stage and extent of NGO involvement and the relation of NGO projects to Bank adjustment loans – are pursued in the analysis of projects in the chapter that follows.

4 World Bank-NGO Project Cooperation: Less than Meets the Eye?

In an April 1988 speech, (then) World Bank Senior Vice President Moeen A. Qureshi spoke of the World Bank's work with NGOs in these terms:

> In the last few years NGO influence on Bank policies has grown.... Where bureaucratic eyes are astigmatic, NGOs provide vivid images of what is really happening at the grassroots.... strong organizations of poor people often help public programs respond to the real needs of the poor.... I have asked our staff to look for more situations where NGOs could help us elicit the participation of poor people in planning public projects and policies.

Qureshi's speech is frequently quoted by NGO enthusiasts within the World Bank to show the range and depth of the organization's official commitment to working with NGOs. Along with other publications and public statements since 1988, it suggests that the Bank is cooperating with increasing frequency with NGOs, turning especially to local and national organizations in borrowing countries, and opening itself to work in all stages of the project cycle.

This chapter examines the 304 projects that the World Bank cites as involving NGOs between 1973 and 1990, focusing on the nature of NGO involvement, the character of the NGOs involved, and particularly the growth in the number of projects with NGO involvement since 1988. The encouraging growth in the number of Bank-financed projects with NGO involvement, especially in the last years of the 1980s, reflects a determined effort by some in the Bank's Operations Division and its management to expand operational collaboration. The progress, however, is undercut by troubling questions about the quality of the collaboration.

The 304 projects usually involve NGOs in implementing one component of a larger project. One quarter of the projects involve NGOs in project design, direct receipt of funds, or in conflict with the World

Bank. The incidence of these 'major roles' increased slightly after 1988, but reports of a dramatic change in the character of NGO involvement are found to be inflated. A supplementary survey of data available for 151 projects approved in 1991 and 1992 finds NGO 'design' often consists of subprojects to be financed from a project-created fund, or compensatory schemes in the context of structural adjustment plans. Examined over time and across regions with an eye for the quality of the NGO participation, the project record suggests some of the potential and limitations in the collaboration. It also raises questions to be pursued in understanding the World Bank's capacity to expand and systematize the collaboration.

DATA AND CONTEXT

The list of 304 projects involving NGOs has been compiled by the unit responsible for NGO relations, the International Economic Relations unit of the Operations Division (OPRIE) (formerly in Strategic Planning and Review (SPRIE); then in External Affairs (EXTIE)). The one- to three-page summaries of the projects collected by this office have been supplemented with other sources, including Project Completion Reports where available, for roughly half of the projects.

An additional 229 new projects were reported in 1991, 1992 and 1993 as involving NGOs. The 1991 and 1992 projects are reviewed more briefly. (Documentation for the 1993 projects did not permit their integration into the analysis.) The available information for the 1991 and 1992 projects was more limited, and the review focused on understanding the role of adjustment-related projects in the numerical expansion of NGO involvement, and on the nature and extent of NGO participation in 'design' of the projects.

Two weaknesses in the data stand out. First, projects are listed and summarized by World Bank staff, then collected in annual progress reports to management and the Board. There is no guarantee that the list is complete, that it is consistent by region, or that NGO involvement is not overstated. Each year the regional vice presidents ask their staff for a list of projects that involve NGOs. The yearly tally thus depends on staff's response to management's annual memos, and countries with interested staff persons and regions where management stresses reporting of NGO collaboration may be over-represented.

Second, project summaries are derived from Staff Appraisal Reports and reflect the project as designed, not the actual course of project implementation, so the data used here represent project plans as negotiated by governments and the Bank. The course of several projects' implementation is discussed in later chapters, but neither the Bank nor this study has attempted to survey the actual course of implementation of the reported NGO projects. One staff person close to the NGO effort estimates that perhaps one third of the projects cited in recent years have 'a significant NGO element.' Another Bank staffer, also a close observer of policy and practiced toward NGOs, notes that if the extent of actual (rather than planned) NGO involvement is reviewed the results will be 'a scandal.'

The 304 projects begun between 1973 and 1990 that the World Bank reports to have involved NGOs should be kept in perspective. Among some 5,000 projects financed in the Bank's history, 6.1 per cent involve NGOs. The 304 projects reviewed are a small minority of the World Bank's operations, and are not at all typical of project lending. They represent the cutting edge of the Bank's relations with non-governmental groups, and of efforts to encourage popular participation in Bank-financed activities.

NGO involvement in most cases touches only a small component of the project. In the $70 million Philippine Health Development III project, for example, $7.4 million is devoted to community health programs initiated by NGOs. So the number of projects and their total dollar value are not accurate measures of the extent of NGO influence on World Bank lending; in actual dollar terms, NGO involvement is much smaller.

World Bank engagement with NGOs since the late 1970s has also coincided with the growth of structural and sectoral adjustment lending. This development has quite properly drawn much wider attention than have the Bank's overtures to NGOs, and has reshaped the institution and its role in the international economy. Adjustment lending sets much of the political and organizational context for Bank-NGO relations. In the late 1980s and early 1990s adjustment was also the immediate context for many Bank and government efforts to enlist NGOs' operational help.

THE VARIABLES: THE NGO PARTICIPANTS AND THEIR ROLES IN PROJECTS

To explore the nature and quality of the World Bank's project interactions with NGOs, one needs to draw some qualitative distinctions among the 304 projects surveyed. The simple typology developed here rests on the stage of project development at which NGOs enter into collaboration, and on three distinctions among the types of NGOs involved. The distinctions that result are broad, and classification of individual projects may be open to discussion. But they do provide a basis for some qualitative judgments about the projects and about the character of project interaction.

Community-based, National and International NGOs

Relationships, communication and division of labor among these levels are essential issues in NGO operations. Distinctions between projects with community-based, national NGO and international NGO involvement, and the various combinations of these groups, will be examined closely. For this survey, organizations with local membership are referred to as community-based organizations (CBO); larger-scale umbrella or coordinating organizations (federations of cooperatives, national associations of credit unions, etc.) are national NGOs, as are locally-based development-promoting organizations.)

Professional development NGOs and interest-based organizations

NGOs may be divided, as Salmen and Eaves (1989) note, according to the extent to which they work in support of a common social good versus a private good. But a related distinction is not treated by Salmen and Eaves: NGOs may be divided between those that are professional, charitable, voluntary, or humanitarian organizations expressly promoting 'development' – here called 'professional' – and those that are essentially organized as an expression of common interests: federations of cooperatives, national labor unions, trade associations, etc.

One might expect interest-based NGOs to be more aggressive and more likely to come into conflict with the Bank in protecting the interests of their members or beneficiaries. They may press demands and mobilize people to express objections, rather than confer about the merits of policies over a conference table, and be less readily swayed by the influence the World Bank holds in professional circles. One might also expect Bank staff to be more comfortable working with organizations of development professionals, who know the 'language' and procedures of donor agencies.

The relation to structural adjustment

NGO projects' relation to adjustment loans proved difficult to operationalize in the project survey. The links between NGO participation and World Bank policy conditions are not always clear and explicit. As a result, I have not attempted to test the relationship between NGO collaboration in projects and the growth of adjustment lending, but only to note the rapid growth, after 1988, of NGO participation in compensatory plans explicitly linked to adjustment programs. The politics of NGOs' relation to the World Bank in the broader context of adjustment lending is discussed in Chapter 6.

NGO Roles in Project Collaboration

The project cycle

World Bank discussions of its own work with NGOs recognize the importance of NGO involvement before the project implementation stage. Involvement in design processes is urged so that project designers can learn from the NGOs' knowledge and experience, and design a project or that responds to NGOs' understanding of local needs and priorities.

A major theme in the sociological theory of complex organizations suggests a second reason to give close attention to the stage of NGO participation. Contingency theory (Thompson, 1967) suggests that a large organization will place priority on protecting its 'core technology' from outside disturbance. The 'core technology' or standard operations that are central to production (in this case, of loans and projects) consists in the World Bank of its project cycle and its methods of gathering information, usually through brief missions to member countries.

The project cycle is a series of steps, strictly adhered to in planning loans, which include project identification, pre-appraisal, appraisal, negotiation, implementation and evaluation. The stages that precede implementation (here collectively referred to as 'design') penetrate more deeply into the World Bank's standard operations than does participation in implementing projects. NGO participation in design, direct funding of NGO projects and significant conflict between an NGO and the Bank are the three categories of interaction in which the World Bank's standard operations are most likely to be significantly affected. The 304 projects involving NGOs can be readily divided into three groups, distinguished by the level and nature of NGO involvement. These categories are summarized in Table 4.1 and discussed below.

Table 4.1 NGO Participation in World Bank-Financed Projects, 1973–90 by Type of Involvement

Major Roles	76
Implementation	177
Minor Roles	51
Total	304

Source: calculated from World Bank project summaries.

NGO implementation

NGO implementation of a World Bank-financed project is the typical mode of cooperation, with 177 projects involving NGOs solely in implementing a project component, or involve community groups, cooperatives, or farmers' associations in organizing and delivering some input or service.

Major roles

Seventy-six (76) of the projects feature interaction that is unusual either because it involves NGOs in project design, includes direct funding of NGO projects by a Bank-financed fund, or involves conflict between project managers and NGOs over the actual or potential impact of the project. This group of projects is referred to as major roles, indicating NGO involvement beyond implementation.

Of these 76 projects, 54 feature NGO participation in design. This figure includes cases where NGOs serve on a project design team, are consulted in appraisal or pre-appraisal, or become involved in changes in a project after funding begins. It includes cases of participation by local representative groups, as well as instances of input by NGO staff with technical expertise where relation to local communities' views is less clear.

Salmen and Eaves (1989) distinguish 'advice' from 'design' participation, to identify cases where an NGO may be consulted briefly during project design, but not participate in a sustained way in shaping a project. I have grouped the 'advice' cases with cases of NGO participation in design, ignoring the difference of degree. A more important distinction, not made in the Bank's categorization, is between participation in designing a project, and NGO design of a subproject, to be submitted for support by a fund established by the project. Such arrangements can be a valuable resource for NGO activities, but they do not draw NGOs into shaping a Bank-financed project. Twelve of the 76 projects involve direct funding of NGO activities. In these projects a component of the World Bank's finance is devoted to a fund, usually managed by a committee of government and NGO personnel, for NGO activities in a sector or region.

Finally, 11 of the 76 projects involved conflict between Bank or government officials and an NGO significant enough to be reported in the summaries. It seems likely that more than 11 projects in the last two decades have raised some conflict with an NGO. These cases involve sustained criticism or protest, and have made their way onto the Bank's list of projects with NGO involvement. Several led to an NGO role in redesign of the project.

These 76 projects are the principal focus of this survey, and some are discussed in later chapters as well. Just as the 304 are distinctive among all projects, so these 76 represent the most intensive project interaction to date. Why focus on a subgroup of 'major role' projects? From an organizational analysis perspective, the projects are important because they challenge the World Bank's standard operating procedures. Direct funding, participation in design, and conflict over a project are all likely to penetrate the Bank's standard operations more deeply than does NGO implementation of a project component.

These projects also represent the kind of interaction with NGOs that the World Bank describes as a goal, and examining them is one way to evaluate its claims to be doing more than using NGOs as implementers or cheap contractors. Comparing claims with actual project performance sheds light on the true extent of collaboration, and on the role of public relations in the World Bank's NGO campaign. Loans that finance social services by NGOs in the context of structural adjustment programs may suggest that some of the interest in NGOs is grounded in the Bank's desire to help borrowers make adjustment programs more politically sustainable. The Bank's response to disputes with NGOs in conflictive cases offers insight into its responsiveness to external pressures and politics, and may suggest preferred strategies for NGOs and other reformers.

Minor Roles. Fifty-one projects involve less significant interaction than the NGO-implemented projects above. These include 11 cases in which the project or NGO component was dropped out before appraisal; five in which contact was only in passing; and 35 projects that contracted with NGOs to provide specialized services that did not involve the NGO in direct contact with local populations, or draw on NGO experience and knowledge from such contact. These projects, most from early in the Bank's reported experience with NGOs, are referred to collectively as 'minor role' projects.

Eleven projects where Bank staff initiated plans for NGO participation but either the project was not approved or the NGO component was dropped before appraisal, are included in Bank's report of NGO participation. Government opposition to the NGO role is sometimes the barrier, illustrating one problem faced in Bank-NGO collaboration. In five 'minor' cases NGO participation involved only fleeting contact, as when a volunteer association trained a blacksmith for a regional development program in Niger; or NGO activities that parallel a Bank-financed project, for example NGO volunteers in Liberia building classrooms simultaneous to a Bank-financed school construction project.

The 35 'contractor' projects require more explanation. The point here is not that NGOs are under contract, as a contract is involved in most of the 304 projects. The issue is rather that the NGO either provides a technical service similar to those a for-profit contractor would provide (drilling wells, building facilities, planning a rural electrification scheme or a railway system), without any direct contact with local populations; or provides services solely to the government (usually training) that focus on technical capacities, and do not involve special content relating to contact with local organizations or communities.

NGO PARTICIPATION OVER TIME: A CLOSER LOOK

Figure 4.1 reports the frequency of NGO involvement in Bank-financed projects by year, since 1973. With some fluctuation, the number of projects reported grew steadily through the late 1970s and the 1980s. Between 1976 and 1988 an average of 15 new NGO projects was approved annually. Reporting that 46 and 48 projects involving NGOs were approved in fiscal year 1989 and 1990, the Bank's NGO unit calls 1988 a turning point, signalling a new posture toward NGOs. According to the latest Bank progress report the trend continued in 1991, 1992, 1993 and 1994, with 88, 68, 73 and 114 new projects approved.

The Increasingly Explicit Link to Structural Adjustment Loans

But there are three troubling tendencies in the quality of this recent project engagement with NGOs. First, in 14 of the 94 projects approved in 1989 and 1990, NGOs deliver compensatory services to soften

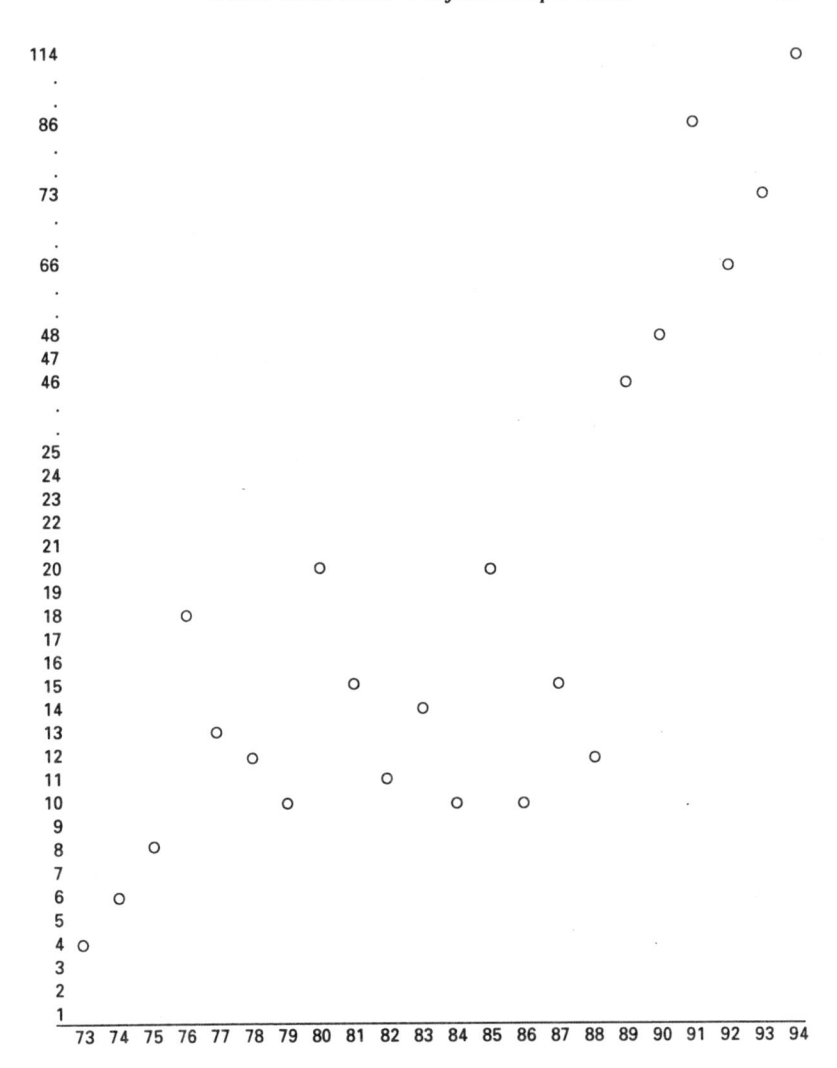

Figure 4.1 World Bank-Financed Projects with NGO Involvement, by Year of Approval

Source: Salmen and Eaves (1989, p. 9); Strategic Planning and Review Department (1989); subsequent World Bank Progress Reports on Cooperation with NGOs.

the effects of an adjustment plan. In Bolivia, Guatemala, Jamaica, Chad, Ghana, Guinea, Guinea Bissau, Madagascar, Mauritania and Uganda, NGOs have been enlisted in special compensatory programs to provide social services to people affected by budget and employment cutbacks or other changes such as the removal of food price subsidies. The World Bank's reports on 1991, 1992 and 1993 project collaboration single out another 14, 9 and 7 newly approved projects as 'adjustment related.' Many NGOs are concerned that this form of interaction amounts to governments and the Bank using NGOs as insurance against the political backlash from harsh adjustment regimes.

NGO involvement in easing the effects of Bank-supported adjustment regimes goes well beyond the cases mentioned here. Some projects in SAL countries have no stated tie to the adjustment program, even though they finance the provision of urban services, housing, and health projects. Such cases – in the Philippines and elsewhere – are more difficult to categorize as adjustment-related.

In other cases NGO compensatory services are not formally part of a World Bank-financed operation. The Catholic Relief Services' (CRS) Compensatory Feeding Program in Morocco was negotiated with the Moroccan government and partially funded by USAID, with only informal participation by Bank staff. In Tanzania, church-related NGOs have been asked by the government to take over the operation of hospitals once run by the government (Interview with Rogate Mshana, 23 September 1992).

Formal NGO participation reflects a wider phenomenon, as NGOs are drawn into Emergency Social Funds and Social Investment Funds and called on to fulfill welfare and relief roles as government agencies retreat under fiscal fire. For some NGOs this has meant increased attention to relief needs, scaled-back development agendas and a greater organizational focus on their role as service providers, rather than as agents of change in civil society.

The trend also sheds light on the politics of the World Bank's increasing project engagement with NGOs. In compensatory programs, the Bank and governments seek NGO assistance in a moment of humanitarian and political need. NGOs become an adjunct to the most important item in the World Bank's agenda: adoption and effective implementation of economic liberalization plans. The significance of this employment of NGOs in politically charged situations by the 'apolitical' World Bank is taken up at length in Chapter 6.

Creating New Community Organizations

A second trend appears in the recent NGO projects: many make farmers' groups, newly organized for purposes of the project, the units for receiving or paying for some input. Establishing new 'beneficiary' groups to play a role in project implementation is not a new tendency, but it is reported more frequently among the most recent NGO projects. Newly created groups are the NGOs involved in 27 of the 94 new projects in 1989–1990 (28.7 per cent), compared to 35 of 210 projects approved through 1988 (16.6 per cent).

In the Eastern Region Agricultural Development Project in the Yemen Arab Republic (1989), for instance, two government agencies will organize 'project beneficiaries' into 'collective units' at the level of tertiary irrigation blocks. The collective units will be responsible for operating and maintaining irrigation canals and for water distribution and water fees. In Bangladesh the BWDB Systems Rehabilitation Project (1990) was to promote the formation of 'Structure Maintenance Groups' and 'Earthworks Maintenance Groups' to do the work of maintaining irrigation structures.

Forming new groups for irrigation systems management and cost recovery undoubtedly has merit on efficiency and financial grounds. But groups created for the project, especially by a national government agency, are neither likely to survive (Oakley and Marsden 1984; OED 1988) nor equipped to play the representative role of existing social organizations. The high incidence of such group formation by project authorities in the newly reported projects suggests that the quality of the Bank's interaction with NGOs has not grown with its frequency since 1988.[1]

What Constitutes an NGO Role in 'Design'?

Third, as noted above, the post-1988 projects do not show the kind of increase in NGO design roles that would indicate a deepening relationship in project collaboration. The Bank's reports about learning from NGOs stress the significance of NGOs' role in project design. So the increase in NGO participation in design, from seven projects annually in the 1980s to 16 in 1988–90, and an impressive 89 in 1991 and 1992 combined, appears to be good news. But when the nature of 'design' involvement is considered, much of the reported surge evaporates. The breakdown of these design projects is summarized in Table 4.2.

Table 4.2 Breakdown of NGO Roles in Project Design, for World Bank-Financed Projects Reported to Involve NGO Design, 1989–90 and 1991–92

	1989–90	1991–92
Reported NGO Design Projects	33	89
Percentage of Total NGO Projects	34%	58%
Sub-projects[a]	11	39[b]
Compensatory Projects	0	23[b]
Reported Total Less Sub-projects and Compensatory Projects	22	35
Percentage of Total NGO Projects	23%	22%

Source: Calculated from World Bank project summaries.

a 'Sub-project' refers not to a project component, but to separate NGO projects that are submitted to a project-financed fund for support.
b Eight of the 23 adjustment 'design' projects are also counted in the 'subproject' category. The double-counting is eliminated in calculating new totals.

Designing NGO sub-projects

In many cases NGOs 'design' only a sub-project, an NGO proposal to be considered and funded by a project-financed authority. NGO design of such proposals should not be conflated with participation in designing World Bank-financed projects or project components. Of the 33 'design' projects report in 1989–90, 12 involve only such sub-projects. (Only one such sub-project arrangement was reported as 'design' before 1989.) The increase in design roles appears to be largely a matter of zealous reporting. If the 12 projects are set aside, the numerical bulge shrinks to annual averages of 7 in 1980–88 and 11 in 1989–90.

Similarly, of 89 'design' projects reported in 1991–92, 39 involve NGO 'design' only of subprojects to be financed by currencies set aside under the project. There is no indication that NGOs influenced the shape of the project, or that the Bank or government opened their planning process to NGO participation.

Designing adjustment-related welfare schemes

The close relation to adjustment programs also produces exaggerated figures for 1991 and 1992. Twenty-three of the 89 'design' projects involve NGOs in adjustment-related programs. NGOs are invited to design not the policy reforms themselves, but food distribution, health care, public employment and other schemes to soften the reforms' impact.

More than half (54 of 89) of the vastly expanded number of NGO 'design' projects in 1991 and 1992 involve either no 'design' at all or advice on design of social service or employment programs to mitigate the effects of adjustment conditions. If the sub-project 'design' and adjustment-related projects are subtracted from the 1991 and 1992 'design' projects, 35 of the 156 projects (22 per cent) remain, almost exactly equal to the proportion over the period 1973–1990.

In addition, some of the reported design projects involve NGO advice on tiny components of large sectoral projects. A Ghanaian women's association was consulted in designing a $300,000 pilot scheme as part of a $230 million transportation project. As part of a $410 million primary education program in the Philippines, NGOs designed part of a $300,000 non-formal summer pre-school program. Two ornithological societies were consulted in planning a $623 million energy sector project in Turkey. It appears that some project Task Managers are zealously reporting cases that stretch one's conception of NGO involvement in project design.

Several of the NGOs consulted make no particular claim to represent primarily the interests of the poor.[2] A professional association of veterinarians in Uganda is the NGO involved in promoting privatization of services to farmers. The Chambers of Commerce in Turkey and Sri Lanka, and the Cairo Businessmen's Associations are the NGOs involved in design of three projects, and the Ecuadorian Association of Municipalities is reported as designing training projects for municipal workers.

There are encouraging tendencies in the 1991–92 projects as well. NGO involvement in appraisal and design stages of energy, natural resources management and other environmentally sensitive projects reflects operationalization of the requirements for Environmental Impact Assessments. In several cases governing committees are established to oversee project components, with NGO participation. 'All of these are to be encouraged. But they do not amount to a major change in the character of project engagement with NGOs.

NGO PARTICIPANTS AND THEIR ROLES

Community-based Groups and NGOs

The World Bank's recent reports on collaboration with NGOs emphasize its increased engagement with national and local, as opposed to international NGOs. Prominent among these are community-based organizations. Of the 304 projects reviewed here, 137 involved CBOs. Eighteen of the 137 (13.1 per cent) involved major roles for the NGOs – design, direct funding or conflict – as do 77 (25.3 per cent) of the population of 304. There is no marked difference in the tendency of projects with CBOs to have a major NGO involvement.

Projects in which CBOs *and* intermediary NGOs are involved are much more likely to involve a major role than are those where CBOs are involved alone. Only 5 of the 62 projects where CBOs stand alone involve a major NGO role. (Discounting 16 cases where the project itself promotes creation of new CBOs, the figure remains modest, 5 of 46.) For projects with joint CBO-intermediary NGO involvement, however, 31 of 75 (41.3 per cent) involve either a role in design (17), direct funding (9) or conflict with the Bank (5). Table 4.3 reports these results.

Table 4.3 Major Involvement in World Bank-Financed Projects, Community-Based Organizations Alone and Community-Based Organizations and Intermediary NGOs Together

	Type of NGOs Involved	
	Community-Based Alone	Community-Based With Intermediary NGO
Total Projects	62	75
Number of Major Roles	5	31
Design	4	17
Direct Funding	1	9
Conflict with World Bank	0	5
Percentage with Major Roles	8.1%	41.3%

Source: Calculated from World Bank Project Summaries.

National and International NGOs

What of the subset of projects that involve NGOs organized above the community level? These consist of all except the projects with CBOs only (62), a total of 242. The World Bank emphasizes its increasing involvement with national – as opposed to international – NGOs (Operational Directive 14.70, 1989, p. 4; Progress Report, 1990, 6; Qureshi, 1988; 'Working with NGOs' in World Bank, 1994c). Its stated emphasis on national organizations may be in part intended to placate borrower governments, who may find domestic NGO involvement less offensive than World Bank engagement with foreign-based NGOs. But cooperating with national-level institutions may also mean working with professionals who are closer to local needs and realities, and may offer an opportunity to help build development institutions in the country itself.

Given the importance the Bank attaches to working with national NGOs, two questions arise about the national and international NGOs involved in projects:

1. How has national NGO participation changed over time? and
2. Do NGOs have major roles more frequently in projects involving either national or international NGOs?

Between 1973 and 1988, newly approved projects involving NGOs relied on national NGOs in 28 per cent of cases, international NGOs in 56 per cent. (Sixteen per cent of cases involved CBOs only). By 1989, 36 per cent of newly-approved projects worked with national NGOs, only 26 per cent with international NGOs. Thirty-eight per cent involved CBOs only (World Bank, 1990 Progress Report, p. 5). Reports from the Bank show this trend toward Southern national NGOs continuing in 1990 and 1991.

These figures also reflect a sharp increase in projects involving only CBOs. CBO involvement without the support of national-level coordinating groups or other supportive NGOs has seldom resulted in more than NGO implementation of Bank-financed schemes.

How important is the involvement of national NGOs for the frequency of major NGO involvement? Table 4.4 summarizes the findings. As anticipated, participation by a national NGO is more likely to be associated with a major role (32.9 per cent of cases) than is an international NGO (17.4 per cent of cases). Even more striking, in 20 of the 32 cases (62.5 per cent) where both national and international

Table 4.4 NGO Involvement in Major Roles in World Bank-Financed Projects, by Involvement of International NGOs, National NGOs, and Both[a]

	Type of NGO Involved		
	International	National	Both
Number of Projects	115	82	32
Number Major Roles	20	27	20
Percentage of Projects with Major Role[b]	17.4%	32.9%	62.5%

Source: Calculated from World Bank Project Summaries.

a Excluding projects involving a CBO only.
b Variation is significant at the 0.01 level.

NGOs are involved, NGOs assume major roles in the project. Several of the 20 are major transportation or energy projects that provoked protest by local unions, peasant's associations, environmental organizations or groups of indigenous people. International organizations, especially environmental organizations, joined the fray, all focusing on the World Bank as a major financer of the projects.

The strong association between combined national and international NGO participation and major NGO roles holds true whether CBOs are involved (13 of 19) or not (7 of 13). Local NGOs with connections to Northern partners or international networks appear to join more readily in contacting local or Washington-based Bank staff about concerns or grievances. Electronic communication networks help move information between project sites, national capitals, and NGO offices in the industrialized countries. Despite the widely shared view that southern NGOs should be the primary participants in an NGO dialogue with the Bank, involvement of northern-based groups is strongly associated with major roles.

Professional Versus Interest Groups

A final distinction among NGOs is between interest-based organizations and professional 'development' NGOs. Interest-based NGOs are involve in a small minority of NGO projects, and their interaction appears not to be qualitatively different from that of development NGOs. Table 4.5 reports the findings.

Table 4.5 Professional and Interest-Based NGOs, and Major Roles in World Bank-Financed Projects

	Interest-based	Professional
Number of Projects	32	186
Number of Major Roles	12	63
Percentage Major Roles	37.5%	35.9%

Source: Calculated from World Bank Project Summaries.

Table 4.6 NGO Involvement in World Bank-Financed Projects, by Region and Year of Approval, 1973–90

	Africa	Asia	Latin America and Caribbean	EMENA[a]
Total World Bank Projects 1947–89	1469	1548	1141	756
Total NGO Projects	160	73	49	22
NGO as % of Total	10.9%	4.7%	4.3%	2.9%

Source: Calculated from World Bank Project Summaries.

a Europe, Middle East and North Africa.
b Regional variation is significant at the 0.01 level.

Regional Distribution

The regional distribution of projects presents two anomalies: the numerical dominance of Africa region projects, and the relatively small number of projects in Latin America and the Caribbean. In some ways, the regional distribution reported in Table 4.6 conforms to expectations based on NGO organization and activity in the regions. That the Europe/Middle East/North Africa (EMENA) region should be the lowest, for example, is in keeping with NGOs' relatively minor role in the Middle East, compared to Asia or Africa (Durning, 1989a).[3] The reputations of NGO sectors, however, would not lead one to predict Africa's numerical prominence and the relatively small number of projects in Latin America and the Caribbean.

The regional rankings are unchanged when NGO projects are considered as a proportion of total projects. Africa rates highest with 10.9 per cent of its projects involving NGOs, EMENA lowest at 2.9 per cent.

Table 4.7 World Bank-Financed Projects with NGO Involvement, 1973–90, by Region and Major and Minor Roles

Region	Africa	Asia	Latin Amer./Caribbean	EMENA[a]
Total NGO Projects	160	73	49	22
Major Roles	32	21	20	4
Major Roles as % NGO Projects	20.0%	28.8%	40.8%	18.2%
Design	26	13	11	4
Direct Funds	5	2	5	0
Conflict	1	6	4	0
Minor Roles	39	9	5	5
Minor Roles as % NGO Projects	24.2%	12.3%	8.2%	22.7%
Aborted	3	4	4	0
Trivial	5	0	0	0
Contracting	31	5	1	5

Source: World Bank, *Annual Report*, 1989, pp. 178–82, and calculations based on World Bank Progress Reports.

a Europe, Middle East and North Africa.

The distribution of major and minor roles, however, deviates from this pattern and offers one explanation for the regional anomalies. Some 40 per cent of all NGO projects in LAC, as shown in Table 4.7, involve NGOs in major roles, while in other regions fewer than 30 per cent of NGO projects are major roles. The character of NGO involvement appears to differ in Latin America from the other regions: Latin American NGOs are reported to participate in projects less often solely as implementers, and more frequently in more influential roles.

The distribution of minor roles is also lopsided: Africa and EMENA each report more than 20 per cent of NGO projects either aborted, trivial, or in contract-style relationships. The EMENA findings, based on a relatively small regional total, reflect the predominance of transport and infrastructure projects in the region's middle-income countries.

In Africa, the large number of contracting projects, particularly in West and Central Africa, implemented exclusively by international NGOs unlinked to local groups, reflects the character of a substantial part of NGO participation in World Bank-financed projects. In several West and Central African countries, NGOs such as the National Rural Electrification Council of America (NRECA) and the British Organization for Rehabilitation through Training (ORT) have been enlisted to provide technical training to government officials and to build roads, railways and schools.

CONCLUSIONS

Much of the work of investigating the real extent of NGO involvement in World Bank lending and interpreting the projects in their political and institutional setting remains to be reported in the next three chapters. A survey of project documents does identify four significant patterns in the involvement of NGOs in Bank-financed projects:

1. The 304 projects are divided among 77 major role projects, 176 where the NGO is solely an implementer, and 51 where NGO involvement is minor. The divisions are based primarily on the depth of potential penetration by an NGO into the World Bank's core technology (design, conflict, direct funding); and the extent to which the NGO involvement offers a chance for NGOs' political roles as representative, watchdog, agent of accountability to be exercised.
2. Projects with major NGO involvement have tended to involve joint participation by community-based, national and international groups. International NGO involvement alone has tended to be less deep, and CBOs alone have rarely engaged in other than implementing and minor roles. Whether this is because of greater political and organizational resources, greater aggressiveness by NGOs affiliated with an international network, or simply the initiative of some Bank staff, is explored in further discussion of project examples (Chapters 5, 6 and 7).
3. NGO involvement has increased gradually since 1981, and beginning in 1989 the number of projects approved annually with some NGO involvement jumped sharply. But problems arise in examining the quality of World Bank-NGO interaction in the new projects, including their close links to structural adjustment programs; the creation of new local organizations to implement project components; the use of 'project design' to describe NGO submission of sub-projects for support by a Bank-financed fund.
4. Africa region projects are dominant, numerically, and relatively few have been approved in Latin America and the Caribbean. But project engagement in Latin America and the Caribbean has tended strongly to involve NGOs in design, direct funding or significant conflict

with the Bank, while implementation and minor contracting roles dominate project cooperation in Africa. Some possible explanations, including varying government capacities, differing proclivities among the Bank's regional divisions, and differing political and policy contexts, are discussed in the remaining chapters.

Categorizing and counting the projects cannot answer the most interesting and important questions about NGO involvement World Bank lending. What is the real extent of NGO participation in project design? How does the combination of national and international NGO involvement come to be associated with very active participation in the projects? Does the growing number of NGO projects reflect a systematic, growing openness in the Bank to more and deeper NGO participation? Is the Bank moving to institutionalize participation of NGOs in project planning and implementation? And how is the trend toward NGO involvement related to the dominant trend in the World Bank during the 1980s, the growth of policy-based structural adjustment lending? These topics are probed through interviews and case studies in the chapters that follow.

5 Moving Money: Organizational Aspects of a Development Model

Introducing organizational theory into the analysis of the World Bank, one risks appearing to excuse its performance as a function of the perversity of large bureaucracies, a quirk of the organizational type. This chapter and the two that follow put forward an organizational analysis that deals not with bureaucratic quirks, but with the form and substance of the World Bank's role in the global economy. The contribution of organizational analysis begins with the premise that organizations are not only created entities and tools of their creators, but also social entities, holding to values and priorities and working to preserve themselves and advance their own interests.

In this chapter I argue that the World Bank promotes and implements a capital-driven development model and investment strategy, and accepts other development mandates only as adjuncts to capital-driven economic growth. This basic mandate and strategy reflect both internal, organizational factors and the interests of powerful actors in the World Bank's political economy. The mandate has led to patterns of staffing, operations and measures of performance that are in contradiction with social and poverty-related objectives that are appended to it. The organizational apparatus that exists to implement a capital- and growth-driven, export-oriented development model is incompatible with the stated goal of working collaboratively and responsively with NGOs.

The capital investment mandate has made efficient disbursement of capital an organizational measure of success at the World Bank, an institutionalized standard of performance that shapes the implementation of new policy initiatives. This effect can be seen in the cases of poverty alleviation policy in the 1970s and the adoption and implementation of structural adjustment lending in the early 1980s. The organizational imperative to 'move money' has implications for NGO involvement in Bank operations and policy formation, as the project record and interviews of World Bank and NGO officials show.

Some Bank officials acknowledge the tension between pressure to disburse funds and the concern for sustainability of investments. But recognizing the tension and adding directives and caveats for staff will not be enough to reorder priorities, without basic changes in the organizational features that are designed to implement those priorities.

THE DISBURSEMENT IMPERATIVE: A PROXY MEASURE OF PERFORMANCE

The imperative of transferring capital has become a principal mandate for the World Bank and for individual staff, who respond in part to institutionalized incentives and priorities. This section argues that the imperative has become the effective standard of success used by the Bank and by many of its observers. The disbursement imperative holds and maintains this standing not simply because of bureaucratic perversity, but because it reflects objectives and interests rooted in the World Bank's role in managing international economic relations. In subsequent sections it is argued that recent reforms of the Bank's portfolio management leave the structures and procedures in which the imperative is institutionalized largely untouched.

The Organizational Mandate

The observation that the World Bank tends to absorb new initiatives into the program of growth-oriented capital investment is not new. Like Mason and Asher (1973), Fatouros (1977, pp. 27–8) notes that policy shifts in the 1970s involved not repudiating former approaches but adding new anti-poverty emphases. Ayres (1983, p. 75) adds that despite the rhetorical emphasis on 'new-style' lending in the 1970s, the 'overwhelming portion of World Bank activities continues to move in the same manner and direction as in the past.'

New issues on the agenda are rendered rhetorically compatible with capital-driven growth, as in 'growth with equity' and 'sustainable development.' But while rhetorical compatibility may suffice for public relations purposes, it has not allowed 'new policies' to be effectively implemented. The 1987 *Annual Report* illustrates this tendency, pledging to integrate 'the core of poverty concerns of the 1970s into the growth and market-oriented concerns that marked the first half of the 1980s.' As Hans Singer (1989, p. 1314) complains in a brief comment on the Annual Report, '...there is no recognition of the possibility that the neoliberal pattern of growth advocated may itself preclude such positive action [against poverty].'

The imperative of moving money has made commitment of funds a proxy measure of organizational success and of staff achievement. Sociologist Judith Tendler (1975, p. 90) argues that moving capital comes to 'define organizational output' both for most development agencies and to the outside world. At multilateral development banks especially it 'can cause a quantity-at-any-cost approach . . .' (p. 56).[1]

The institutional tendency to define success in terms of money moved is in keeping with the tendency in official development circles to assess the adequacy of the industrial world's aid effort by reference to amounts of money or per centages of GNP devoted to the cause. At least since the Pearson Commission Report (1969), international authorities have tended to advocate greater amounts of aid and investment, deducing the level needed from GNP growth targets (Tendler, 1975, pp. 91, 124). As Tendler notes, under this standard almost any increase qualifies as a positive step.

Macro-economic development models have softened some of their prescriptions for capital-led development, and some of the economists involved in these theoretical changes have promoted their ideas within the World Bank. But the ensuing changes – modified sectoral priorities, greater emphasis on technical assistance and institutional change, and discussion of social issues – have been appended to Bank operations with the assumption that they can successfully refine and supplement its mandate to promote development through financial intermediation and technical assistance. Sociology advisor Michael Cernea (1989) argues that 'financially induced development' continues to be the norm at the Bank, despite his belief that finance is often the least important of a complex set of inputs needed for widespread improvements in well-being.

The transfer of capital remains a major factor in the World Bank's assessment of aid and development finance. Net transfers from 'the developing countries as a group' in the late 1980s were a source of distress and a sign of the failure of both private and public effort to promote recovery and development (World Bank, *Annual Report* 1990, p. 29). Capital is the World Bank's greatest resource, and capital flows and the amount of its own lending should be indicators of its contribution to development. But recent evidence suggests that the availability of capital and the institutional need to disburse it can drive planning decisions and produce perverse results.

When lending capital is plentiful, as since the 1987 IBRD general capital increase, projects, the primary vehicle for moving capital, become the World Bank's scarcest resource. Supply rather than demand drives the movement of capital. The search for acceptable activities for investment, according to some staff, is energized by the imperative to find projects that conform to government and World Bank priorities, and that can be shown to meet the Bank's economic, financial, social and technical standards (Asia staff no. 3).

The extreme difficulty the World Bank has in withholding loans for even the most problematic projects illustrates the strength of the mandate. Strict procedural standards for financial and economic return of investments, as well as environmental and social measures, are 'finessed' when political and internal pressures require that a loan be made. Worrisome loans are often justified on the grounds that through its involvement the Bank may exert some influence to improve a flawed plan or project. A US Treasury Department official is quoted as saying: '[T]here is no project too destructive, and too costly, that the World Bank will not throw hundreds of millions of dollars at to try to make it better. In fact the worse the project, the more urgent the justification for the Bank's involvement' (in Rich, 1990, p. 321). The Environmental Defense Fund's Bruce Rich argues that this pattern of amelioration through investment has perpetuated destructive projects that might otherwise have withered away for want of foreign financing.[2]

Individual Incentives

Careers at the World Bank have long been built primarily by designing projects that win Board approval. It is commonplace in insider discussions that staff advance primarily by identifying, designing, negotiating and preparing projects that the Board will approve and that further the investment program in a country (Van de Laar, 1980, pp. 236–7; Ayres, 1983; Tendler, 1975; Watson, 1985; Hellinger, Hellinger and O'Regan, 1988).

McNamara introduced management devices that institutionalized this quantity-driven program. Five-year planning documents and 'annual country allocation exercises' set country and sectoral lending targets that are 'benchmark[s] for judging staff performance and individual promotion' (McKitterick, 1986, p. 47). Targets 'put heavy pressure on professional staff to rapidly generate a sufficient volume of projects' (Van de Laar, 1980, p. 222). A former Latin America country economist reports coming under pressure to continue a lending program, despite the staffer's warning that further lending to the country would be unproductive and would almost certainly not be repaid (Finance staff no. 1). The country fell into arrears to the Bank within a year of this episode.

Such resistance to targets by individual staff is by all accounts rare.

Much more common, according to several operational staff, is the tendency to press one's project forward, engaging in advocacy on its behalf under the guise of analytic review and evaluation (Asia staff no. 3).

Internal papers by Caroline Moser (1987) and Michael Bamberger (1986) agree that the project cycle, the focus on cost recovery and speedy project preparation, and the requirement that projects be definitively appraised and budgeted before implementation, all limit staff's incentive and ability to finance projects with extensive community participation. In a paper written for the World Bank, Nagle and Ghose (1989, p. 10) cite a 1985 review of participation in World Bank-funded projects in which:

> project staff ... interviewed contended that there were no incentives for pursuing social and institutional aspects of a project including community participation, except where absolutely necessary. They said that the Bank's norms reward quick development of projects and disbursement of funds.

Nagle and Ghose (1989, p. 11) interviewed a staffer who had:

> worked on three participatory projects in Africa ... [and] sees the current reward system as the biggest obstacle to developing more participatory projects. He said the Bank does not reward a staffer who wants to spend time and effort to go to project sites to work with beneficiaries to bring about their participation in the project.

For individual staff, as Van de Laar (1980, pp. 236–7) notes, '[n]o amount of exhortation ... that small, simple and labour-intensive solutions in project design should be sought can overcome what the bureaucracy sees as a major purpose of its own activities: to quickly spend its budget allocations.'

The findings of the 1992 Wapenhans report gave these concerns new official standing (see Chapter 2). And in the period since, Wapenhans the Director of the Operations Evaluation Division has circulated an informal proposal for a new project cycle. A working paper draft acknowledges the problems associated with the present project cycle and argues that the Wapenhans reforms cannot be adequately implemented without a substantial overhaul of the cycle. A new cycle based on four stages – listening, pilot, demonstration, implementation – is proposed.

Some Bank managers argue that less sweeping changes – annual portfolio reviews, marginal increases in time allocated to project supervision – can correct the problems diagnosed by Wapenhans. Short of such a redesigned standard operating procedure, efforts to lessen the disbursement pressure – what Wapenhans refers to as the 'approval culture' – will find itself up against the big issues of the Bank's development model and its debt-management mandate.

Lending to Finance Debt Servicing

The desire to move money is sometimes treated by the World Bank's observers as a function solely of a bureaucratic compulsion (Crane and Finkle, 1981; Ness and Brechin, 1988). Bureaucratic and organizational factors play important roles in establishing and perpetuating the mandate, but capital-based investment in practice rests on profound theoretical and ideological models and programs, and on powerful interests that shape the Bank's management of countries' commercial and official debt.

Major private banks, the US government and leaders of international corporate interests have shaped the Bank's role in transferring capital for debt servicing and repayment, particularly in the early 1980s. A 1982 conference sponsored by the Brookings Institution produced an unusually public record of talks between commercial bankers, corporate leaders and the World Bank. Bankers and leaders of such transnational entities as Bechtel, Inc. who participated in the conference, stressed their keen interest in the Bank's efforts to maintain the solvency and debt servicing schedules of debtor countries and to insure the profitability of private investments to these countries (Fried and Owen, 1982).

US officials involved the World Bank in the development of the Baker and Brady Plans for managing the debt crisis, and have called upon the Bank to play a leading role in the plan. Both plans relied on a basic scheme: transfer enough capital to finance debt servicing and avoid crises between individual debtors and private creditors, while the World Bank encourages new economic policies, more open to foreign investing and marketing (Loxley, 1986; Gibbon, 1992).

The World Bank sought increased capital allotments in order to play these roles while maintaining project lending. Rich argues that the capital increases given the IBRD in 1988 intensified the pressure to build careers by constructing portfolios of large loans. After lobbying for additional lending capital from member countries, the Bank found its lending ability threatened by political and economic crises in three major borrowing countries, China, Brazil and Argentina. These worries seem to have increased the pressure to disburse funds to other borrowers. If adjustment lending (the Bank's least staff-intensive vehicle for disbursing funds) were reduced, the pressure to disburse capital would become even greater (Rich, 1990, p. 318).

REDUCING UNCERTAINTY AND PROTECTING THE MEANS OF PRODUCTION

The organizational impulse to move money and the individual incentives to perform have been widely observed. Insights from the sociological study of major organizations in industry and the service sector help explain why maladaptive processes and organizational structures at the World Bank are so entrenched.

Structural Contingency: Reducing and Managing Uncertainty

Structural contingency theory focuses on the relation between an organization and its environment (primarily other firms and markets). Emphasizing the organization's desire to minimize uncertainty in its environment, and to protect the standard operations that are the core of its productive process, it offers two insights into the World Bank's management of pressure and of new policies.

Every organization copes with a 'task environment,' the markets, individuals and other organizations it deals in the course of doing its work. Sociologist James Thompson showed that the task environment, largely beyond an organization's control, is the chief source of uncertainty and the greatest threat to organizational performance and control.

Organizations' vulnerability to perturbations from the environment can be shown to be central to their behavior (Pfeffer and Salancik, 1978, pp. 24, 34). The organization is a 'market for influence and control' in which internal and external actors put forward their demands and interests. An organization weighs and balances these demands, and interest groups evaluate its effectiveness in terms of their own interests. Actual or perceived dependence on other actors or markets drives much of an organization's behavior.

If coping with uncertainty is the organization's central problem, uncertainty reduction is the basic logic of organizational behavior, strategy and structure. To reduce uncertainty, organizations protect the core of their productive technology, the processes by which raw materials are processed into output, from change in the environment. This core includes machines, skills, knowledge, training, strategies, procedures and special characteristics of inputs and outputs (R. Scott, 1985). Organizations will act to limit uncertainties (variations in supply, demand, inputs), whether their product be automobiles, college graduates or international loans and development projects.

Structural changes are sometimes used to protect the core productive technology. An organization can change its boundaries to embrace a part of the environment that is imposing constraints, as through vertical integration. 'Boundary-spanning units' that handle relations with important actors in the environment are another structural option for protecting the core technology from contingencies. An organization may divide a diverse, heterogeneous environment into homogeneous segments and establish separate units to handle them. A school district's 'tracking' of students into skill levels is an example, as is the division of elementary and secondary schools.

Self-assessment is a final way to reduce uncertainty. How an organization 'keeps score' of its own performance is fundamental when there is ambiguity about standards of desirability in the organization's field of activity, or uncertainty about the cause-effect relationships involved in its activities (Thompson, 1967, pp. 84–5). Each organization seeks to negotiate and establish a clear domain of action, agreed to by actors in its task environment, and to describe and represent their own activities in terms of socially accepted goals. In setting standards for its own work, an organization responds to the most important interests in its task environment, attending especially to the most visible portions of its own work.

Uncertainty, 'Core Technologies' and the World Bank

Applying structural contingency theory to the World Bank requires some reflection about the nature of its key inputs and outputs and its task environment. Capital is a key input, and member states and international capital markets that supply capital can subject the World Bank to political and financial uncertainties. But the supply of projects suitable for World Bank finance may be a greater source of uncertainty than is the supply of capital. Theoretically, the Bank assesses and finances projects proposed by member governments, assisting in design and financing those that its Board approves. But almost as soon as lending began, staff perceived that the flow of suitable project proposals would become a constraint, and began to assume a greater role in identifying and preparing project proposals (LePrestre, 1982; Mason and Asher, 1973). As lending grew in the 1970s, acceptable project proposals became the most critical input (Tendler, 1975; Van de Laar, 1980), and they remain both a key input and a part of the product.

If capital and project proposals are the major inputs, the primary 'output' consists of the packages of financial, technological, social and logistical arrangements that make up projects and program loans. The production process is fraught with uncertainties, requiring cooperation of government officials, other international or bilateral agencies, and, to a greater or lesser degree, the people and communities to be affected by the project. Projects are affected by factors as diverse as electoral politics, commodity prices and the weather.

In principle, strict standards of quality govern the product, defining operationally what are sound investments. The core of these standards is economic and financial: internal rates of return must be acceptable, and borrowers must be acceptable investment risks (Baum, 1978). The processes that guide identification, planning, appraisal and implementation of projects serve to assure the World Bank of the quality of its output. Criteria of economic, financial, technical and social soundness offer standards that define and certify projects' quality. The project cycle provides a prescribed set of steps that guarantee that the project has met these tests. These criteria and the project cycle make up the core of the World Bank's work processes: the skills, knowledge and processes that go into producing loans and development projects. More specifically, the standard operations – 'core technology' – includes the following:

1. *The project cycle guides identification, design, review, approval, implementation and evaluation of all projects.* The consistency of this multi-year process by which projects are identified based on country economic strategies, planned in detail in advance, appraised for economic, financial, institutional and technical soundness, negotiated with the borrower, implemented and evaluated, is a hallmark of World Bank lending (Baum, 1978; OED, 1990).
2. *A highly trained staff of economists, planners, engineers and social scientists is dominated by neoclassically trained economists.* The Bank seeks to build a staff of career employees, minimizing competing loyalties (Van de Laar, 1980, p. 100).
3. *A system of brief missions to borrowing countries which obtain information, assess needs and supervise projects.*
4. *An apparatus for research, publication and review of information elaborates and disseminates its theory and practice of planning and lending.*

5. *A high degree of centralization affects all aspects of its work.* Despite its global operations and impact, the World Bank maintains the vast majority of its staff, information processing, decision-making and analysis in its headquarters.

The organizational imperative to disburse capital depends on the regular and stable operation of this system. The desire to protect it from change and uncertainty therefore has implications for any policy change that affects the amount of staff time or work needed to 'move' a sum of money. The following sections review the very different courses of two major policy initiatives: anti-poverty lending in the 1970s and structural adjustment lending in the 1980s. Adoption of the new anti-poverty initiatives, appended awkwardly to the capital-investment mandate, was not as smooth or complete as the adoption of policy-based adjustment lending, which supports the Bank's development doctrine, facilitates the transfer of capital and increases the organization's leverage.

The Case of 'Poverty Lending'

Much has been written about the extent and limits of the Bank's anti-poverty emphasis under McNamara, and its durability after McNamara's departure in 1981 (Ayres, 1983; OED, 1988; Van de Laar, 1983; Sanford, 1984; Taskforce on Poverty, 1983; Stryker, 1979). Two sources, World Bank staffer Robert Ayres and the Bank's Operations Evaluation Division, draw more directly than most on interviews and internal documentation. They show the poverty alleviation campaign to be a case of adopting a new priority without downgrading existing mandates or making substantial changes in core technology or internal incentives. Further, it exemplifies the World Bank's ability to segregate a sector or category of lending – 'poverty lending' in this case – and protect its larger scale loans from more intensive scrutiny.

The organizational dynamics of poverty lending emerge at three levels: in the ideological and theoretical basis for the poverty policies; the structural and procedural aspects of implementation; and in project appraisal and the World Bank's assessment of its own work. These are discussed in turn in the following sections.

The theory: redistribution with growth

Robert McNamara became President of the World Bank in 1968 determined to address poverty directly and on a grand scale. The mandate for 'poverty orientation,' which contributed to a wave of attempts to articulate anti-poverty strategies in the 1970s, sparked internal debate over its conceptualization and implementation. Two schools competed for approval: Basic Needs and Redistribution with Growth (RWG). Basic Needs theory called for a floor of social services and income-generating aid for the poorest in the population, aimed at redistributing income, a significant reorientation of the Bank's program of capital-led growth.

RWG, the option that prevailed, proposed targeted investment to sectors in which poor people are concentrated, especially agriculture, but left the basic strategy intact. Avoiding income distribution issues, it 'did not represent a paradigm shift' (Ayres, 1983, p. 90). RWG articulated an anti-poverty strategy that shifted investment toward agriculture without challenging the basic concept of development through growth-oriented investment, and without altering the World Bank's basic mechanism for disbursing funds (see, for example, *Focus on Poverty* 1982).

The result, argues Ayres, 'was a rather tenuous gluing together of some markedly divergent approaches. Poverty-oriented emphases sometimes seemed to have been pasted on to the prevalent ideology without... altering its fundamental slant. This... enabled the Bank to do anything it wanted to do...' (p. 75).

'New-style' lending, old-style organization

The new poverty lending priority, even as articulated in RWG, did call for some substantial changes in lending. Stress on poverty and rural development resulted in new sectoral emphases. McNamara persistently emphasized these changes, and his commitment of the Bank to eradicating poverty and 'the worst manifestations of human indignity' suggested a substantially new organization. But while funds flowed to new sectors and to projects that looked unlike most previous World Bank investments, the structural features that shaped how work is done survived largely unaltered.

The OED (1988) summarizes the implementation of 'new-style' rural development lending in these terms: '[Management apparently] assumed that the Bank's operation was suitable for implementing the new strategy.... [and] that the Bank's standard project processing procedures were adequate and appropriate.' Standard procedures and assumptions were largely unaltered, reflecting the durability of a core technology that relies on technical expertise and illustrating resistance to change in these key organizational features.

New-style projects were largely designed and overseen by a separate Rural Development unit. Management's early effort to establish rural development units in the regional offices was dropped in the face of regional opposition and a separate central division was established in 1973 (OED, 1988, p. 49). (In contrast, environmental staff were integrated into regional units in the late 1980s, a move the Bank says indicates the high priority now given to environmental policy.) The Rural Development Division's staff were structurally set apart from the mainstream of operational work. According to Schechter (1987, p. 202) the new staff hired to work on RWG strategies 'became something of a parallel staff, working alongside more senior staff, some of whom were not as committed to massive expansion and developmentalism.'

The framework for developing projects within the project cycle was largely unchanged. Ayres (1983, p. 66) attributes a 'lack of imagination' in identifying projects partly to the failure to introduce interdisciplinary teams. Although the need for interdisciplinary work was recognized, sectoral divisions remained unchanged, and taskforce work was not widely used.

Information gathering, supervision and decision making remained highly centralized in Washington (OED, 1988, p. 56). Development needs and project ideas were appraised through brief overseas missions and more lengthy analysis and negotiation in headquarters. 'Bank operational staff and consultants are expensive and are not expected to spend prolonged periods of time in borrowing countries and their outlying project areas,' notes OED (p. 56). Ninety-four per cent of professional staff remained stationed in headquarters, and important decisions were almost all taken there (Ayres, 1983, p. 65).

Critics such as Gran (1988) treat this as evidence of willful ignorance of these aspects of economic life in poor countries that defy explanation under the World Bank's ideology. The persistence of a centralized, narrow information regime is consistent with Thompson's and Wildavsky's (1986) assignment of information selection biases to the hierarchical organizational culture (see Chapter 7). OED and Ayres describe the effects with typical understatement. For OED (1988, p. 56) the highly centralized process resulted in the application of project models to new situations without adequate adaptation. Ayres (1983, p. 65) observes that 'it is difficult for this mission-oriented approach to provide the sustained picture of rural and urban development processes that appeared a requisite for the Bank's decision-making in these areas.'

The project cycle, too, was under pressures that restricted the time available for developing complex rural development projects. The need to allocate sufficient time for project development has been widely recognized, particularly when the project aims to benefit groups that are not already well-organized and prepared to undertake the activities proposed (Bryant and White, 1982; Korten, 1980). Even in project supervision, where new-style lending was fully expected to require more staff time, OED (1988, p. 17) reports that the additional time was not allotted. The scissors effect created by growing amounts of capital to lend and restricted staff resources meant that project staff 'could not afford the luxury of [designing a project] for a slow start-up' (p. 56). Schechter (1987, p. 56) argues that 'staff managing many new-style projects chose to concentrate on putting through the traditional kinds of projects rather than assuming the heavy burden of helping the borrowing countries identify and work out complex, time-consuming new projects.'

Management had evidence from studies by the LAC office that new-style projects were absorbing more staff supervision time than 'conventional' projects (Ayres, 1983, p. 127). Yet in the face of evidence that these time requirements are inherent in the nature of the projects, the 1978 *Annual Report* optimistically asserted that '[d]elays in disbursements can reasonably be expected to fade as borrowers and the Bank gain experience in project execution' (p. 8).

The absence of structural changes to accommodate the new initiative was matched by a paucity of efforts to integrate poverty and rural development concerns into the skills, values and incentive structure of the professional staff. OED (1988, p. 49) notes a failure to 'sell' the new approaches to staff despite widely expressed 'coolness' toward them. Nor was any 'particular effort made to train staff in the finer points of the [rural development] strategy' (p. 48).

This ambiguity with respect to training and promotion of new-style policy, together with implicit messages sent by leaving other aspects of standard procedures intact, left room for uncertainty about management's commitment to a new style of anti-poverty lending. Staff opposition to the change suggests that explicit, energetic promotion through rhetoric, training, and structure would have been required to effect a major change in lending procedures:

> The absence of these instead allowed uncertainty about 'the kinds of achievements that would bring rewards to staff members. Sometimes it seemed that poverty alleviation in rural areas took precedence. But other times emphasis seemed to be placed on the aggregate amounts of loans processed or on the aggregate amount of incremental

agricultural production likely to occur.... Such conflicting signals often contributed to internal controversy' ('Bank official,' quoted in Ayres, 1983, p. 10).

Some important managerial changes did accompany the anti-poverty campaign. Two planning tools, the Country Program paper and the annual country allocation exercise, were introduced as McNamara promoted a programming, planning and budgeting regime developed at Ford Motors and the Pentagon (McKitterick, 1986, p. 47):

> ... a five-year lending program for the Bank/IDA in a given country [was developed] against a detailed statistical analysis of each sector of the country's economy. The annual country allocation exercise drew on these five-year plans where possible and set targets for the staff for each country and each sector within each country. Attainment of these annual targets became the benchmark for judging staff performance and individual promotion.

The organizational innovations that accompanied the anti-poverty campaign, then, only heightened the focus on the quantity of lending rather than the process of participatory and poverty-oriented lending. Meanwhile the organizational structure, project cycle and information system all remained essentially unchanged in the face of the new identity proclaimed by McNamara. The durability of these features illustrates the strong tendency of a core technology and information system to resist change.

As with anti-poverty lending in general, other social issues encountered considerable ideological, structural and procedural obstacles to integration into the World Bank lending program.[3] In the absence of strong pressure from without, or compelling need to change in order to satisfy and retain an important constituency, these internal organizational obstacles were sufficient to keep social concerns at the margin.

The Case of Adjustment Lending

Adjustment lending was introduced as a short-term, emergency solution to immediate balance of payments problems and the debt crisis (Development Committee, 1990, pp. 14–15). Adjustment lending to any country was to continue for three to five years. Speeches and reports introduced the new policy with an urgency comparable to the launching of anti-poverty lending.

Adjustment lending responded to pressure from the Reagan and Thatcher governments, which controlled 24 per cent of voting power on the Bank board and 'relentlessly attack[ed the Bank] for being insufficiently pro-market' (Cypher, 1989a). Criticism by conservative members of Congress and pressure from the US Administration to participate in the 'Baker Plan' for debt relief also helped motivate management's adoption of policy-based lending (Bacha and Feinberg, 1986, p. 340).

Commercial banks stimulated the adoption of policy-based lending in two ways. First, their retreat from additional lending in the early 1980s helped to create the political and financial crisis that motivated the Baker Plan, and choked off the flow of capital for debt servicing by debtor nations. Second, there is evidence that commercial lenders themselves pressed the World Bank to step into the breach with measures that both financed debt service and motivated policy changes (Hamilton, 1989). For international banks and corporations, adjustment lending represented a more direct approach to opening economies to transnational investment (Cypher, 1989a, p. 61).

Internally, adjustment lending had much to recommend itself. Adjustment's export-oriented program was responsive to the widespread criticism among staff of import-substitution strategies (Bacha and Feinberg, 1986, p. 340). Some staff also consider the 'Asian Miracle' economies of Taiwan, South Korea, Hong Kong and Singapore to be models of free-market development, whose emulation the Bank should encourage (Cypher, 1989a).[4]

Discontent among donors with the impact of project aid also had an influence, and quick-disbursing policy-based loans, especially large loans to major debtor nations, were an attractive vehicle for moving money. SALs have in fact been efficient disbursers of capital: the average amount of adjustment loans was more than 25 per cent larger than the average project loan in 1987 and 1989. (In 1990, SALs and project loans were of roughly equal average size; in 1994 SALs were some 13 per cent larger (calculated from Annual Reports 1987, 1989, 1990).)

Policy-based lending offered new challenges and rewards to staff economists with macro-economic expertise. It was also a flexible tool, adaptable to sectors, and applicable where economy-wide programs could not be negotiated or implemented. Sectoral adjustment loans (SECALs) and 'hybrid loans' made policy-based lending a viable option for many country programs (Development Committee 1990, No. 23, p. 18).

Contingency theory offers a helpful characterization of the policy change. Adjustment lending can be seen as moving the analysis and design of policy at the country and regional level – already part of the core technology – into the forefront of lending activities. Ayres (1983) describes three levels of World Bank activity: participation in the 'international marketplace of ideas' through discussions of macro and sectoral policy; national policy dialogue; and project lending. He notes 'slippage' and compromise with each step away from the abstract (ideas) toward the concrete (project lending). Adjustment lending moves the policy-making apparatus from the background into the center of the core technology by offering loans directly in support of policies the Bank endorses or designs.

Especially when compared to anti-poverty lending, where foot-dragging led to very slow and incomplete adoption, adjustment lending was quickly incorporated into the World Bank's lending program. While organizational and professional factors apparently shaped the pace and extent of adoption of anti-poverty lending, the overriding importance of disbursement and of the Bank's role in debt management led to rapid incorporation of policy-based lending.

I return to both cases in Chapter 6, to discuss how the World Bank's standards of self-assessment influenced the course of policy change. Standards and methods for measuring and certifying its own performance – pre-appraisal of projects and calculation of economic and financial rates of return through cost-benefit analysis – remained stable in the face of new and potentially challenging kinds of lending.

NGOs, DISBURSEMENT AND STAFF TIME

Working with NGOs, unlike adopting anti-poverty lending in the 1970s or adjustment lending in the 1980s, requires that a new set of actors be incorporated into the lending process. The anti-poverty campaign introduced a new priority but made no fundamental change in lending apparatus. Adjustment lending introduced a new kind of loan, and with it new opportunities for disbursement and influence.

The World Bank's engagement with NGOs is related to both poverty lending and adjustment. It gives new rhetorical life to the anti-poverty commitment of the 1970s, as the Bank publicizes its engagement with the development profession's premier poverty fighters. It is tied to adjustment lending by the prominence of NGOs in programs to soften the effects of adjustment on the poor. But the policy of collaboration with NGOs is distinct in that it purports to engage the Bank with a new and different set of actors and interests.

The World Bank has publicized its work with NGOs as part of an effort to demonstrate a continued commitment to poverty-oriented lending. The meteoric rise of adjustment lending provoked questions from several quarters as to the status of anti-poverty lending (Sanford, 1984; Stokes, 1986). Bank documents make it clear that these questions were a matter of concern. The Bank's Operations Evaluation Division (OED, 1988, p. 15) raises the question of whether the 'poverty focus' is waxing, waning or wavering, noting indicators that suggest 'a decline in the share of World Bank activities specifically targeted toward poverty reduction.' The OED concludes that the poverty focus is intact, but cites only research activities, 'positions' and policy statements such as those of a 1986 poverty task force.

As with previous policy emphases, the issue of poverty eradication under structural adjustment, for the Bank, is one of balancing growth, recovery, and protecting the poor (Development Committee, 1987; 1990). The 1987 *Annual Report* commits the Bank to assisting governments in designing adjustment programs 'that to the extent possible... protect the poor, notably through improvements in the efficiency and targeting of social expenditures'. Singer (1991, p. 15) worries that this 'ominous' language reflects no 'moral imperative or even high priority for the protection of the poor.'

World Bank reports and public documents on poverty and on NGOs link the NGO effort to its anti-poverty policy both implicitly and explicitly. NGOs, for example, are mentioned repeatedly in Chapter 4 of the 1990 WDR ('Promoting economic opportunities for the poor') and identified as an important option in ending exclusive reliance on government agencies, a change needed for 'successful programs' in rural infrastructure and technology (World Bank, WDR, 1990, pp. 67, 70; see also World Bank, 1990d).

In view of the close relation between anti-poverty and NGO policy in the World Bank's constellation of policy priorities, it is not surprising that the issues raised in interviews about collaboration with NGOs closely parallel those that defined and limited the 1970s anti-poverty campaign: the imperative of moving money, limitations on staff time and energy, the tendency to substitute expertise and effort for listening and learning; and the failure to institutionalize procedures and incentives that would promote the new policy widely and systematically.

'Finessing it'

The pressure of time and money is the most-discussed theme in my interviews with World Bank staff. Many cite what a senior Asia economist called 'the disbursement imperative' as a key limit on innovative lending.

'There is no incentive to innovate,' argues one staffer (Policy staff no. 3), when one rises by moving money quickly. A Finance staffer agrees that the disbursement imperative 'dominates decisions at the Bank,' (Finance staff no. 1), and McKitterick (1986, p. 47) claims that in 200 interviews of Bank staff, not one 'said he got promoted for saying "No.". . . What count[s] is getting the appraisal report done in time to meet the target.'[5]

Limited staff time per project surfaces even more often than the disbursement imperative. Working with NGOs takes time, and senior project staff from Latin America and EMENA stressed that they lack the staff to canvass and build relations with NGOs. Two Operational staff stressed the need to hold down one's 'coefficients,' the work-weeks per project figures reported in Project Completion Reports (LAC staff no. 1; LAC staff no. 2). Frequent complaints of overwork, also noted by Thomas (1980, p. 173), were typified by a senior agriculture specialist's lament about restricted mission size and chronic overstretching of project task managers (Policy staff no. 5). Several Operations staff asked how NGOs might be contacted by someone with more time (NGO experts, Resident staff, consultants) (Africa staff, October 6, 1989; Africa staff no. 3; LAC staff, 6 October 1989).

But Operations staff from Asia, Africa and Latin America regions who described extensive contacts with NGOs consistently said they themselves had spent time in the country meeting and talking with NGO representatives in order to develop relationships with them. Information collected in a central office could be helpful, they argued, but forays by NGO specialists could not substitute for building personal contacts between country staff and local NGOs.

Some frustrated staff say the World Bank lacks the 'agility' needed to work with NGOs, and operations staff from three regions describe cynicism about social requirements, seen as 'baubles' to be hung on 'Christmas tree projects,' a reluctance to 'genuflect' toward new issues (Finance staff no. 1; Policy staff no. 3; Africa staff no. 3; LAC staff no. 2; Asia staff no. 3).

But the most frequent response to the time/money crunch was described by a senior Asia economist as finessing it (Asia staff no.3). 'Finessing it' occurs when too much is required to be done in too little time while preparing a project. One says the right things, proposes (for example) organizing the requisite number of irrigation groups, and does one's best, knowing that the work described would require more than the time allotted. Reluctance to delay or scrap a project was noted by Thomas (1980, p. 174) who found that when a project has been appraised 'it becomes very difficult for the staff to avoid implementing it. "Management puts us under pressure to ignore little problems, but then no one has the guts to say no when the project is a bad one."'

'Finessing it' also describes most staff's response to the time and money crunch faced by the organization as a whole. With staff limited, capital increased and new commitments to staff-intensive environmental, social and NGO measures, most operational staff acknowledge the crunch but finesse it. Official documents often claim to be doing more of all things (for all people) at one time, as in a 1990 publication: '[The World Bank] is focusing more than in the past on economic policies at the national and international levels and, at the same time, on the poverty and environmental aspects of development' (1990d, p. 17).

OED (1988, p. 55) cites the same tendency in reviewing rural development strategies. When 'lending volume remains the main performance measure,' staff are encouraged to 'discount... the value of experience in favor of drive and commitment. The latter qualities are conducive to keeping a lending strategy alive... in the face of misfortune, but obviously they court serious dangers.'

The 1992 review of project quality and implementation (Wapenhans Report) makes this staff-wide focus on designing new lending, rather than overseeing the quality of existing loans, a matter of official concern. It sees priorities as reversed, with quantity of lending overpowering concerns about quality, and staff pushing internally conceived projects on borrowers. Staff responding to interviews say (71 per cent) that they are 'overwhelmed by responsibilities for which they have little or no pre-Bank experience or in-Bank training' (World Bank, 1992, p. 19).

But in the wake of Wapenhans, and while some Bank managers are asserting that procedural reforms will relieve the pressure to lend, the Bank has announced significant cutbacks in administrative budget for fiscal years 1996 and 1997. The across-the-board 6.5 per cent cuts in internal (not lending) budget respond to member countries' understandable concerns about high costs. But they also make it difficult to be optimistic about the implementation of innovative and participatory methodologies that are demanding of staff time, and thus money.

A great deal of evidence, then, points to a conflict between the mandate to move capital and new issues that place labor-intensive demands on staff. The tension limits the real significance of commitments to social issues. Staff with specific concerns about poverty impact and participatory development process – who identify themselves as a minority – say the effort to involve NGOs in operations depends on the individual efforts of a few highly motivated staff (Africa staff no. 1;

Policy staff no. 6). One Africa staff economist asked with some frustration: 'Is it more important to get resources to poor people, or to move money? Maybe we'll see this changing at the Bank... Maybe the Bank will be prepared to do a project without every cent preappraised' (Africa staff, 6 October 1989).

Many NGO sources, including several involved in intensive project collaboration with the Bank, make the same observation. A European NGO executive notes that 'in day-do-day operations, individual staff members, especially the task-managers, have immense freedom of manoeuvre, providing that they deliver the goods.' He observes among some staff great '... readiness to cooperate and take account of the views of NGOs, a readiness which would vary from one staff member to another' (G. Meier, letter, 2 July 1990). An NGO staffer in the Philippines engaged in the Philippines Health III project said pointedly that she saw the initiative as coming from the project task manager himself, 'not the World Bank' (interview, 21 November 1989).

Staff do note sub-regional and sectoral exceptions to the time/money crunch. Some social sector project staff noted that the disbursement imperative applies less to health, nutrition and population than to agriculture, industrial and infrastructure loans. Some say that pressure is self-selecting by sector, and that professionals who wish to can choose jobs that put them under relatively little pressure, and find creative ways to use project appraisal resources that build contacts with NGOs (Africa staff no. 2; Africa staff no. 3). An Africa country economist acknowledges that the stereotype of an 'inflexible bureaucracy fixed on moving money' is based in fact, but notes that the organization is not monolithic (Africa staff no. 1).

West Africa staff, for example, had free rein from their regional director in the late 1980s to pursue collaborative projects with NGOs under the Social Dimensions of Adjustment (SDA) program. The Southern Africa Department is the geographic unit that has now moved to the forefront in promoting innovative work. The Department's stated approach to programming, management and policy dialogue calls for resident missions and country staff to consult extensively with interested groups, to slow down operations and dialogue where necessary to allow for government deliberation and initiative, and to apply a variety of assessment methodologies to improve the breadth and depth of the department's information about clients' priorities and needs.

Likewise, the Economic Development Institute's training and capacity-building program with NGOs has been a small exception. Priority is given to 'building trust' through participation in identifying training needs and designing programs. But the EDI programs have the advantage of involving only funds from individual donors' trust funds, not Bank lending resources.

Still, the propensity to commit funds quickly remains a problem for NGO collaboration Bank-wide, even in projects or project components that are small, by World Bank standards, and in the social sectors. The Health Development III Project in the Philippines, with a $7.4 million component to finance NGO primary health care services, aimed to build on progress made in the Aquino government toward a policy of cooperation with NGOs in social sector work. The greatest concern of two experienced UNICEF officials, however, was that the Bank would introduce funds without allowing time for pilot project experimentation and for the training necessary for government regional health personnel to allow working arrangements to grow successfully. Without enough time for a slow start-up, these health officers feared that government-NGO working relationships could not flourish (interview, December 1989).

Budget and time constraints have also been faced more directly in the environmental sector. Kenneth Piddington, then chief of the Bank's environmental office, noted in a 1988 internal memo that the organization had to face 'resource implications of internalizing environmental review to project development.' He noted as well that he was not 'satisfied that the resource implications have been properly worked through. . . .' Regional environmental staff mention funds available for consultants during project preparation, and a perceived flexibility when project preparation is delayed by environmental assessments or debates (SAC staff no. 2; Asia staff no. 5).

Even these exceptions, however, highlight the extreme limitations placed on the World Bank by its treatment of social needs as addenda to the growth imperative. The Bank's NGO liaison office makes a critical distinction between sectors and projects where cultivating participation is 'worth the effort,' and those where it is not. Participation is 'worth the effort' when projects 'are designed to help a specific group of people;' require beneficiaries to pay some costs; or need active beneficiary commitment in order to work (Strategic Planning and Review, 1989, p. 14ff.). In promoting participatory strategies internally, large-scale projects and those thought to produce broadly enjoyed benefits are exempted. Where participation has costs in terms of staff or community residents' time or 'delays and changes in project design, development of community organizations and people-responsive structures . . . benefits may not be as high' (Strategic Planning and Review, 1989, p. 14).

To be sure, thinking among participation advocates within the Bank has advanced a good deal since 1989. It is true, as Stiefel and Wolfe note, that the Bank has conceptualized participation and reviewed its own performance more rigorously than other international organizations, including some of those to whom the rhetoric comes more readily than to the Bank (222–3). Still, in practice, one can only imagine the Bank's lending apparatus adapting to the delays of extensive participation if the practice were limited, by sector or otherwise. The 1989 language expresses the present thinking more candidly than Bank spokespeople would today: participation is 'worth it' in irrigation and probably in other sectors to be determined, and probably 'not worth it' in health and several others.

So these tensions resurfaced in 1991 and 1994 seminars on participation, held as part of the Bank's 'learning process' on participatory development. Bank staff and external participants raised questions about the organization's ability to incorporate more participatory methods when its lending and staff are driven by the mandate to move money. The Bank's review of some 35 participatory projects is seeking to determine whether participation has in fact required more staff time and slowed disbursement. (The content of the workshops and the Learning Process recommendations are discussed in Chapter 7.)

Recognition of this tension by the staff cadre that supports participation, of course, does not resolve the issue. Now that the concern raised by outside critics has been broached by the official review of lending quality – the Wapenhans report – the World Bank will have to choose to confront the tension outlined here. The Bank can re-tool, radically reshaping its lending process and project cycle to meet the challenges, or it can finesse it. The latter option is the ingrained response of a majority of middle level professional staff, according to one staff promoter of participation and NGO strategies. A major contingent of these staffers assume that they can weather the present round of proposed changes as they have previous reforms (interview June 1994). The durability of the Bank's mandates and procedures seem to make the latter more likely. The result will depend in good part on how vigorously and effectively the Bank's NGO critics can press the issue.

'First-level' and 'Second-level' Issues

Some staff complain that the multiple policy directives they receive from management – regarding the environment, poverty, appropriate technology, women in development, NGOs – force them to weigh and

Organizational Aspects of a Development Model 109

discern which are to be taken seriously. Such requirements distract staff from what many consider to be their central mandate, and are sometimes perceived as bureaucratic or politically-inspired requirements that complicate their work and reduce their effectiveness. McKitterick (1986, p. 47), for example, argues that 'under McNamara the Bank... became a "development agency" with a multiplicity of purposes.... Bank staff lost any coherent sense of institutional purpose....' The Wapenhans report (1992) finds this expanding scope of responsibilities to be a continuing problem for the quality of investments.

Yet no staffer I have spoken with has had any difficulty discerning which issues are to be assigned highest priority. Among the multiplicity of issues to which project staff might give attention, several staff describe a simple hierarchy of issues that they say is generally understood.

Two topics have become 'first-level' issues: national economic and pricing policy and the environment. One ignores these issues in project planning, a senior economist said, only 'at the peril of one's career' (Policy staff no. 7). Their status seems to be recognized by a broad range of staff. Other issues – gender, indigenous peoples, etc. – are 'second rank' issues that may earn 'brownie points' when included in a project, but will not be noticed if they are omitted (Policy staff no. 7; LAC staff no. 2). Operational collaboration with NGOs remains a second-level issue: the Bank's NGO liaison unit acknowledges that although staff are aware of official policy in favor of collaborating with NGOs, most on staff know little about NGOs (SPRIE, 1990, p. 15).

Staff describe two kinds of factors that can boost an issue to first-level status: an issue rises through external pressure or through advances in theoretical and empirical work by Bank staff. Internal expertise and external political pressure were woven together in a sometimes contradictory web of explanations given for policy changes.

One environmental staffer interrupted my question to assert emphatically that pressure from without is what moves an issue along in the World Bank. There are, in this economist's view, staff who recognize themselves the importance of environmental concerns in Bank-financed operations previous to NGO and other public campaigns on the subject. But it is external pressure, from NGOs, the US Congress and the Executive Directors, that elevated the issue.

An economist in private sector operations attributes the rise of the two first-level issues to quite distinct dynamics of change. Environmental issues gained their status, he notes, through outside pressure. Environmentalists seized successfully on 'a few bad projects' and conducted an effective campaign. Macro-economic policy conditionality and cost recovery, on the other hand, became central to Bank lending on their merits, because staff determined that they were 'the right thing to do' (Policy staff no. 7).

Although other staff acknowledged the effectiveness, and some the necessity of external pressure on environmental issues (Policy staff no. 3), World Bank staff tend on the whole to perceive policy change as developed through reasoned deliberation and discussion by their expert colleagues.

The role of environmental NGOs in advocacy with the World Bank has been described in some detail elsewhere (LePrestre, 1986; Rich, 1985; Schwartzman, 1989; Rich, 1994), and my interviews produced no reason to doubt the widely held view that pressure inspired by the reporting and lobbying of national and international environmental NGOs was the key to changes that have been made in environmental policies and regulations at the World Bank.

Environment and the Bank: From Threat to Organizational Asset?

Documentation collected at the Environmental Defense Fund's MDB Information Center, by the Bank Information Center, and in World Bank files chronicle campaigns of correspondence, communication with the media, documentary films and television programs and lobbying of the World Bank and Northern parliaments, largely led by environmental NGOs based in the North, and carried out by networks of international, Southern national and local groups.

The result, an aggressively 'green' World Bank that carves out new responsibilities for itself in the management of international environmental issues, should have been no surprise to observers of the Bank or to students of organizational sociology. Put on the defensive by a vigorous critique, whose demands have included lending slowdowns or moratoriums for large infrastructure projects, the Bank took the initiative, gaining control of the Global Environment Fund (see Chapter 2), then seeking unsuccessfully to augment funds for the tenth replenishment of IDA by proposing a $5 billion 'earth increment' for environment-related projects.

Environmental advocacy and pressure from major donors created a tension with the Bank's overall mandate. As *The Economist* noted, its role as 'a compulsive lender sits uneasily with its new job as custodian of the environment' (2 September 1989, p. 44). An improved environmental policy might call for less rather than more lending. But while carrying out environmental assessments and requiring national environmental action plans, the Bank has successfully turned a potential threat to its disbursement capacity into an asset through the GEF and projects labeled as environment-specific.

The Bank's move into the center of global environmental action is reminiscent of its response in the late 1950s to calls for an institution to meet the capital needs of countries – notably India – that could not borrow from the IBRD. The Bank moved quickly and effectively to put the newly proposed UN fund under its own control, and the IDA was born (see Libby, 1975a). Thirty years later, when global environmental issues became a significant challenge to the Bank's operations, it took advantage of its size, scope and resources to expand its mandate and absorb a troublesome issue into its own structure.

CONCLUSION

Historically, the World Bank has adapted its mandate in order to survive: in so doing it created a development mandate and established a niche for itself among international and national organizations. More recently, the development mandate has proven to be quite stable, and new proposed objectives have been appended to the mandate of financially induced capital-led development. The organizational structure and process that have served capital-induced growth-oriented development strategies do not adapt to the requirements of more process-oriented, participatory operations.

The implications for NGOs and the World Bank are made more explicit in the next chapter, which discusses contradictions within and among the organizational myths that underpin Bank operations.

6 The World Bank and Apolitical Development

Much of the World Bank's influence depends on its success in representing itself, its activities and the 'development' it promotes as 'apolitical.' World Bank officials have long been aware of the importance of the apolitical image: President Eugene Black wrote in 1962 that '[w]e ask a lot of questions and attach a lot of conditions to our loans. . . . [W]e would never get away with this if we did not . . . render the language of economics morally antiseptic. . . .' (in Swedberg, 1986, p. 388).

This chapter explores the apolitical image, shows how this image empowers the World Bank, and argues that the Bank's engagement with NGOs, along with other factors, stretch the image's credibility. Two myths underlie the apolitical image: the myth of the primacy of member countries' sovereignty; and the myth of development as an apolitical, technical process achieved through gradual economic change, political stability, and integration into the global capitalist economic system. These myths constitute a formidable barrier to cooperation with non-governmental organizations. Where the World Bank does engage NGOs, the relations strain its apolitical image and confront the myth of sovereignty and of apolitical development with the highly political nature of the Bank's work and influence.

Engagement with NGOs is one of several ways the myth of apolitical development is being stretched at the World Bank. The Bank's emphasis on 'governance' issues and pressure from without and within for greater attention to civil and political rights in borrowing countries are challenging the Bank's underlying myths (David Gillies, 1993; Jerome Levinson, 1992). In these areas as with NGOs, the realities of a changing world confront myths and structures that have served the Bank through previous changes.

The World Bank is neither apolitical nor a neutral servant of the wishes of its member states, but an organization with a measure of autonomy, considerable power over many of its borrowing members, and a variety of ways to exercise that power. Many of those channels of influence are effective only in the presence of the sovereignty and development myths: development plans with profound political and distributional implications can be promoted forcefully if their basis is agreed to be apolitical and scientific. And when real economic choices are sharply constrained by debt and the absence of financial and institutional alternatives, emphasizing borrowers' formal sovereignty softens the hard realities of power relations in their dealings with the Bank.

Tensions between the apolitical image and a highly political reality, and between the technocratic myth of development and the economic and social realities of poverty in borrowing countries, form a contradictory foundation for liaison with NGOs. As bases for World Bank operations, the sovereignty and development myths are fragile, but have been held together successfully through the Bank's dealings with governments and with quasi-governmental bodies. The tensions and contradictions are sharpened by current efforts to involve NGOs in Bank-funded operations, by a new 'popular participation learning process,' and by the attacks of some of the World Bank's NGO critics.

THE WORLD BANK AND 'APOLITICAL' DEVELOPMENT

The World Bank goes to some lengths to represent its own activity as above politics. This description of dispassionate analysis of technical problems by objective professionals is typical:

> ... a loan proposal or a policy question that reaches the Executive Directors ... has been very thoroughly discussed and analyzed by a group of trained professionals recruited on a broad international basis, with differing points of view, wide international experience, and an ever increasing sensitivity to the individual culture and problems of member countries (World Bank and IDA, Questions and Answers n.d., p. 6).

The claim of freedom from political considerations has been called a 'principal element of the mythology of Bank lending...' (Ayres, 1983, p. 71). Thomas' interviews of Bank staff show that the mythology also contributes to staff's preference for the Bank as employer over a bilateral aid institution.

The Apolitical Image and Economic Orthodoxy

Legal scholar A.A. Fatorous (1977, pp. 23–5) argues that the apolitical and technical image is the most important dimension of the Bank's operating ideology, the dimension by which it 'frees itself from the common constraints on non-intervention that the international legal order imposes on public actors.' Any remaining constraint is removed 'by the fact that any final action taken... is incorporated, or allowed for, in an agreement with the country concerned. [This] consent legitimizes all aspects of the decision the Bank may have successfully imposed.'

This freedom from international legal constraints, along with the breadth of its working mandate, fosters considerable independence, or relative autonomy of action. Not only the World Bank itself, but the 'development' it promotes is represented as apolitical, as progress that will follow from correct policies and institutions. Conversely, the strict separation of the economic and political allows the Bank (and other international financial agencies) to operate without having to 'confront the full implications of their actions within a society' (Levinson, 1992, p. 62). So long as 'country performance' is conceived of overwhelmingly in terms of the Bank's preferred economic indicators, the Bank is free from having to give formal consideration to political and civil rights in borrowing countries.

Sectoral lending patterns have changed since postwar reconstruction, but three factors remained constant in the conceptualization of development. Development is technical, driven by capital investment, and almost always furthered by more contact with the global economy.

Development is treated not as a complex, problematic process where what counts as 'development' depends upon circumstances and on the interests of all groups involved. It is, instead, progress that will proceed in a more-or-less predictable fashion if enough of the missing ingredient – technical skill, capital, correct prices – is supplied. Some NGOs argue that the Bank must 'take the side of the poor' in designing and negotiating policies and projects (Bangkok NGO-World Bank Committee Meetings, 1989; noted in Strategic Planning and Review, 1990, p. 20; Addendum to the Report of the Participatory Development Learning Group, World Bank, 1994g). But 'taking sides' makes no sense if development depends on technically correct measures and on policy guidance that determines scientifically the best route for all participants.

The tendency to de-politicize development is not unique to the World Bank. David Goldsworthy (1988) illustrates the lack of political-mindedness in development theory and practice throughout official and private development agencies, and in much academic discourse. The presence – Goldsworthy would argue the primacy – of values, interests and power considerations in all situations of underdevelopment and social change is inconvenient for World Bank operations, incompatible with the myth of sovereignty, and an obstacle to rapid and effective disbursement of resources.

Politics has no place, formally, because economic science supplies reliable answers to policy questions. Ayres (1983, p. 4) argues that the World Bank relies on 'a dominant ideology' of neoliberalism, emphasizing economic growth through:

> ... capital accumulation [and]... export expansion and diversification. Ingredients of neoliberalism derivative from these basic goals [are] highly prevalent in Bank documents, publications and interviews with Bank staff and officials. [They] include fiscal and monetary probity; 'getting prices right'. . .; a sound currency; external economic equilibrium; export dynamism; economic stability; and, through all of these things, a favorable investment climate.

Orthodox theory serves as a sure, scientific basis for policy, and as intellectual and ideological justification for the World Bank's activities. The 'vast majority' of staff interviewed by Ayres:

> ... reject the notion that these emphases indicate an ideology at all. In their view, as expressed in repeated interviews, all of this is neutral. It is simply sound economic and financial management, technocratically orchestrated and [universally] applicable . . . (1983, pp. 74–5).

Economic doctrine helps the Bank shape discourse about development around technique and science rather than values and politics. The presentation of economic theories as scientific formulations shields them from criticism (Sassower, 1988, pp. 167–8), permitting the Bank to exert financial leverage to promote not 'its way,' but a certifiably 'correct way.'

For a generation, officials returning to government posts after training courses at the Bank's Economic Development Institute (EDI) have testified to the status afforded to World Bank development models. A Sudanese official typified the responses to a survey by Ronald Libby (1975b, p. 174), saying that the Bank's '"scientific approach to the problems of development is the best and only way to progress."' EDI participants call the Bank '"the most qualified to assume the general development of a country at any stage of its economic and social growth. Technicians of the World Bank . . . are the best the world over"' (Haitian official in Libby, 1975b, p. 174).

Setting the Standards, Defining the Myth of Development

The idea of apolitical development is important to the World Bank for two reasons. One has already been raised: interventions in national economies can be justified if development policy is a matter of correct technical decisions. A second role is more complex. By defining the 'development' it is to support, the World Bank has established standards of success in a field where there is no consensus about what constitutes successful development.

Carlsson, Köhlin and Ekbom, in a study of the organizational and political dimensions of economic evaluation, show that an agency's use of economic analysis follows from its 'ultimate, though often unofficial goals' (p. 185). In the Bank, refinements such as social cost benefit analysis are not used, and traditional cost benefit analysis becomes a tool not for learning more about projects' economic impact, but for certifying their value and facilitating the disbursement of funds. This function of economic analysis is essential because the World Bank must operate both as an international financial institution and a development agency.

Its creditors require evidence that investments meet standards of financial viability. This standard, as measured by economic rates of return, has become part of the Bank's definition of development. World Bank publications acknowledge other dimensions: World Development Reports regularly take up issues such as poverty and human resources (1980, 1990), agriculture (1982), population (1984), and the environment (1992).

Recent sociological theories of organizations, however, suggest that the World Bank's working definition, as embodied in the processes by which it carries out its version of development, may be more important than stated definitions. A pattern of actions that conforms to – or succeeds in establishing – socially accepted standards for organizations, can certify 'success' where consensus on concrete measures of success is elusive. Organizational theorists Dimaggio and Powell write: 'Politics and ceremony ... pervade much modern organizational life' as organizations compete not only for economic fitness, but for social fitness, 'political power and institutional legitimacy' (1983, p. 150).

The pattern of actions involved in World Bank lending reveal an operational definition of 'development.' As acted out in the lending process, development is marked by three characteristics:

1. It can be planned and managed, as evidenced by the project planning and pre-appraisal process.

2. It is 'bankable,' as evidenced by the apparent bottom-line reliance on internal rates of return and cost-benefit ratios in appraising potential investments.
3. It is 'technical,' achieved by adopting 'right' prices, institutions, and technologies.

The World Bank plans and manages development through a standardized project design process, with each project planned in light of a national development plan and needs assessment. The Bank's Operations Evaluation Department (OED) observed planning procedures in the most poverty-oriented, new-style rural development projects of the 1980s. OED (1988, p. 51) calls the standard process 'definitive appraisal', in which project planning involves a single definitive pre-assessment 'with all that this implies with respect to rigidity... and perhaps later slavish adherence to questionable objectives and design.' Appraisals consist of a 'short country visit by a team of staff (and often consultants) followed by a lengthy period of drafting and reviews at headquarters. In some cases follow-up visits were made to complete the appraisal, but most of the work was done at headquarters' (OED, 1988, p. 50).

As the development myth expanded to include explicit attention to equity issues and small farmer production, the project design and development apparatus failed to change with it. In OED's view, the problem with a definitive pre-appraisal or 'blueprint' is that it finds itself 'at odds with some of the realities of sustainable rural development.' Legal, technical and other factors make it difficult to change project plans to respond to changing circumstances, so 'to "live with" the appraisal design is the easiest course. The existence of an appraisal report tends to "cement" the original design in place' (OED, 1988, p. 51).

The definitive appraisal is deeply rooted in the World Bank's management and operating style. It is associated with 'the "bankability" notion of development financing,' in which profitability must be demonstrated conclusively before a planned investment is approved. The appraisal report:

> is in effect the product and chief measure of output for both individuals and units at several levels. Thus in operating units... the grey cover appraisal report is an objective in itself, second only to Board approval.... The appraisal is thereby seen as an endpoint rather than a beginning. Sometimes after the grey cover stage, staff disengage from an operation, and this adds further discontinuity to the process (OED, 1988, p. 51).

Definitive appraisal and the system of planning and incentives in which it is enshrined is fundamentally out of step with 'sustainable development.' Such social and economic change is a long-term process, but 'the incentive system for staff and the prime measures of their performance are based mainly on convenient short-term measures towards the long-term goals – appraisals, Board approvals and [dollar] amounts committed' (OED, 1988, p. 51).

Some observers attribute these rigidities, and the tendency to formalize and depoliticize development, to the need to tread carefully through the geopolitics and ideologies of the Cold War. Technocratic approaches to theory, planning and assessment were necessary, the theory goes, to make the Bank's intervention as inoffensive as possible to a range of ideologies, among borrowers and donors alike. This view offers the hope that in a post-Cold War era, there may be a loosening and opening at the Bank.

But whether they originated as a kind of protective covering from Cold War pressures or from some other dynamics, these characteristics have taken on a life of their own. They depict, to various interest groups, not only the World Bank's political acceptability, but, as organizational sociologist John Meyer writes of organizations in general, its rationality and its command of its field of activity. Ideas, expectations and ideologies are fleshed out in formal structure and visible work patterns that uphold the principle of rationality, a collective normative principle of modern life that is 'a legitimating moral force external to any particular organization.' Meyer's theoretical description fits the World Bank perfectly: 'Organizations ... are liturgical structures, celebrating wider principles [technical rationality] in part by ignoring many aspects of experiential reality' (Meyer, 1984, pp. 190–2, 197).

The World Bank's apolitical posture, and the planning and assessment approaches that accompany it offer a mode of operation compatible with industrialized country and banking interests; they are a strategy for organizational survival in a highly uncertain field of work; and, it is argued in the next section, they are a source of power and influence in daily operations.

APOLITICAL DEVELOPMENT AND THE WORLD BANK'S INFLUENCE

The World Bank has successfully promoted its notion of development among bilateral agencies, some development professionals and many borrower government officials. The Bank exerts influence through (1) the 'global marketplace of ideas,' (2) advice and lending that encourages changes in national economic policy, and (3) development projects (Ayres, 1983, pp. 19–22). Intellectually, its reputation for technical competence and its international status give it considerable clout. Publications such as the WDR 'attract... worldwide attention,' (Lipton, 1987, p. 200), and the Bank has shaped opinion on issues such as the Green Revolution (Stryker, 1979, p. 331), basic needs strategies (Streeten, 1979) and market-based agricultural pricing (Balassa, 1984; World Bank, 1981).

Intellectual Influence: World Bank as Tutor and Model

Richard Stryker (1979, p. 325) outlines the dimensions of this intellectual leadership, calling the World Bank:

> ... the leading international institution for development financing and for elaborating new development strategies. [Its] influence... extends well beyond any quantitative accounting of its operations. Its country reports, evaluating borrowers' economic and policy performances; its expertise in designing and evaluating development projects; its coordinating role in aid consortia and inter-agency activities...; and the efforts of its President to stake out a broad ranging leadership role,... not just as a financial body but as the central and most innovative source for elaborating and operationalizing development strategies – all these, above and beyond its financing weight, make the Bank an increasingly formidable international actor.

Stryker's description, which pre-dated the growth of the Bank's policy-formation role in the 1980s, could be made even stronger today. Policy advice, dispensed through loan conditions, training, informal relationships and employment of national staff at the Bank, secures a working influence in key ministries. The Bank's clout in shaping ideas, policies and institutions would of course be vastly diminished without its financial leverage. But the influence it exerts through means other than financial leverage, while not independent, merits more consideration.

First, the borrower-creditor relationship creates an avenue for ongoing influence on institutions and procedures in government. The ability of lenders to shape institutions and practices has been noted at least since the 1970s. A set of actions explicitly or implicitly called for in relations between Bank and borrower, a 'code of conduct' that includes introducing 'appropriate accounting, disbursing and other business practices,' changing or creating institutions and accepting the authority of 'certain economic policies and laws...' (Howard, 1977, pp. 2–3). A cooperative relationship grows out of a loan, 'which establishes a continuing... relationship whereby the [lender] can affect...the policies of the [borrower]...' (Fatouros, 1977, p. 30; see also Libby, 1975). Through positive working relations, the prestige attached to close contact with Bank personnel, and training programs for borrower government officials, relationships are built that integrate a cadre of state personnel into an international network of financial, economic and other technical experts. British economist Michael Hodd (1987, p. 342) citing Keynes, argues that:

> the power of vested interests [is] vastly exaggerated compared with the gradual encroachment of ideas. For... African countries, the prevailing [economic] orthodoxy may have originated with the defunct economists and academic scribblers who developed neo-classical theory. But the more immediate influence is likely to be an African technocrat in continual close contact with the research departments of the IMF and the World Bank.

This ongoing informal contact is reinforced by opportunities for formal training at the World Bank's Economic Development Institute (EDI). The EDI training program helps build a cadre in national ministries sympathetic to the Bank's approach to development and finance (see Chapter 2). The EDI evolves, as its director notes, 'to meet World Bank needs, or needs created by World Bank programming.' At present it focuses on senior policy seminars for 'ministers, deputy ministers and permanent secretaries,' focusing on 'high priority and politically sensitive development issues' (De Lusignan, p. 30), and one- to two-month seminars for mid-level government officials. Some 1,000 government officials participated in training activities in 1983, 3,000 in 1992 (World Bank, *Annual Report*, 1992, p. 91).

Libby's (1975b, p. 198) survey of EDI alumni and a non-EDI control group from the same countries shows the EDI training strategy to be effective. Responses to questionnaires and interviews on subjects such as aid administration, coordination and economic bases for development planning:

> suggest... the presence of a World Bank constituency of development administrators in client LDCs. They represent a source of sup-

port for Bank operations..., support the autonomy of Bank projects and informally solicit World Bank sponsorship of aid coordination groups for their countries.

Donor Coordination: Managing the Aid Regime

Personal and intellectual influence are reinforced by leverage available to the World Bank through its coordination of donor programs in some countries and its power to certify countries' creditworthiness to commercial lenders (LePrestre, 1982, p. 91). Consultative and Coordinating Groups for national aid programs are a forum for Bank influence on state policies and on bilateral donors (World Bank, *Annual Report*, 1990). The World Bank convened and chaired donor coordinating groups for 26 member countries in 1992 and 1993 (World Bank, *Annual Report*, 1993, p. 20). It promotes coordination with private banks and donor agencies by cofinancing more than half of its new projects (World Bank, *Annual Report*, 1992, p. 91). Cofinancing expands the World Bank's catalytic financial role, but two-thirds of cofinancing in 1992 was by other multilateral and bilateral agencies, suggesting that cofinancing does at least as much to disseminate Bank lending approaches as it does to mobilize resources otherwise not available to finance development. (Another one-quarter of cofinancing in 1992 came from export credit financing.)

Coordinating donor strategies is an important and quiet dimension of the Bank's influence. The World Bank has long asserted more authority than does the OECD, which sometimes plays a similar facilitating role. 'While in theory the Bank's role is "merely" technical and is intended to provide the data on which the donor countries' representatives can base their judgment, in reality it comes very close to making itself judgments and evaluations on behalf of the donors' (Fatouros, 1977, p. 33).

In the 1980s the coordinating role expanded, and its influence increased, through a process that Peter Gibbon (1992, p. 3) describes cogently as part of the rise of a new 'aid regime.' With reduced aid flows and the rise of adjustment lending, aid coordinating bodies took on new roles. They evolved from 'occasional meetings between recipients and bilaterals for purposes of coordinating pledges of new aid with donor lists of new projects,' to serving as 'mechanisms for the ... review of recipient's [*sic*] progress with policy reforms.'

Bilaterals lacked independent sources of economic data and interpretation, 'the new regime... involved a decisive subordination of the bilaterals,' and a more active role for the World Bank as chair. 'Nor was there any real international forum where proposals could be made for revising IMF or World Bank recommendations, even if a will existed to do so' (Gibbon, 1992, p. 3).

In all of these settings the World Bank exerts influence – formal and informal, personal and institutional – that helps to perpetuate its view of development. Conversely, the view that development is a matter of technical expertise, not conflicting values and interests, provides the World Bank with a message that minimizes and legitimizes its intrusiveness.

THE MYTH OF SOVEREIGNTY

The World Bank's myth of sovereignty confronts a real-life problem: The institution does not conduct its affairs in deference to the sovereignty of (some of) its member states. Many borrowing countries are – or perceive themselves to be – in a position of weakness when they meet with the World Bank's representatives. Moreover, the Bank's history of association with the US government challenges the sovereignty myth.

The Appearance of Sovereignty

'Sovereignty' is upheld (and World Bank discretion maintained) by the Bank's formal system of governance, and by important structural and operational features. Four of these features are reviewed here. In each case, formal procedures, which represent the sovereignty myth, are contrasted with the reality of day-to-day operations, in which influence is exerted and the discretion of sovereign members is often limited.

1. *Members' sovereignty in relation to the World Bank is represented by the Governors and Executive Directors (EDs).* Governors delegate authority over day-to-day operations to the EDs, who must also approve each proposed loan. Voting rights, allocated in proportion to countries' capital contributions, set out the formal power relations in the direction of the World Bank. But in reality, it has long been true that 'few, if any, matters of importance are decided by a mere tally of votes.' Management uses 'continuing consultations and informal contacts' to avoid confrontations and reach consensus 'before a loan is

formally submitted for approval' (Fatouros, 1977, p. 114). EDs act only on questions put to them by the President, and expanded lending has eroded EDs' power, making them little more than a rubber stamp in all but exceptional cases (Ascher, 1983, p. 421; LePrestre, 1982, p. 149; McKitterick, 1986, p. 51; Ayres, 1983, p. 66).

The Executive Directors have taken more active management roles in several issues in the last two years, asserting themselves on the nature of internal reforms following on the Wapenhans report, and the establishment of an independent appeals panel. But the Bank's formal governance institutions remain, for most members, a forum for acting out rather than asserting sovereignty.

2. *Development policies are publicly promulgated in ways that portray members' sovereignty.* National development plans are ritually presented as government-initiated proposals, even when drafted and negotiated by World Bank staff. The World Bank's role is as creature and servant of the state, which retains control over policy decisions. In Broad's (1988) detailed account of the negotiation of the first Philippine Structural Adjustment Loan in 1980, protracted negotiations and pressure by the World Bank produces a new set of government policy statements, represented solely as the government's initiative. The policy-making role is often subtler and less coercive, but always the ritual of sovereignty is played out. As leader of Consultative Groups for national policy assessment and aid coordination, the Bank works with government officials to prepare development plans. The final product is 'so extensively "processed" by the Bank that they are often perceived by the recipient country's officials as being the Bank's proposals, rather than their own' (Fatouros, 1977, p. 33).

A paper by the Southern Africa division director, proposing measures to restore government initiative and ownership over economic policy, is unusually candid in acknowledging the extent of donor influence. Calling for steps to 'put the government back in the driver's seat,' Director Stephen Denning notes the need for 'creating a space where [g]overnment can think' (1994, pp. 6–7). 'In an environment where donors may be perceived as pressing their own development policies and the services of their own experts on Government, some respite may well be needed for the Government [*sic*] develop its own sectoral policies and priorities' (p. 7). Government officials, Denning notes, 'do not always feel that they are fully in control of donor assisted programs in their ministries,' partly because of 'the major role that donors and donor-funded consultants play in designing, preparing and implementing such assistance' (p. 6).

3. *The procedural fiction that projects are conceived and controlled by borrowing governments is also scrupulously upheld.* Project identification, according to the World Bank staff operating manual, is 'in principle' borrowers' responsibility, but in practice the Bank should be involved (OMS, 2.12, 1978, p. 1). A 1990 paper reminds NGOs that the Bank 'provides financial and technical support to projects, but does not take direct responsibility for their preparation and implementation' (World Bank, 1990d, p. 6).

Other observers, including Swiss economist Bettina Hurni (1980, p. 109), generally friendly to the World Bank, are more candid: '[T]he psychological and material gap between most borrowers and their creditors . . . makes the principle of "borrowers' full responsibility" for projects somewhat theoretical.' Libby (1975b, pp. 115, 120) concludes that 'despite the independent, formal legal status of Bank projects, they are largely conceived, implemented, supervised and protected by the Bank', which retains rights of supervision and review, by contract. A staff economist calls it 'a pity' that, in 1990, Bank staff still develop most projects through most of their stages (Policy Staff no. 7).

The establishment of autonomous government bodies to manage projects was long a favored way to maintain World Bank influence in projects and preserve the projects' autonomy from government ministries. Fatouros notes that autonomous implementing agencies allowed projects to avoid civil service requirements, employ expatriate staff freely, minimize partisan political pressures, and supervise financial accounts and project execution. Lending through intermediary institutions helped make the World Bank 'one of the main external "institution builders" in the Third World' (Hurni, 1980, p. 100). The approach has largely been abandoned (Hellinger, 1987), but recent social service projects in several countries undergoing structural adjustment have created and worked through autonomous agencies.

4. *The Bank assumes a mediating posture.* 'Bank officials . . . see themselves (and their institution) as . . . "in the middle," . . . trying to effect a compromise' between creditor and debtor countries (Ayres, 1983). Political scientist Philippe LePrestre (1982, p. 269) notes that the World Bank 'presents itself as the defender and promoter of Southern interests, appeals for more aid, acts as a go-between, and harnesses its intellectual and financial resources toward alleviating the burden of underdevel-

opment. [It] . . . enjoys, and cultivates, the basic support of its clients.'

This mediating posture, however, is a difficult and contradictory one in light of the Bank's role in adjustment and debt management. The Bank is precluded, for example, from advising a client country to repudiate any part of its debt, or to seek to bargain collectively with other debtors for a better 'deal' from creditors. The Bank offers its borrowers debt management arrangements on the creditors' terms, with the promise of continued borrowing as inducement, and no alternatives in sight. The mediating role, then, has built-in limitations. The Bank is positioned in the middle. But while it speaks for the creditors as a group, it cooperates in a strategy to prevent common action by groups of debtors.

The sovereignty myth is rooted in reality: governments do own the World Bank. They repay or guarantee loans, and their representatives approve loans and policy changes. Technically, a country can limit the World Bank's influence by forgoing credit or by honoring agreements selectively. But sovereignty is sharply limited in everyday operations. The emblems of sovereignty in the Bank's structure and procedure discussed above symbolize sovereignty even as they permit the Bank to exercise influence and a measure of autonomy.

The World Bank's relative autonomy of action is widely recognized, although there is not agreement on where the discretion is lodged within the organization. Nathaniel McKitterick (1986, p. 45) believes that the 'President of the World Bank has always been one of the independent leaders in international life; the Bank runs the way he wants it to.'

Much discretion, however, rests with the staff that make up a 'highly qualified technostructure' (Hurni, 1980, pp. 81–2). Hurni notes that when projects are presented to the Board, 'the Executive Directors show great confidence in the ability of the technostructure. . . .the technostructure provides the intellectual and technical inputs necessary . . . and the decision-making process is designed to support it in an objective, nondiscriminatory way' (1980, pp. 81–2). Sovereignty of most members with respect to the World Bank, then, is limited by the weak accountability of staff to the Board and to the nations they represent.

The pressure of debt, reduced capital flows and the lack of organized alternatives make agreement to World Bank policy conditions almost unavoidable for most borrowers. Borrowers' formal control over policy and over project development in reality permits World Bank influence through Consultative Groups and its supervisory role in project implementation. The Bank's apolitical public image, a sign of borrowers' sovereignty, in reality facilitates the exercise of influence over development policy.

Sovereignty and policy-based lending

The myth of an apolitical World Bank serving its sovereign member states was strained when explicitly policy-based lending was initiated in 1980. Structural adjustment loans afforded the Bank a more prominent position in shaping national economic policies that are highly politicized in many countries.

To be sure, the Bank had long exercised influence over policy. As reported by its retired agriculture chief:

> Senior Bank officials have ready access to the decision-makers in nearly all countries.... [E]conomists and technical staff (backed by a vast information system) provide the material for any ensuing 'dialogues' with governments. ... [I]ts growing ability to conduct informal dialogues about policy, strategy, programs and projects and to promise financial support for projects that fit into mutually agreed priorities has made the Bank unique (Yudelman, 1985, p. 11).

But quiet 'development diplomacy' became more public and overt with the advent of policy-based lending. Former World Bank economist Elliot Berg and Alan Batchelder argue that structural adjustment loans are 'the price to get the Bank to the "high policy table" in the recipient countries' (quoted in Cypher, 1989a, p. 60). Paul Mosley (1987, p. 6) argues that the Bank offers SALs and promises economic results to persuade governments ... 'to buy out some of the restrictive practices by which they ... hold the state together,' typically protective tariffs, exchange rates, quotas and the like, for national industry; patronage and civil service jobs for the middle class; price controls on food and other commodities for consumers; and state marketing systems for commercial agriculture.

Adjustment Lending: The Politics of Conditionality and Implementation

Negotiating and implementing SALs brought the World Bank to a new level of national economic policy making, with two implications for the organization. First, its political profile rises as it is identified with macro policy regimes previously associated principally with the IMF.

Second, supervising policy implementation presents new enforcement challenges to project staff and to management. Because adjustment addresses the structure of production and micro-economic policy, it threatens some groups' interests more fundamentally, and its long duration allows opponents time to organize in opposition (Joan Nelson, 1989, p. 110).

Despite its aversion to public participation in 'political' activity, the World Bank has found it necessary to attend to the volatile political issues that arise in the process of adjustment. The Bank has long enjoyed an image as more benign, less coercive and more generous than the IMF (Broad, 1988; Cypher, 1989b). It was, before the advent of adjustment lending, primarily known as a source of project finance, rather than designer and monitor of economic reform programs.

The political difficulties adjustment schemes confront are reflected in the remarkably weak implementation record of World Bank adjustment loan conditions over the first eight years of adjustment lending. For 51 SALs and 15 Sectoral Adjustment Loans (SECAL) reviewed in the World Bank's 1988 report, an estimated 60 per cent of all conditions were 'fully implemented during the loan disbursement period.' Conditions dealing with energy policy were most likely to be fully implemented, export finance and tax reforms least (Country Economic Department, 1988, pp. 7, 60). The review reports an 80 per cent rate when 'partial implementation' is included, and tries in other ways to present the situation in the best light, but many of the 141 pages are devoted to explaining to the Executive Directors why implementation has been so poor. Mosley's (1987) findings corroborate the Bank's: 60 per cent of conditions have been implemented, in 37 SALs in 21 countries. Mosley, Harrigan and Toye (1991) find similarly weak implementation (54 per cent) in a review supported by case studies (p. 136).

Why is the implementation record of loan conditions so poor? One might expect this powerful representative of international finance to impose its will more effectively on borrowing countries in dire economic straits. In some cases, notably the 1981 SAL to the Philippines, national economic policy and administration has been successfully reworked. But gaps in implementation elsewhere call for explanation.

The implementation and enforcement of SALs is limited by contradictions in the World Bank's bargaining position that render it unable or unwilling to use sanctions to enforce SAL conditions. The Bank has sanctions available to ensure implementation even of politically painful conditions: payment is in tranches, and further payments or new loans may be conditioned on compliance (Development Committee,

1990a, p. 18). SALs have also gained some of the status of IMF Extended Financing Facility agreements, certifying countries' creditworthiness to commercial lenders.

But for a variety of reasons, the World Bank may prefer to give a borrower the benefit of the doubt rather than invoking sanctions for non-compliance. These reasons include the need to move money, geopolitical interests of member states, the desire to cultivate borrower countries' political support, and management's interest in legitimating policy-based lending with their own staff, with industrial country governments and with the financial community. These are among the factors that impede vigorous enforcement of SAL provisions, and that define some of the limits.

Mosley, Harrigan and Toye's case studies of SAP negotiation and implementation confirm some of this. For instance, not only is the Bank reluctant to use non-lending as a sanction for poor implementation, but borrowers wishing to avoid or evade conditionality are 'aware of ... the Bank's "disbursement dilemma..."' (p. 300).

Winning technocratic hearts and minds?

Mosley (1987) speculates that full compliance in most countries is of secondary importance to the World Bank. The long-term impact on the staff of Planning and Finance Ministries, he suggests, may be as important as short-term compliance with specific measures. The Philippine experience supports this hypothesis. By cultivating technocrats within the Philippine state who were sympathetic with its economic program, the Bank won implementation in the 1980s of a program of economic change that had eluded the IMF throughout the 1970s. The national bureaucracy was 'seeded' with a corps of 'young, graduate-educated technocrats,' Western trained, who became 'the World Bank's counterparts on the inside' during negotiation and implementation of the SAL (Broad, 1988, p. 61, 73).

Training at the Economic Development Institute (EDI) has a part in this process. EDI graduates returning to the Philippines can expect a promotion, and there is great demand to be sent, as 'bureaucrats who cannot claim the status of "technocrat" increasingly face job insecurity' (World Bank memo quoted in Broad, 1988, p. 102). The EDI offers the World Bank a source of influence more subtle than financial leverage. In adjustment lending as in other programming, influence among professionals and movement between the Bank and governments is a driving force in shaping administration and economic policy. This trend entails conformity of staffing, policy and sometimes structure of key planning bodies in borrowing countries to that of the Bank.

In some countries, adjustment lending allows the Bank to reinforce the objectives of governments already committed to adjustment programs. In others the financial leverage afforded by policy-based loans increases the Bank's influence, especially in the context of indebtedness and decreased capital flows from other sources. And in many countries, the process of negotiations and the opportunities they present for training, influence and persuasion help the Bank build an internal constituency for national policies consistent with its development program. Throughout the process of negotiating and implementing SAL agreements, the doctrine and trappings of sovereignty keep the Bank formally in a subordinate and apolitical role.

The Bank as Governance Institution

This has remained true even as the Bank's negotiation, implementation and supervision of adjustment plans has become increasingly intrusive. Legal scholar Jonathan Cahn (1993) documents the extent of administrative, regulatory and legislative changes required by sectoral and structural adjustment loan agreements. Increasingly detailed conditions have made the Bank 'a governance institution, exercising power through its financial leverage to legislate entire legal regimens and even to alter the constitutional structure of borrowing nations' (p. 160).

Like political theorist Robert Cox, who describes an 'internationalization of the state' through its expanding accountability to the Bretton Woods institutions (1987), Cahn sees the effective sovereignty of nations severely compromised. Less powerful states, he argues, become 'satellites in a new empire, extensions of much broader policy dictates established with only slight reference to territorial boundaries.' The Bank's conditions 'blur the distinction between international and domestic, public and private law, making World Bank influence pervasive at all levels of the law's domain' (p. 187).

Sovereignty and NGOs

While deploying resources to influence government policies and institutions and to privatize whole sectors of state activity, the World Bank takes a gingerly approach to NGOs. From the earliest official statements on NGOs, guidance to staff has been dotted with cautionary references to sovereignty, and with lists of 'weaknesses and disadvantages'

(Ernest Stern, Senior Vice President for Operations, memo to Operational Vice Presidents 27 March 1981). In recent documents staff are repeatedly instructed to safeguard 'the privileged relationship with governments;' they are reminded that 'all overtures to NGOs are with the consent of governments,' and that activities must conform to 'government's policies towards NGOs' (SPR, 1989, p. 3; Qureshi, 1988; Salmen and Eaves, 1989, p. 65; OD 14.70, paragraphs, 1, 7(c), 8 and 10). The earlier Operational Manual Statement (OMS) was revised in 1989 to stress 'the need to proceed in conformity with the relevant governments' (Ducksoo Lee, memo to Vice President for Operations, Moeen Qureshi, 1989). Dropped was the suggestion that labor unions be consulted when a project threatened to close down a factory (Draft OMS, 15 January 1988, p. 7).

Subordinating NGOs' political role to service delivery

NGOs are approached cautiously because their values-oriented and sometimes politicized nature threatens the apolitical expertise on which the World Bank's fundamental myths are based. Many NGOs see development as a matter of values and democracy, of siding with the poor and organizing around political and social issues (Brown and Korten, 1989). Implicitly, through their 'grassroots' ethos, and sometimes explicitly in their advocacy work, NGOs propose accountability to affected groups and communities as an alternative or a complement to sovereignty as the informing principle for World Bank relations to borrowing countries.

This potential as a vehicle for accountability in relations with the World Bank is recognized frequently by NGO leaders (DeGraaf, 1987; Hellinger, 1987; Brodhead, 1989; BRAC, 1989), and some Bank staff whom I interviewed (Policy staff no.3; LAC staff no.2). This dimension of the NGOs' work, rather than the reputation for economic efficiency as service deliverers, is considered of paramount importance by many NGOs. This political role is presented emphatically in one discussion paper written for Bank staff as the key distinctive to be nurtured and appreciated in NGOs (Brown and Korten, 1989), and its importance is recognized in official World Bank statements (Qureshi, 1988; World Bank, 1990d; Strategic Planning and Review, 1989).

But in projects and operations involving NGOs, there is little evidence that staff consider the representative – as opposed to the service-delivery – role. The caution with which staff have approached NGOs is reflected both in the roles assigned to NGOs in Bank-financed projects, and in the kinds of NGOs staff choose to associate with.

The subordinate role assigned to NGOs was typified in the late 1970s and early 1980s by the prominence, especially in Africa, of contractor-style projects in which NGOs were contracted to build roads and schools or supervise railway construction. Bank reports on NGO collaboration argue that in the late 1980s the NGO role grew to be much more substantial. But many examples of projects with minimal, subordinate roles for NGOs may be found in the last few years. Bank reports describe the Kwango-Kwilu technical assistance project in Zaire (1978) as involving NGOs and firms in a mixed capital company created to coordinate and promote rural development efforts. The company, CODAIK, was found by the Project Completion Review (PCR) to be dominated by government representatives, and the role of private sector representatives was, in the end, minimal (PCR, p. 3).

Many other recent projects assign NGOs a minimal role. In the Guinea Education Sector Adjustment Credit, approved in 1990, NGO involvement consists of an ongoing program of school construction by French volunteers. In Honduras, the Agricultural Credit IV project (1988) extends a small line of credit to rural credit unions, which are expected to 'explain the system' to newly formed 'groups of farmers.' In Argentina, the First Housing Sector Project (1988) uses newly formed housing cooperatives as a way to cope with extremely long lines awaiting government housing assistance. Applicants registering together as housing cooperatives receive some priority when assigned places on the waiting list.

Not only are NGOs subordinated to government programs in these project roles, the choice of NGOs for collaboration is also constrained by Bank staff's cautious approach. The concerns encountered in interviews with operational staff were summed up by the concern of an agriculture specialist that NGOs may be 'religiously or politically tainted' (Policy staff no. 5). A senior Africa economist involved in NGO projects warned colleagues in a training session to beware of NGOs with a 'Point of View,' driven by a political agenda or strong value commitment (6 October 1989). NGOs' uneasy relations with some governments is a concern expressed repeatedly in interviews and staff memos (Hans Wyss memo to Moeen Qureshi, 1988; Asia staff no. 3; Policy staff no. 3).

Not only their presumed politics but also NGOs' contrast with familiar, interest- and profit-driven behavior are of concern to some staff economists. An economist working in South Asia worried that NGOs that receive outside support will never 'become entrepreneurial' and self-supporting (Asia staff no. 3). An economist in private sector operations told me he prefers to work with firms because 'we understand firms, they are guided by profits. NGOs are less predictable' (Policy staff no. 7). When NGO members of the NGO-World Bank Committee argued in 1989 for loan conditions to promote participation and 'democracy' in development planning, World Bank staff gave a spirited defense of apolitical lending and respect for diverse political forms (personal observation, NGO-World Bank Committee, Bangkok, 1989).

NGOs and internationalized advocacy campaigns

Staff are particularly uncomfortable with 'advocacy NGOs,' which have in some cases linked Southern and Northern organizations in a network that presses the multilateral development banks (MDB) on issues where they are vulnerable to criticism. A World Bank (1990, p. 4) pamphlet on NGO relations credits environmental NGOs with helping to 'sensitize public opinion and development practitioners, including the Bank,' and indigenous and international NGOs together with focusing 'the attention of the Bank and its member governments to the environmental and social costs of some large-scale projects.' Controversy and conflict between the Bank and NGOs, especially in environmental issues, is reported elsewhere in similarly antiseptic language (World Bank, *Annual Report*, 1987, p. 62; World Bank, *Annual Report*, 1989, p. 95; Strategic Planning and Review, 1990, pp. 9–10).

But staff's opinions of advocacy NGOs and the international networks through which they work are generally less friendly. Although interaction with such cause-oriented groups or networks of international and local NGOs occurs only in a small minority of the World Bank's NGO-related projects, 'advocacy NGOs' are frequently the first subject raised in conversations with operational staff. Some US-based NGOs in particular are accused of practicing an isolated, confrontational style of politics (Policy staff no. 3). An Asia staff economist calls advocacy by policy NGOs 'out of control, out of hand, run amok,' and suggests that advocacy groups are 'unprofessional, not knowledgeable' (Asia staff no. 4). Staff also challenge policy NGOs' knowledge of Bank operations, complaining some of their vocal critics 'don't do their homework' and rely on out-of-date images of World Bank atrocities (LAC staff no. 2; Africa staff no. 2).

Networks of NGOs that extend advocacy on national policy issues

The World Bank and Apolitical Development

beyond national borders raise the political dimension of working with NGOs in a particularly sensitive way. The Sardar Sarovar Dam Project and Singrauli Thermal Energy Project in India, for example, have provoked protest from local groups and national environmental organizations that captured the attention of the Environmental Defense Fund in the United States and other environmental NGOs based in the industrial countries. Their campaigns, through public protests in India, correspondence and meetings with World Bank officials, public information efforts in the United States and Europe and lobbying of donor parliaments, have drawn considerable attention to domestic Indian policies and the World Bank loans that support them (Patkar, 1989; Udall, 1989).

The success of such internationalized campaigns in India, Indonesia, Brazil, the Philippines and elsewhere, has been mixed. Some projects have been modified, and some gains have been made in World Bank policies toward the environment and native peoples' rights, and in staffing for these sensitive areas. The Sardar Sarovar project has become the central test case, with many NGOs charging that the Bank not only failed to implement its own policies for resettlement of displaced persons, but then refused to respond to many of the findings and recommendations of an unprecedented independent review that the Bank itself established. Some made the World Bank's performance in this case grounds for a campaign to reduce government appropriations to IDA-10 (see Chapter 3).

Regardless of the immediate success of the campaigns, however, environmentalists such as Stephan Schwartzman of the Environmental Defense Fund feel that the international networks of information and political activity they have created are lasting achievements (interview, 9 May 1990). In the case of local organizations in the Brazilian Amazon, while influence on the local level has been limited, 'the alliances made... have gained an unprecedented voice and influence for Amazonian organizations internationally' (Schwartzman, 1989).

Generally, its close ties to the state and its unwillingness or inability to implement projects through non-government groups that can mobilize participation in projects, distribute benefits equitably and promote lasting and replicable social change render the World Bank unable to assist 'development' as many NGOs see it (Hellinger, 1988; Annis, 1987). But the Bank has not hesitated to embrace and involve NGOs in the implementation of compensatory projects to buffer the political and social effects of Bank-supported structural adjustment plans.

NGOs in Compensatory Projects

The challenge to political stability that sometimes accompanies stabilization and adjustment regimes is also a challenge to the World Bank's sovereignty myth and its apolitical image. Food price and fuel price increases, public sector layoffs and reduced imports have provoked demonstrations and resistance in so many countries under IMF stabilization that the term 'IMF riots' has been coined to describe the phenomenon (Cypher, 1989b).

The World Bank has not adopted its sister organization's stance. Rather than leaving it to cooperating governments to manage social dislocations or political resistance, the Bank has worked with several governments to develop plans to limit the social and political costs of adjustment. These increase the plans' likelihood of success and buoy the World Bank's image as the 'kinder, gentler' lender.

NGOs are a widely-discussed option in designing such plans (Demery and Addison, 1987; Zuckerman, 1989; Joan Nelson, 1989; Ribe, Carvalho, Liebenthal, Nicholas and Zuckerman, 1990). NGOs are not always involved: compensatory plans in Chile, Costa Rica, South Korea, Senegal and elsewhere have entailed little NGO action, as government programs with donor assistance blunt the effects of unemployment, food price increases and currency devaluations (Zuckerman, 1989). Nor are programs financing compensatory services the only measure available to the Bank and borrowing governments. Increased World Bank investment has also accompanied some countries' adjustment programs. Ghana's sustained adjustment program, for instance, helped make it the largest recipient of IDA funds in sub-Saharan Africa, and the third largest in the world, behind only China and India.

But compensatory programs became a more prominent adjunct to adjustment strategies in the late 1980s. In the years 1988–92, the World Bank approved at least 37 new compensatory plans involving NGOs. The Bank cited no project before 1988 where NGO involvement was explicitly 'adjustment-related', but 42 such projects are reported in the years 1988–93.

The spate of new NGO compensatory arrangements seems to have two sources in the World Bank: the reported success of the Bolivian Emergency Social Fund (ESF) and the campaign of research and publication in the Bank's Africa division around the Social Dimensions of Adjustment (SDA). The Bolivian ESF has attracted considerable attention within the Bank. A September 1989 colloquium on the Bolivian experience was well-attended by Latin America region staff, and many staff in training sessions during the following month indicated their region's or country office's interest in similar plans.

Publications of the SDA project highlighted the potential role for NGOs in softening SALs' regressive distributional impact (Serageldin, 1989; Alderman, 1990), and SDA manager Ismail Serageldin, who also directed West Africa operations, reportedly encouraged work with NGOs in his region. Ghana's Program of Action to Mitigate the Social Costs of Adjustment (PAMSCAD), an early example of compensatory measures in Africa, engaged NGO participation, but not without difficulty. The SDA itself has since been absorbed into a technical unit on poverty, and its research program reduced in scope.

Some NGOs have hesitated to get involved in Bank-financed adjustment programs, and the NGO Working Group on the World Bank has suggested conditions for NGO participation in such schemes (NGO Working Group on the World Bank, draft, 1989). But NGOs present no recognizable, unified position on this or almost any other issue, and many have accepted opportunities to use government funds to meet pressing needs that are hoped to be short-term. Bolivia's Emergency Social Fund (ESF), financed by the World Bank and other donors and administered by a semi-autonomous government agency created for the purpose, financed projects proposed and initiated by NGOs and by local governments and firms. Job creation was the principal aim of the ESF and of the Social Investment Fund that has succeeded it.

NGOs play a more prominent role in more recent special compensatory funds in Chad and Guinea. Chad's 'Social Development Action Project,' approved for World Bank finance in 1990, aims to stimulate employment generation through training for unemployed people; to improve poor people's health and living conditions; and to reinforce the government's institutional capacity to design and monitor programs to improve social conditions' (World Bank Project Summary). Volunteers in Technical Assistance (VITA) agreed to provide management training to government officials and manage a micro-credit program. A French NGO (Association Française des Volontaires de Progrès) was to train officials in the Ministry of Labor and Employment. The role of local NGOs in creating and proposing subprojects was not specified.

Guinea's 'Socio-Economic Development Project' was also approved in 1990. The IDA credit, available to NGOs for projects, is to complement an existing government program for local government initiatives. About one-half of the $11.9 million credit finances strengthening the Social Policy Division in the Ministry of Planning. The other half – nearly $6 million – is to be allocated for NGO projects, 'because the

Government did not yet have either the data or the capacity to deal with the various social problems' (World Bank Project Summary). All sub-projects are subject to IDA and government approval.

NGO participation in adjustment-related projects has been defined here as narrowly as possible. In some countries other projects are surely related, more or less directly, to adjustment programs. But in most countries the location, timing or sector of NGO projects suggest no particular relation to the SAL. A 1986 Bank-NGO project in Guinea funds livestock improvements, related only in the broadest sense to the country's adjustment program (Guinea Livestock Rehabilitation Project; from World Bank project summary). In other cases the link to adjustment is clearer: while livestock improvement in Guinea had no immediate relation to the adjustment program, projects in health and urban enterprises certainly do (Health Services Project, 1987; Conakry Urban Development Supplemental Finance Project, revised in 1986).

More broadly still, NGO participation in any World Bank-financed operation is relevant to the adoption of adjustment lending in the 1980s. NGOs are part of the 'human face' that the Bank sought to project as it broadened its policy-based lending and defended its environmental record and reputation.

The World Bank's low political profile and carefully cultivated apolitical identity has been called into question by policy-based lending. By raising the level of the Bank's political engagement, adjustment lending has created an opening for NGO involvement, but it is an opening largely defined by the Bank's needs as it seeks to help governments implement adjustment plans.

DEFENDING ADJUSTMENT AND MANAGING INFORMATION: STRAINING THE SOVEREIGNTY MYTH

Discussions between the World Bank and various groupings of NGOs have covered a wide range of topics, from energy, water and forestry policies to adjustment, popular participation and information policy. The Bank's responses to NGOs on two of these – adjustment and information policy – highlight the contradictions between its myths and the reality of its policy and influence.

Unequal Adjustment, Leverage and Sovereignty

NGOs have criticized World Bank adjustment policy for unfairly placing the entire burden of global adjustment on the poor countries who can afford it least; and for promoting strategies that flood the market with export goods as countries desperately try to export and trade their way out of debt.

First, it has been argued that the Bank has helped coordinate a global adjustment regime that has placed all of the burden and hardship of change on the poor, debtor countries. The *NGO Position Paper on the World Bank* (1989), and earlier discussion papers (Clark, 1987; Brodhead, 1989) call on the World Bank to press for adjustment by all nations to deal with problems that are global in scope. Others have noted this 'unbalanced adjustment' as well (Overseas Development Institute, 1986; Griesgraber 1994).

Second, some have argued that the Bank acts in bad faith when it encourages non-traditional export strategies, sometimes focused on producing and marketing the same products, in many highly indebted countries. Two NGO members complained vehemently in the 1989 NGO-World Bank Committee meeting that Bank-supported export promotion policies were moving numerous nations into non-traditional export markets when the market could not absorb their combined production at favorable prices.

World Bank representatives at the meetings responded with three lines of argument; two directed to the 'unequal adjustment' argument; one to the critique of non-traditional export strategies. First, they pointed out that the Bank has indeed called upon the United States to reduce its budget deficits, and upon other industrialized countries to resist protectionist pressures and adopt other measures in keeping with the World Bank's vision of an expanding global economy. Speeches by (then) President Conable were cited, as was a World Bank/IMF Development Committee publication on the subject (Development Committee, 1989; see also Raison, 1986).

NGO discussants, however, argued that these calls for sensitivity to global needs in industrial-country economic policy making were no more than gentle sermons, while adjustment in the poor countries was planned and promoted by Bank staff and backed by the financial leverage of project and policy-based loans.

One World Bank representative then advanced a second line of argument: The Bank cannot be expected, he explained, to criticize too sharply the countries that guarantee or provide the lion's share of its funding. 'These are our bosses,' he noted, and there are limits to what the Bank can do.

The third theme advanced by the Bank representatives was addressed to the critique of export-oriented strategies as flooding limited markets by encouraging similar strategies among many countries aspiring to join the ranks of the 'newly industrialized countries' (NICs). The World Bank's job, one representative argued, is to promote efficiency. If the Bank identifies the strategy that best exploits a country's comparative advantage, the best it can do is help that country to be as efficient as possible in carrying out that strategy and producing those goods and services. If more than one country pursues the same strategy, the benefits will depend on how efficiently each carries it out.

These three responses – present in many Bank statements and discussions – lay bare contradictions embedded in the sovereignty and development myths. Sovereignty, it becomes clear, is mediated and limited by power relations. Adjustment is a joint responsibility of industrialized and underdeveloped countries in theory, but in practice the Bank is powerless to implement the portions of its advice that apply to national economic policies in the North. Left with the option of one-sided adjustment or no adjustment at all, the Bank promotes an adjustment strategy in the South that cannot succeed in the absence of cooperative policies in the industrialized world.

The apolitical, strictly technical nature of World Bank advice is further eroded by the problems of over-used non-traditional export strategies. The Bank's debating strategy is to bring this discussion back to the national level: as advisor and financier, the Bank helps each country implement a plan as efficiently as possible. The size of each market and room for expanded supply may be examined and debated. But the logic of the policy is to encourage each country to produce a product, or to create the environment for international corporations to produce the product within its borders, more efficiently and cheaply than others. This is the nature of competition in the international market, but when competitors' strategies are all guided by a single advisor, the result is a buyers' market where sellers have been directed by non-market forces toward strategies that depress prices.

Privileged Information, Sovereignty and NGOs

NGOs have criticized the World Bank for restricting access to information about projects under consideration. Without early access to project papers as new investment ideas are first considered, NGOs argue, local organizations and communities cannot contribute to the project's development, or react to projects they wish to change or oppose. NGOs in the NGO-World Bank Committee made this demand fundamental to the development of cooperative relations with the Bank, and others, especially US-based environmental NGOs, have pressed the case vigorously. Trust and accountability are impossible, it is argued, when project ideas were kept secret until planning is so far advanced that little influence was possible for NGOs or community groups (NGO-World Bank Committee, 1987 Meeting).

World Bank representatives long responded that the sovereign rights of its member countries required that information remain confidential, held only by government officials and the Bank. The policy implied that the Bank is accountable to citizens solely through their national government. Some NGOs persisted, demanding a more open information policy as a foundation for cooperation, and, in 1987 the Bank agreed to open a considerable amount of project documentation to NGOs. Monthly Operational Statements, listing projects under development and describing briefly any potential for NGO involvement, are available to any NGO. In addition, a 'List of World Bank-Financed Projects with Potential for NGO Involvement' is sent periodically to an extensive mailing list of NGOs in the North and in the South. NGOs are encouraged to review the list and contact World Bank staff about projects in which they are might want to participate.

But most actual project documents remained restricted. NGOs based in Washington developed informal access to documents through sympathetic staff members and Executive Directors who encourage review and comment on proposals. They also mounted a campaign for greater disclosure, often with support from the US government, whose own freedom of information policies make it more sympathetic than some other members.

In 1992, under threat of IDA funds being withheld by a key committee of the US Congress, the Bank's Board agreed to a new information disclosure policy. While the new policy expands the list of documents that are to be routinely available, and makes them available both in Washington and in each Bank office, even this measure falls short of the principle, set forth in the Bank's Operational Directive on the subject, that presumes information to be public in the absence of compelling reason to keep it private.

The most critical shortcoming in the new policy is the substitution of a new summary for public information, called a Project Information Document (PID), for several actual project documents. The working documents remain restricted, and the public gains access to a presentation drafted specifically for public consumption. PIDs, furthermore, are not prepared until the project's development is fairly advanced, rendering them useless to NGOs wishing to be involved in design and pre-design stages.

Despite the limitations, which NGOs continue to attack, these developments in information policy offer a new perspective on the doctrine of the primacy of Bank relations with governments, and on how this 'sovereignty' doctrine is used. First, under pressure, the Bank found a way to modify its governments-only policy. By disseminating some information about projects still under discussion with governments, the Bank acknowledged a legitimate role for NGO comment, and demonstrated that there is room for change in its interpretation of its members' sovereign rights.

Second, the hesitancy with which the Bank approached information-sharing with non-for-profit organizations contrasts with its openness toward private banks and firms that might be interested in a project as potential investors or as bidders to provide services. For such commercial concerns the Bank has long provided information on projects under development, as well as manuals on how to bid on World Bank-financed projects (summarized in World Bank, n.d., *Guide to International Business Opportunities*). The privileged information the Bank hesitated to provide to NGOs was readily available to for-profit firms who wished to invest in projects. (Even the newly-created public information facility was used far more frequently by for-profit companies than by NGOs in its first year.)

Third, the difficulty of obtaining full information, both descriptive and evaluative, extends to the Bank's Board. Proposals for special evaluative units reporting to the Board were made by Executive Directors during the first half of 1993, as the Board seeks to improve the reliability and independence of its own information base.

A final point of contention over information relates to the role of Northern-based NGOs as recipients and users of project and policy planning documents. Bank staff distinguish between making information available to persons likely to be affected by a project, and to Northern-based NGOs (Beckmann, quoted in Stokes, 1988; Policy staff 2; representatives at the 1989 NGO-World Bank Committee meeting). In so doing they echo the reluctance of some governments to have information in the hands of foreign-based NGOs who are critical of their environmental and social policies.

But advocacy NGOs often work most effectively in networks that move information quickly between Washington, the capitals and remote rural areas of the South, and coordinate action based on the information. Affected persons do not frequent resident representatives' offices in their capitals, much less Bank headquarters, and Northern NGOs claim a legitimate role as conduit of information. The Bank remains reluctant to undermine the confidentiality of its relations with borrowing governments by handing documents to NGOs. In information policy as in other matters, the sovereignty myth remains a constraint on the extent of interaction with NGOs.

CONCLUSIONS

The myths of development and sovereignty play three important roles in the World Bank's organizational life. They represent a basis for World Bank activity by defining its goal in terms the Bank is able to meet. Second, by shaping widely-held standards of development, the myths articulate a standard of performance, a way to certify that the Bank is achieving adequate results. Finally, while apparently defining the limits of the World Bank's power and domain by subordinating it to governments and assigning it an 'apolitical' mandate, the myths open avenues of influence and facilitate the exercise of political power.

Growth-oriented lending, policy advice, and technical assistance on project implementation are the primary services the World Bank has to offer. These serve well if 'development' is defined as a function of growth and of objectively 'correct' policies, institutions, prices and technologies. By rendering these choices as engineering, economics and technological problems, the myth of development allows the Bank to promote and finance changes of great political import.

The primacy of state sovereignty is being challenged, both at the World Bank and in the wider world. Advocates within and outside the Bank have made progress in bringing human rights, governance, military spending and other issues into the rhetoric of the Bank. But the myth that its economic advice is apolitical continues to be a significant factor, facilitating the Bank's aggressive intervention in all matters of economic planning and policy, contributing to the Bank's limited vision of the policy options and frustrating NGOs and others in society who require openness and accountability in policy making.

The importance of these myths to World Bank operations means that changes which threaten them, including operational and policy cooperation with NGOs, will be approached with caution. Despite progress in the dialogue and operational collaboration, experience to date confirms the expectation that NGO roles will be shaped to conform to the myths of development and sovereignty.

7 Organizational Culture and Participation in Development

The preceding two chapters review organizational barriers to change – the aversion to uncertainty, the disbursement imperative and the powerful myths of apolitical development – and outline their relations to external interests and pressures that shape World Bank policy. A third set of constraining factors, which together form an organizational culture, are the subject of this chapter. The Bank's organizational culture sharply limits popular participation and NGO involvement in its operations, and constrains the organization's ability to learn from experience. The organizational culture integrates and reinforces elements of the mandate and myths discussed in the previous chapters.

'Organizational culture' is made up of values, ideologies, practices, myths and ceremonies that give an organization internal identity and coherence. Each organizational culture features – and depends upon – a systematic selection and filtering of the information that makes up the organization's picture of its world, and that provides the basis for decision-making. The World Bank's culture is hierarchical and grounded in division of labor, technical expertise and comparative advantage. The culture is pervasive and dominant, but there are small, sometimes vigorous 'undergrounds' working against the grain of the culture. NGO representatives tend to meet the members of these minority groups, often as the dissenters seek external allies. Some of their efforts are documented in this chapter.

Still, the organizational culture dominates and structures thinking and action at the Bank: it filters information thoroughly, limiting the capacity to learn and to practice 'participatory' development. The organizational culture, central to the Bank's operations, contrasts with its publicly espoused image and contradicts and limits efforts and claims to increase the quality and influence of NGO participation in its programs.

The argument is analogous to that of the previous two chapters: a hierarchical and technocratic organizational culture that dominates attitudes and procedures at the World Bank renders the Bank's policies almost impervious to critique – external or internal – that does not begin from accepted organizational and theoretical premises. Despite the efforts and intentions of individuals, this organizational culture makes meaningful growth of NGO influence, and progress on the broad NGO agenda, extremely difficult. The information bias of the culture dominates planning, implementation and evaluation of policies, as this chapter observes in the cases of rural development lending, structural adjustment lending and the ongoing dialogue with NGOs. It promotes intellectual insularity and an emphasis on control of the implementation of investments, and limits the potential for organizational learning.

ORGANIZATIONAL CULTURE

Organizational culture is the internal counterpart of the myths of institutional theory. Conforming to pervasive myths allows an organization to legitimate itself in the view of the larger society. Organizational culture refers to values, ideologies, practices, myths and ceremonies within an organization that give it meaning, identity and coherence internally.

A literature on organizational culture, often strongly applied, proliferated in the 1980s. Peters and Waterman (1982) reflects this applied bent most strongly, but the theme of culture as managers' secret weapon also appears in Schein (1985), and in Deal and Kennedy (1982). 'Culture' has also been used loosely within the Bank, since the 1992 Wapenhans report, to describe the overemphasis on disbursements and project preparation ('approval culture') that Wapenhans criticizes. With its popularity has come ambiguity about the meaning of 'culture.' I distinguish two dimensions of organizational culture.

In its most widely used sense, organizational culture portrays for individuals the organization's basic values, the kinds of people who are most respected in the organization, the kinds of information that are taken seriously in decision-making, and the routes by which one may rise in the organization. Deal and Kennedy (1982, p. 15) treat organizational culture as embracing values that define success for employees, heroes who act out these values; rites, rituals and ceremonies that 'show employees the kind of behavior that is expected of them;' and a cultural network that transmits the culture among participants. This is roughly the meaning of 'culture' in the Bank's current usage.

A second approach to organizational culture highlights systematic biases in how organizations search out and select information. All organizations – firms, voluntary associations and agencies – selectively convert raw data from their environment into information on which decisions and actions are based. Michael Thompson and Aaron Wildavsky (1986) argue that organizational cultures are characterized and sustained by distinct 'information biases' that limit and shape how information is obtained and selected for decision making. As an organization's lower echelons 'filter and compress the data for the higher, detail is removed and order added. The choice of what data are actually transmitted is formally found at the top but informally left to the lower levels' (Thompson and Wildavsky, 1986, p. 275).

Culture, then, is the framework by which data are gathered and constructed into a coherent view of events and circumstances. Each type of organizational culture (hierarchy, market, sectarian or egalitarian) tends toward a distinct kind of information 'search behavior.' The hierarchical culture, for example, typically emphasizes efficiency, specialization and division of labor and justifies inequalities on grounds of efficiency and effectiveness.

A study of the World Bank's organizational culture affords a perspective that contrasts sharply with the organization's official image. Bank officials and many public documents portray the institution as learning, changing and responsive, eager to collaborate with NGOs, including in early stages of project work. Former Vice President Warren Baum (1978, p. 24) praises its '... response to the lessons of experience.... Mistakes ... are not often repeated. The lessons of experience are built into the design and preparation of future projects. The project cycle is working as intended.' Among official documents and papers by senior managers, Yudelman (1985), Israel (1978), and the organization's pamphlet on information disclosure (n.d.) express similar views.

Official documents treat interaction with NGOs as a case of the World Bank's openness and responsiveness. Growing collaboration with NGOs (Strategic Planning and Review, 1989, p. 17), frequent consultation in project design (World Bank, 1990d, p. 8; *Annual Report*, 1989; 1993, pp. 94–5), and learning from dialogue and collaboration with NGOs are stressed: 'NGO input is often crucial in [project] design and implementation' (World Bank, 1990d, p. 11). The Bank's promotional materials for the fiftieth anniversary characterize the Bank as a set of global 'partnerships,' including with NGOs and with 'the worldwide academic and research community' (World Bank, 1994f).

In contrast to official sources, most staff I interviewed (and some internal documents) assess the NGO role more soberly: it depends on individual initiative (Africa region staff no. 1; Finance staff no.1. Policy staff no. 3), is 'still *ad hoc* and dependent on circumstances', and ... relatively rare[ly involves a] say in the formulation of the project concept and its strategy' (Cernea, 1988, p. 32). ' ... most Bank staff are still relatively unfamiliar with NGO activities and capabilities,' even according to the unit charged with building Bank-NGO relations (Strategic Planning and Review, 1990, p. 15).

Theories of organizational culture also suggest an alternative view of the culture of the World Bank. Hierarchies emphasize efficiency, specialization and division of labor, justifying inequalities on efficiency grounds. Technical rationality expresses itself in a division of labor, rationalization of work, and emphasis on predictability in the production process. Hierarchies' information search is biased accordingly:

Hierarchies are concerned with maintaining the existing order. [... their legitimacy rests] on science and expertise; the right person in the right job most capable of making the right decision. So hierarchies search for new information to do a better job of holding together the existing social order. [They] are slow to discard old truths, returning to the old until the new can be comfortably accommodated with the existing order (Thompson and Wildavsky, 1986, p. 283).

INFORMATION BIAS AND ORGANIZATIONAL LEARNING: THE CASES OF RURAL DEVELOPMENT AND STRUCTURAL ADJUSTMENT

The information generally selected for consideration in policy-making in the Bank excludes many political and socio-cultural considerations that shape the realities of social and economic change in the countries of the South. Factors that fit the realities defined by the myth of development, and that are susceptible to its influence and control, are treated as the only relevant considerations. Staff's control over information buttresses dominant paradigms by selecting information that is consistent with them.

When a project or national economic policy performs unsatisfactorily, staff appear to choose from a narrow menu of explanations, featuring weak government commitment, poor management, and inappropriate macro-economic policy. Poverty persists and economies languish, in the world of the Bank's culture, for reasons beyond its influence. Other explanations for project failure are generally absent from World Bank papers. One searches in vain for a project or country strategy review that calls a government ministry too corrupt to manage an investment, acknowledges that local power is so skewed that a project cannot benefit the relatively poor, asks whether vital knowledge about coping sustainably with rural conditions resides in sources that the Bank has not tapped, or acknowledges that people did not cooperate in a project that they could not control. These 'answers' are untenable because they undercut the World Bank's mythology. They cannot be embraced within the existing framework, so they go largely unrecognized or unreported. When reported, they are bracketed as extraneous, exogenous, uncontrollable.

The Case of 'Rural Development' and 'Sociological Issues'

A comparison of two series of internal evaluations of rural development projects in the 1970s and 1980s documents this process of information selection (OED, 1988). One set, known as Project Performance Reviews (PPRs) and Project Implementation Reviews (PIRs), are formal parts of the project cycle, sent to senior management. They treat management, financial, disbursement and implementation problems. PIRs are 'selective, both as to projects and general problems.... [They] provide good insights into what managers felt were important issues...' (OED, 1988, p. 52).

'Lessons Learned' papers, circulated informally among staff, note sociological issues more often, and occasionally criticize World Bank and borrower 'communication and cooperation.... In contrast, PIRs largely avoid self-criticism of Bank procedures...' (OED, 1988, p. 53). Information is selected to favor technical and administrative problems and to filter out sociological, political and organizational issues.

In rural development lending as in other operations, the information chain's lower strata continued to rely on official views of development needs and priorities. Policy statements stressed involving 'beneficiaries' in project design, but OED (1988, p. 60) concludes that guidelines on participation had 'limited operational impact. Beneficiaries were not assigned a role in the decision-making process, nor was their technological knowledge sought prior to designing project components.'

The Case of Structural Adjustment and the East Asian Miracle

The intellectual history of structural adjustment within the Bank is replete with similar selectivity and purposeful management of information. A major World Bank research project completed in 1993 reinterprets East

Asia's economic successes and provides a window on how the East Asian 'Miracle' has been stylized and presented to support an economic program.

The study's findings are that getting 'the fundamentals' right is indispensable to broadly-based growth, but that in some cases certain state interventions did work in East Asia. The report is distinguished by significant omissions. First, there is not one paragraph about the environmental or natural resource costs or advantages of the strategies reviewed. Although the region's natural resource endowments are mentioned, there is no discussion of real resource costs, sustainability, pollution issues in chemical and steel industries. Even in the review of policy lessons for growth in the present world economy, resource use and costs are unmentioned (pp. 23–4).

Second, the Bank itself is virtually absent as an actor in the study, despite its energetic promotion and finance of the East Asian strategies. The authors' models account for the growth impact of various packages of interventions, but the Bank and other donors are absent from the account, and lessons for growth-producing policies in the 1990s are derived without reference to the major international actors.

But the way the Bank's spokespeople have promoted and interpreted the findings is even more telling. In a *Financial Times* interview the project's research director, John Page, presents as bold and new the central findings: that the Asian economic powers followed varied paths to rapid growth, including, at times, aggressive state intervention and protection of certain domestic industries. "'If we're right", says Mr Page, "the economic policy arsenal has many more weapons than we suspected"' (*The Financial Times*, May 1993, p. 15).

But economists outside the World Bank have argued throughout the 1980s that the Bank's stylized image of the East Asian miracle was distorted. Yale economist Colin Bradford (now Chief Economist at USAID) reviewed the literature in 1986, and argued that the World Bank and IMF misread the East Asian experience, producing a stylized version that supported their adjustment and stabilization models (see, for example, WDR, 1983, pp. 57–63; WDR, 1985, pp. 54–5; Krueger, 1985; Agarwala, 1983.) Bradford cites major published studies of Taiwan, South Korea, Hong Kong and Singapore from the late 1970s and 1980s that highlight the variations the Bank is now 'discovering.'

The Bank not only ignored independent, dissenting research as it created the stylized East Asian experience, but employed its caricature of that experience to justify an approach to structural adjustment that did not succeed, and indeed was never tried, in Asia.[1] Manfred Bienefeld

(1994) considers the East Asia case an example of the 'conflict between the historical record and today's neo-liberal policies.' The Bank's interpretation of the record demonstrates a clear preference for global integration over the 'conscious building of individual, internally coherent economies' (p. 42).

Moseley, Harrigan and Toye (1991) argue that the whole history of Bank-sponsored adjustment in low-income countries has ignored the lessons of East Asia and other industrializing areas. Citing Fei and Ranis, they note that successful postwar industrialization has involved a period of state protection of infant industries, protection that was removed gradually over time. By discouraging protection and state management of investment in the low income countries, Bank-style adjustment is 'a gratuitous obstruction' to the pattern of policy evolution that has produced the very few successful industrializations since World War II.

Similar selectivity is evident in the World Bank's 1988 evaluation of adjustment lending. The global implications of country-based policy recommendations and the domestic political reactions to adjustment both extend beyond the range of factors the Bank wishes to admit into its analysis. But their exclusion means that self-assessment is done in a fictional world that differs sharply from the realities with which client governments must cope.

The evaluation tends to focus solely on the 'correctness' of prescribed policies, given the supply and demand responses forecast by its models, and assuming full implementation. When actual results fail to meet expectations, exogenous factors – slow supply response to new demand for investment, persistent global recession, poor terms of trade – are often invoked to explain the disappointing performance and remove any question of the appropriateness of the adjustment program.

By treating debt and global economic setbacks in this way, rather than as part of an integrated set of domestic and international barriers to development it is possible to segregate economic shocks and explain away the failure of adjustment plans. The alternative would be to recognize such failures as the result of a package of services inappropriate to prevailing conditions.

Assessments of growth-related indicators using computerized general equilibrium models rely heavily on projections of global economic conditions. The systematic optimistic bias of these estimates, documented by Cole (1987), affects SALs and their assessment, as the Bank's ten-year review notes, '... projections of outcomes during the adjustment phase were optimistic. Not only the persistence of the negative external shocks but also the lags in implementation and supply response were underestimated' (1988, p. 79). This systematic bias reflects an optimism about economic recovery that can be traced throughout neo-liberal thought and policy on debt management (Corbridge, 1993, pp. 32–4).

An internal memorandum by an analyst in the Policy Analysis and Review Unit (SPRPA) highlights this problem (Earwaker, 1989). Noting that the advent of SALs had made global economic projections central to Bank lending, Earwaker (1989, p. 1) argues that 'to the extent that projections are based upon overly-optimistic assumptions they will exaggerate the likely effectiveness of a proposed package of policy reforms in achieving the targeted adjustment.'

Such estimates have long lacked realism, he argues, because of 'a disposition to favor scenarios' that show the country needs World Bank finance, and that prospects for repayment are satisfactory. But with adjustment lending, where short-term performance is essential to making the case for adopting otherwise unpopular policy measures, economists have employed assumptions that produce 'a rate of GDP growth that is constrained only by the imagination of the task manager and the requirements of the lending program' (Earwaker, 1989, p. 2, 3).

In planning and evaluating adjustment measures as in other programming, the organizational culture carries out a purposeful selection of information. It permits the organization to focus its attention, and the attention of its observers and borrowers, on factors that it officially recognizes, and that are consonant with its myth of development.

Canadian scholar John Mihevc (1993) and Susan George and Fabrizio Sabelli (1994) have both compared the Bank to certain religious institutions in this respect. For Mihevc, the enunciation and pursuit of the basic principles of economic liberalization mirrors the zeal and single-mindedness of fundamentalist theologies and religious bodies, holding certain 'truths' as privileged and reinterpreting and constructing a reality to fit them. George and Sabelli push the metaphor further, 'this supranational, non-democratic institution functions very much like . . . the medieval Church. It has a doctrine, a rigidly structured hierarchy preaching and imposing this doctrine and a quasi-religious mode of self-justification' (p. 5). Religious fundamentalists and admirers of Medieval Catholicism may be troubled by the characterizations, but the observations surely sum up many aspects of the behavior and thinking at the Bank. These tendencies, unfortunately, have strong implications for how and what the organization learns.

CULTURAL, STRUCTURAL AND PROCEDURAL LIMITS ON LEARNING

Hierarchical organizational culture links together many features that limit the World Bank's capacity to listen, change and learn. These features – conceptual, procedural and structural – limit the ability of individual staff and of the organization to establish working relations of collaboration and accountability with NGOs.

The Nature of Organizational Learning

Michael Cernea (1987), World Bank rural sociology advisor, notes that governments and donors find it easier to focus on infusions of capital than to inquire into the causes of failed development strategies and unsuccessful projects. New strategies are launched with fanfare, but Cernea (1987, pp. 9–10) is 'struck by how little interest there has been in learning the true reason for failure . . .' of previous strategies. The factors that impede such systematic organizational learning are explored in this section, and they are shown to limit the World Bank's ability for genuine interaction with NGOs.

Theories of organizational learning stress the role of routines in forming an institutional memory and of common assumptions in underpinning these routines. Barbara Levitt and James March (1988, p. 320) argue that organizations learn 'by encoding inferences from history into routines that guide behavior.' An organization's routines are vehicles that preserve and transmit its experience, a kind of collective memory.

'Routines' as Levitt and March understand them include 'the forms, rules, procedures, conventions, strategies and technologies around which organizations are constructed, and through which they operate,' as well as 'the structure of beliefs, frameworks, paradigms, codes, cultures, and knowledge that buttress, elaborate and contradict the formal routines.' Because routines are independent of individuals, they can survive turnover and the passage of time.

Routines change either through trial and error experimentation or through deliberate organizational search for new methods. But experience gained in either way is always interpreted through actors' own frames of meaning. In drawing lessons from experience:

> the facts are not always obvious, and the causality of events is difficult to untangle. What an organization should expect to achieve, and thus the difference between success and failure, is not always clear. Never-

theless people in organizations form interpretations of events and come to classify outcomes as good or bad (Levitt and March, p. 322).

The common assumptions and understandings that make such judgments possible are extremely difficult for an organization to change or re-learn. Chris Argyris (1987, p. 84) distinguishes two types of learning. One occurs when an error is detected and corrected 'without questioning or altering the underlying values of the system.' The second, systemic learning,[2] goes beyond correcting immediate problems, to confront the values and expectations that guide and drive actions in the organization. Systemic learning involves 'the important issues of competence and justice,' and often raises 'indiscussible' issues.

Here the organization confronts its own myths, by which it defines success for itself, in a field where what 'works' is not self-evident. Systemic learning challenges the factors that provide stability and self-identity in an organization. It calls organizational myths or core technologies into question, and may demand a new kind of information search. All of this is likely to undermine other goals, including those that underlie the organization's system of incentives. Declaring a new policy will probably not be enough to effect the changes required, if actors with informal power bases are not convinced of the merits of the change. In the World Bank, the key variables, valued by individuals and institutionalized in the organization, include neoclassical economics, the doctrine of sovereignty and the supremacy of technocratic policy formation.

Most organizations find systemic learning extremely difficult. Frames of reference and organizational myths create clarity for an organization in the face of the ambiguity of success and failure. These established patterns of perception and analysis reach deep into organizational structures and individual psyches, and it is difficult to build or to accept a case for change when organizational standards and procedures are all based on widely-held standards of success.

Established theories and procedures are often not only encoded in patterns of thought and frames of reference, but also institutionalized in organizational routines and enshrined in professional expectations and norms. Features as general as rational-technical bureaucratic organization and as specific as the use of cost-benefit analysis in appraisal are buttressed by doctrines, myths, habits and expectations in the organization and beyond. Much experience in an organization goes unrecorded or is reported selectively, further strengthening the *status quo*, especially in fields that do not feature strong competitive pressure to change.

These features do not mean that organizations are rigid, allowing no change. On the contrary, the ability to tolerate 'deviant memories' and to admit variance from established procedures, without allowing precedents to be established, is vital to an organization's survival. An organization bolsters the 'short-term flexibility and long-term stability' of its routines if it is able to tolerate such variation (Levitt and March, p. 327).

These theories suggest that learning in an organization is limited in three broad senses.

1. *Learning by the individuals does not equal learning by the organization.* Individual staff or even units within a larger organization may be able to absorb lessons from experience and change behavior in further programming, without the lessons being accepted and 'learned' in the same sense by the organization. The distinction between individual and organization here is critical, because one person or group – outside or within the World Bank – could work for years to reshape a particular investment without any assurance of a broader impact.
2. *Systemic learning is difficult in a hierarchical organizational culture:* a lesson may be appreciated and perhaps acted upon in a particular case, without being 'learned' by examining assumptions, structures and procedures that may require change in order to avoid the errors. Learning in this sense is not just cognitive, it requires systematic action and correction.
3. *Systemic learning is more likely to follow from a new coalition gaining the power to define problems and solution and articulate values, than from a cognitive paradigm shift among individuals* (LePrestre, 1993, p. 16).

Information and Limits on Organizational Learning: Three Cases

How do these problems for organizational learning manifest themselves at the Bank? Three cases illustrate some of the dynamics.

1. *Deliberate manipulation of information as a power base in the organization: program lending in Malaysia.* Management specialist David Hulme (1989) documents learning and 'deliberate non-learning' at the Asian Development Bank (ADB), the World Bank and Malaysian government agencies during a series of rubber estate projects in the 1960s, 1970s and early 1980s. Agencies sometimes fail to learn a lesson because

of inadequate evaluation methodologies, but more often because some participant in the project planning discourse does not want to consider a particular lesson. 'Actively "not learning from experience" is as much a part of organizational process as "learning from experience"' Hulme, 1989, p. 2).

In a series of rubber production schemes in Malaysia, the ADB clearly recorded important lessons about scheme size, site preparation, market adaptation, need for 'settler capital', cropping patterns, the difficulty of procuring land for projects; problems with certain types of settlers; and local staff's management capacity. But while some issues were considered in planning successive projects, others were systematically ignored. The selective learning 'was based not upon an ignorance of certain lessons, but on their avoidance and suppression' (Hulme, 1989, pp. 6–9).

Planners in the government and the banks treated lessons 'not as neutral pieces of information ... but as strategic resources that are a potential source of power and influence over future planning discourse.' Lending targets and planning agendas were central: lessons that could be incorporated into a rehabilitated and expanded settlement scheme were adopted, while those that threw the project format into question or threatened to delay approval (in this case, land availability, settler selection and management capacity) were ignored or glossed over (Hulme, 1989, pp. 10–11).

Although Hulme focuses primarily on the ADB, the World Bank co-financed the third of the three schemes. An unpublished World Bank report on land-settlement schemes notes that many unsatisfactory land settlement projects initiated since 1975 '"can be faulted on the basis of lessons learnt elsewhere at the time of their commencement"' (Hulme, 1989, p. 12).

In Hulme's case information is suppressed by influential participants. In other instances at the World Bank, not only is information and learning a tool in advancing individual and organizational interests, but some learning is effectively prohibited by beliefs and assumptions that are fundamental to organizational myths and that are maintained by strong information selection biases.

2. *'Learning' without policy change: adjustment and women.* The Bank's evolving awareness of the differential effects of recession and adjustment on women and men shows how understanding can be advanced within the organization without the reappraisal of assumptions and policies that constitutes organizational learning. After the initial period in which

poverty and social effects of adjustment were virtually ignored, the Bank adopted 'protecting the vulnerable' (women, children, the aged) as the substance of its concern for women's welfare under adjustment.

Research sponsored within the Bank during the 1980s documented and deepened the understanding of the effects on women. Caroline Moser and others within the Bank confirmed the effects on women's role in the productive system. Women's work typically included both work that conventional national income measures account as productive, and the unpaid work of household and community maintenance.

This documentation helped some within the Bank appreciate the ways in which women's expanded workloads were the central feature of the 'coping strategies' through which communities and households managed the strains of adjustment. But the documentation of the dimensions of the feminization of poverty – informalization, reduced access to health services, resort to cheaper, labor-intensive foodstuffs, family violence, restricted political roles – has not led to the conclusion that gender equity questions inherent in the present pattern of adjustment need to be addressed. Adjustment strategies have not been redesigned to reduce inequities, nor have planning processes been broadened to give women an expanded role in their design. Rather 'coping mechanisms' have been utilized to maintain existing adjustment programs. In effect, the architects of the Bank's adjustment policies have been content to make women 'more efficient beasts of burden' (Nzomo, 1992, p. 107) in bearing the strains of economic adjustment.

3. *Institutional self-deception and the disbursement mandate: infrastructure lending in India.* In recent experience in India, selectivity and suppression of information have contributed to some of the World Bank's most notorious 'problem projects.' Its handling of the independent review of the Sardar Sarovar dam project provoked a high-profile controversy the Bank would surely have preferred to avoid. Behind the controversy lies a history of external protest and internal selectivity in handling information that amounts to a pattern of institutional self-deception.

The Singrauli energy projects, including a thermal power plant, coal mine and the associated energy grid, were supported by three IDA credits and an IBRD loan made between 1977 and 1987. The project provoked criticism, in India and among international environmental NGOs, for its environmental impact and the conditions under which some 20,000 persons were relocated from the project area. Extensive dissent and protest by Indian and other NGOs is documented in letters and petitions collected in the Environmental Defense Fund's MDB Information Center.

Yet the Project Completion Report on the 1977 IDA Credit to support the Singrauli Thermal Power Plant, written in 1987 (Report No. 6784), includes not one word about the relocation issue, nor about the extensive legal and political conflict in India over the project. Instead, after an analysis of project implementation and production and sale of kilowatt-hours of electricity, the report officially closes the books on the investment by judging it 'entirely successful' because the generating units were completed and electric power is being generated and sold to consumers. This treatment, ignoring the issues raised by relocation and environmental impact in its official assessment of the investment, does not inspire confidence that issues of concern to NGOs have been integrated into the Bank's standards of performance and self-assessment.

The storm of protest over the Sardar Sarovar project became impossible to ignore, even in World Bank documents. The Bank-commissioned Independent Review found that the Bank appraised and approved the loan without regard for its own requirements for treatment of displaced populations, and despite technical and planning flaws (*Sardar Sarovar*, 1992).

World Bank support for the massive project began with a $450 million loan in 1985. According to the independent review, World Bank resettlement policies and the Indian government's own environmental requirements were ignored, and information underestimating resettlement needs, misrepresenting hydrological conditions and failing to take into account other projects upstream were not checked by Bank planners. These failings led to widespread displacement, protest, and repression. In the face of these problems, which grew into a human and public relations catastrophe, the Bank remained involved and sought incremental improvement in the Indian state and national governments' performance. The Review judged this strategy unsuccessful and urged the Bank to 'step away' from the project.

In a rare vote, the Executive Directors in October, 1992, approved management's recommendation to disregard the Review's recommendation and continue funding Sardar Sarovar. The Indian government was given six months to rectify certain problems related to forced relocations. In March 1993, the Indian government announced that it would terminate the loan agreement and complete the project without World Bank support.

Finally, after two extraordinary events – the Independent Review and the Board vote – the Bank stood its ground on relocation standards, and provoked the loan's termination. But what is remembered from the nine-year episode was encapsulated in India Program Director Hans Vergin's words to the NGO-World Bank Committee in November, that the Bank was never bound to carry out all of the Review's recommendations. In so saying he added to the list of experiences and lessons the Bank felt free to disregard: previous experience in Brazil during disputes over infrastructure projects; objections from Indian NGOs about improper resettlement, environmental damage and human rights abuses; its own highly touted resettlement policies and environmental procedures; and the history of noncompliance, by two of the Indian states involved, with agreements made by the national government.

The factors at work read like a checklist of the Bank's organizational traits, reluctance to give up on an investment once begun; determination to keep major loans flowing to a major borrower; shortchanging social and environmental considerations in a process driven by 'engineering and economic imperatives' (*Sardar Sarovar*, p. xxiv); citing as justification the Indian government's sovereignty, while manipulating the governing boards that represent sovereign control over Bank investments. The Sardar Sarovar debacle is not unique. According to the independent review, the problems it uncovered 'are more the rule than the exception to resettlement operations supported by the Bank' (*Sardar Sarovar*, 1992, p. 53).

CULTURE, LEARNING AND CHANGE

Selectivity, Socialization and Intellectual Insularity

A powerful socialization of staff and a tendency to intellectual insularity in the World Bank's research and analysis help to reinforce the selectivity in its handling of information. The insular intellectual environment has been noted by friendly and critical sources alike (Mason and Asher, 1973, p. 66; Hellinger, 1988). 'Even by Washington standards,' writes Ayres (1983, p. xiv), the Bank has a reputation as private and reticent.

Self-suppression of dissent

Thomas' research (1980, p. 119) identified the principal sources that staff consult for information or advice. Remarkably few say they turn to external publications (27 per cent) or visit the country involved (28 per cent) when they need information. Many more refer to 'Bank sources' or host country officials (41 per cent each). The inward tendency is even stronger 'in making a difficult decision,' where only 21 per cent name a non-World Bank source (Thomas, 1980, p. 146). This inward orientation and 'remarkable consensus among . . . staff on what information is important to them . . .' reflect socialization 'into a way of looking at the environment which encourages them to focus on specific information' (Thomas, 1980, p. 118).

Staff also act individually to filter and restrict the dissenting views that are aired. Thomas asked professional staff how they react to decisions from which they personally dissent, and elicited a sketch of a hierarchy in which individuals not only readily implement decisions they dislike, but rarely make a sustained effort to record their dissent. 'When I dislike a decision,' 48 per cent of respondents said 'I just implement it' anyway; 29 per cent voice disagreement but implement it, 26 per cent record their dissent formally, 19 per cent appeal to others on the issue, and 7 per cent 'don't participate.'

Respondents stress the need to go along with decisions when 'one agrees with the basic goals' (Thomas, 1980, p. 151). 'People try to understand the Bank's viewpoint, rather than the individual's. Anything is okay if it's consistent with Bank guidelines.' Thomas finds that there is 'overriding support of the staff for Bank operations,' noting comments such as this: 'The Bank provides a systematic way to analyze problems you don't get any other way. It's good exposure to the complete and practical problems of development' (Thomas, 1980, pp. 150, 181). Thomas concludes that staff have a high level of respect for the Bank's privacy and autonomy. But its inward-looking intellectual world, intellectual conformity and relative lack of dissent also reflect a profound socialization of staff.

Socialization

Ayres (1983, p. 39) describes a socialization that promotes continuity, conformity and:

> the norms and ambience of neoclassical economics. . . . Even the socially conscious might in large measure succumb. . . . Too great a concern with poverty in the economic and sector work program would, to some extent at least, have been perceived by many important individuals within the Bank as deviant behavior.

A social services sector officer in LAC sees the Bank as governed by dominant ideas, 'first and foremost, neo-classical economics.' The pervasiveness of economic theory in everyday discussion amused this respondent, as economists in cafeteria lines discuss and frame their choices of menu and service options in terms of marginal gains, preference structures, and other jargon of the trade (LAC staff no. 1). Socialization takes place in all international agencies, but its 'relatively small size, the likely predispositions of persons working for and with it [and] the common influence of the "financial community,"' make the effect particularly potent at the World Bank (Fatorous, 1977, p. 19).

Sociologist Robert Chambers (1987, p. 4) agrees that 'normal professionalism' − a profession's dominant patter of 'thinking, values, methods and behaviour' − adds stability, and resists change at the World Bank. He appeals for change in the 'normal professionalism' of staff through opening new lines of information and experience in making policy.

But powerful organizational and political-economic factors that sustain the professional culture makes such changes unlikely. Arguing that the Bank hires 'only one kind of economist,' neoclassical, Guy Gran (1986, pp. 277–81) charges that 'assumptions, definitions, terms of reference, analytical methods and subjects for discussion in Bank learning and policy formulation are primarily those reflecting the guild behavior of one particular form of Western positivist social science.'

Gran's assertion is no longer completely true: one can now find a few economists in the Bank with decidedly heterodox views on macro-economics and natural resource economics. But as one social scientist at the Bank noted, the institution resembles an English village in that the only way to be truly accepted there is to be born into it. Mid-career recruits to the Bank are normally hired as 'advisors,' and can ascend to become ever-more senior 'advisors,' but not to management positions. They, like their ideas, are kept institutionally at arm's length.

The impact of criticism on individual staff is mediated by their own intellectual, institutional and professional allegiances, their motivations and the socialization process and internal consensus developed among staff. But the intellectual and institutional power of neoclassical economic theory plays a role as well. As intellectuals and professionals, many staff hold themselves more directly accountable to professional standards than to management's directives and assume responsibility to shape and amend policy as they implement it (Ascher, 1983, p. 427). Economists' credentials and adherence to neoclassical theory give them, within the World Bank, an almost unassailable position from which to judge new mandates.

Insularity

The analytical framework that results suffers from both the lack of cross-disciplinary input within the Bank and from the tendency not to stray far outside its walls. Gran decries the 'insular literary universe' where outside work is rarely cited, and 'any hint of self-critique or irreverence gives way to bureaucratic imperatives' under repeated revision of written work. The selectivity is purposeful; since independent scholars, peasant groups, local NGOs cannot be controlled, 'what they say has no validity. Any other learning method would produce unbearable cognitive dissonance' (Gran, 1986, pp. 277, 285). Several staff interviewed demonstrated this by finding ways to ignore or categorize their critics among the NGOs as ill-informed, attacking outdated images of the Bank (Africa staff no. 2; LAC staff no.2).

Former Bank Vice President Willi Wapenhans (1994), in an essay for the Bretton Woods Commission, criticizes the weak flow of research information into the Bank:

> Relatively little effort is made to engage the intellectual community around the globe... The absence of such efforts creates the perception that the Bank's operational research is exclusive, self-serving, and of insufficient objectivity (p. c-297).

Attitudes toward the 1992 internal review 'Effective Implementation' (the 'Wapenhans report') reflect this insularity and the limits of organizational learning. Preston, in a self-congratulatory memo, says the Bank should take pride in 'its willingness and ability to undertake [such a] frank and critical self-evaluation' (memorandum to Executive Directors, 'Portfolio Management: Next Steps,' 31 March 1993). In reality the critique is entirely internal, retrenching and re-applying the traditional standard of 10 per cent rate of return on investment to identify unsatisfactory performance in projects. In so doing it reaffirms the myth of development success as measured by banking standards, sidestepping criticism and pressure on participation, poverty, human rights and environmental issues by redefining the problem in its own terms. Non-compliance with adjustment conditionality becomes an implementation problem, to be solved by more 'client-oriented' implementation and supervision. Project delays and economically unsustainable projects become managerial problems whose solution lies in more supervision time and a broader view of the administrative burdens that country portfolios place on government officials.

The report dwells for two pages on learning processes in the Bank. It identifies three distinct cycles of learning, all narrowly focused on implementing established objectives, rather than on appraising their validity: in-country portfolio performance, distinctive sectoral experience, and 'the professional learning cycle' of training, exposure and dissemination ('Effective Implementation', pp. 23–4).

A few observers are more optimistic about the Bank's capacity to learn. But each of these assessments acknowledges, implicitly or explicitly, that limitations such as those discussed above set boundaries for learning. Montague Yudelman (1985), former head of agricultural programs at the Bank, views the growth of agricultural lending as an evolution of theory and priorities, driven by the work of some staff economists. He notes that agricultural lending increased as distributional issues gained prominence in development theory.

But the belated recognition that income and resource distribution is a critical issue even in the presence of strong economic growth troubled the Bank again two decades later. After the early experience of adjustment lending in the early 1980s, Zuckerman (1989) reports that equity issues associated with adjustment finally became an issue among staff. The lesson that might have been learned in the 1960s seems not to have penetrated the World Bank's basic perspective on its role in development.

Hurni (1980, pp. 65, 82) praises the Bank's internal planning as highly reflective and self-critical. But she observes 'a gap between the World Bank's research and intellectual approach and its practical actions in the field...' (Hurni, p. 103). The sophisticated research apparatus is applied almost exclusively to those issues that are tractable for the Bank as an institution.

'Expertise', 'Control' and 'Quality'

Alongside the dominant intellectual role of neoclassical economic theory, two foundations for the organizational culture emerge from interviews of Bank staff. These ideas are the technical expertise and superiority of staff; and 'control' of lending operations to maintain their 'quality.'

Many staff identify the self-image of technical competence and superiority as an important feature of the Bank's culture. Many of the marks of this attitude are impressionistic, and evidence of it anecdotal.

None the less, the prevailing sense of superiority to other donor agencies and to counterparts in borrowing government ministries is widely remarked upon by observers, consultants, and sometimes by staff themselves.

A recent anecdote illustrates the dimensions of this organizational ego. Dr Michael Irwin, who served briefly as Director of Medical Services at the World Bank after 32 years as medical director for the United Nations, resigned early in 1990 in response to what he characterized as a staff 'overconcerned with its prestige, and... preoccupied with... salaries, benefits, and "grade creep"' (Irwin, 1990, p. 37). In an incident that led to Irwin's resignation, the new medical director suggested in a letter to the Bank's in-house magazine that staff consider giving up the first-class air travel to which they were entitled. The suggested provoked a storm of protest, calling Irwin 'terribly ill-informed or frighteningly insensitive,' dismissing his office as an unproductive burden on the organization, and branding his suggestion as 'unfortunate and damaging to morale in the... Bank.' One writer called this perquisite 'the most tangible expression (and some would say the "final expression") of the institution's esteem and consideration [toward staff]... ' (Irwin, 1990, pp. 34–6).[3]

The widely-remarked elitism (see Mason and Asher, 1973; Irwin, 1990; Hurni, 1980; Van de Laar 1980) of Bank staff is not simply a function, of course, of well-appointed offices, generous salaries and first-class air travel privileges. The Bank's influence, prestige and other rewards attract technically skilled, highly (if narrowly) qualified professional staff. Professionals who have reached prestigious posts in international development or finance, staff generally share a social and intellectual background that includes advanced training in a handful of American and European universities (van de Laar, 1980). The influence through financial and other clout, the physical and financial perquisites of their employment, and an institutional culture that assigns high status to their intellectual and technical skills, all contribute to a certain lack of humility.

Dimensions of organizational control

The organizational need to control the use of its loans arose early in the World Bank's history, as staff and management sought to balance the notion that projects are initiated and planned by borrowing governments, with the need for project plans that met technical requirements and satisfied the financial institutions from which the World Bank borrowed that its loans would be productive and therefore repayable. Libby (1975b, pp. 45–7) argues that as a World Bank 'development doctrine' was developed in the late 1940s, 'technical assistance' emerged as the concept and tool that reconciled the need for control with borrowers' reluctance to surrender such control. The problem was solved, in Libby's view, by 'subsuming issues of control under the rubric of "technical assistance".'

Former Bank Vice President Wapenhans (1994) details the development of what he considers excessive Bank technical assistance in the design of projects. Wapenhans argues that involvement of Bank staff in project design compromises the Bank's ability to appraise the project and make a credibly disinterested decision as to whether to finance it (p. 296).

The organizational emphasis on 'quality' and 'control' of lending continues to shape staff's interactions with outside actors. A LAC staffer called 'quality' an 'obsession' that degenerates to simple consistency and conformance (LAC staff no. 1). Focused on control and 'quality,' staff find it difficult to delegate control of a project component to an NGO. For this reason one staff economist calls technical expertise the World Bank's greatest strength and weakness (Africa staff no. 3).

QUALITY, CONTROL, UNCERTAINTY AND NGOS

The Problem of 'Certifying' NGOs

Maintaining quality and control also minimizes uncertainty in lending operations, and the threat of uncertainty is an unwelcome implication of cooperating with NGOs. The hundreds of NGOs in most borrowing countries are unknown quantities to most staff, and as a West Africa economist pointed out, there is no easy way to 'certify' NGOs. The absence of a straightforward standard for determining that a NGO is legitimate and acceptable leaves staff with what is widely perceived as a politically risky and time-consuming process of selecting organizations that can be 'effective partners' technically, and inoffensive politically to the borrowing government (Africa staff no. 1).

One result is that staff are likely to contact an NGO that has collaborated on projects with another major donor. In the Philippines, Bank missions contacted two NGOs, Philippine Business for Social Progress and the Davao Medical School Foundation/Institute for Primary Health Care, because of their experience implementing USAID-funded projects

(Asia staff no. 1). This practice of relying on a few NGOs with experience relating to major donors (and comfortable relations with the government) is understandable. But narrowing the range in search of security entails losses, as the Bank misses the experience of other innovative prospective NGO partners.

The risks involved in working with NGOs surface repeatedly in interviews, staff stress the need to distinguish 'serious NGOs' from 'fly-by-night operations' (Policy staff no. 9); to recognize government-based NGO fronts (Africa staff no.1); to distinguish NGOs created solely to respond to a new fund (Policy staff October 6, 1989); and to sort out 'effective partners' for Bank-funded operations (LAC staff, October 6, 1989). The Operational Directive on NGOs, like some other official statements, gives a curiously long recital of NGOs' weaknesses and dangers (OD 14.70, 1989). A staffer in Strategic Policy and Review argues that NGOs must be seen as partners, not risks (Policy staff no. 3). But abhorrence of uncertainty and preference for clear, consistent duties and rewards militates against it.

NGOs, Policy Change and Uncertainty

This resistance to uncertainty is institutionalized in the relative inflexibility of key structural and procedural characteristics of the Bank. The project cycle is the most important of these procedural elements. According to Thomas' (1980, p. 110) interviews, most staff believe the exacting requirements and consistent, reliable process for project development and review are important for 'effective operation'.

Staff have structured and defined outside participation so as to minimize disruption of the process, and to preserve certain stages strictly internal. In India, NGO members of the now defunct national NGO-World Bank consultative body were told that their involvement in discussion of project ideas is welcome and solicited, but that 'appraisal is primarily the responsibility of the World Bank team. . . . this responsibility could not be shared' (Second Meeting of the World Bank-NGO Consultation Committee (India), Summary Record, 1989, p. 7). Exclusive control of appraisal keeps the important stage in which the project's worth is documented and certified within the domain of the Bank, maintaining the primacy of its expertise and its standards of 'quality'.

When popular or NGO input into project design interferes with the pace of project development and information review, it disrupts standard operating procedures that help to define and guarantee successful 'performance' by staff. Interruptions in these processes are widely viewed as risks, disruptions and problems, rather than contributions or opportunities for improved project design (Policy staff no. 3; Policy staff no. 6).[4]

The project cycle's well-defined process for project design, review and implementation assure staff that effort expended to develop a project will yield 'performance,' that is, an approved loan. In the absence of intervening events – a change in government or dramatic economic disturbances – staff have a reasonably consistent guide to satisfactory performance in designing projects. Project approval by the Board remains a *de facto* measure of accomplishment. Under these circumstances, staff are unlikely to resist new policies that enhance the probability of achieving desired outcomes.[5]

But new policies that implicitly redefine performance – guidelines on the environment, poverty, appropriate technology and women in development – can affect staff's perceptions about whether effort expended will yield performance that is agreed to be successful. New policies may be perceived as bureaucratic or politically inspired, slowing project preparation and reducing staff's motivation and satisfaction. New mandates implicitly redefine 'performance' in the organization, giving staff reason to resist or ignore redefinitions of 'performance' or 'success.'

The reluctance of most staff to adopt social measures of welfare in using cost-benefit analysis for project appraisal illustrates this resistance to changes that modify standards of performance. The social weighing of benefits, designed to adjust cost benefit analysis as an evaluative tool to take into account distributional issues, was never widely put into practice. Staff economists argued that it introduced a false precision, because reliable data on the distributional issues were unavailable or impossible to gather. But these same obstacles have not prevented the projection of growth and other macro-economic variables, in order to plan and 'sell' adjustment plans, despite the conjectural nature of much of the data and the (at best) mixed track record of such projections (Earwaker, 1989).

More recently, World Bank anthropologist Lawrence Salmen charged that the staff's failure to adopt a participatory beneficiary assessment methodology – which Salmen has promoted within the Bank – reflects an entrenched organizational culture. He characterizes the intellectual culture as top-down, deductive, favoring economic rather than sociocultural discourse, quantitative, impact- rather than process-oriented, abstract and theoretical. Salmen concludes that 'many Bank staff and borrower-government personnel feel they know what needs to be known regarding a development activity, including the people's perception' (Salmen, 1992, p. 21).

Environmental staff designing procedures for environmental impact assessments (EIA) confront related problems. EIA requirements for projects deemed likely to have environmental impact include consultation with affected organizations in the borrowing country (World Bank, 1990c). But making this requirement effective, and avoiding evasion or perfunctory compliance by appraisal teams is an issue that environmental staff are considering. How many NGOs must be consulted? How extensive is the consultation to be, and what results are required for the project to proceed? (LAC staff no. 2).

Integrating concerns about gender roles and equity has been, as Kardam (1989) concludes, hampered by the absence of a strong internal constituency at the World Bank. One reason is the wide range of issues and techniques involved in assessing and seeking to change the impact of Bank-financed projects. Issues such as intra-household distribution of income and resources and the socio-cultural obstacles to economic opportunity for women are foreign to the economics training of most staff, and incorporating them into project appraisals is not only politically tricky, time-consuming and contrary to the thrust of the development myth, it also undercuts staff's expertise by posing issues they are ill-prepared to address.

Professional socialization, internal and individual motivation and the World Bank's structure and core technology all contribute to the strength of its organizational culture. This culture shapes the interpretation of new input and limits organizational change. In practice, this means that Bank staff who promote change, and advocates from without, face powerful, pervasive resistance.

Exercising 'Control' in World Bank-NGO Experience

The World Bank's need to structure and control the working relationship with NGOs is captured in a small change in the language describing the Operations Manual Statement (OMS) on NGOs. Tentatively entitled 'Operational Collaboration with NGOs' in a 1988 draft, its finalized version is instead 'Involving NGOs in Bank-financed Operations' (OMS draft, 1989; OD 14.70, 1989). The dynamics of individual working relationships vary, but the official policy is not collaborative but tightly controlled, making room for NGO involvement on the World Bank's terms. Other themes encountered in interviews and documents

– 'professionalism,' closely directed 'participation,' government and World Bank formation of local organizations, and careful interpretation of resistance to Bank-supported projects – are all dimensions of the Bank's control of its work with NGOs.

Pervasive attitudes toward professionalism and voluntarism help to set the boundaries for NGO contributions. One Asia staffer summed up the premium placed on professionalism, asserting that '[a]s long as they're based on voluntarism, they'll never be able to do the real development' (Asia staff no. 4). The same staffer argued that the appropriate role for the World Bank was to build on NGO successes, find ways to expand and 'professionalize' NGOs.

Even staff more sympathetic to NGO activities noted that their 'young, idealistic, inexperienced' staff made field collaboration difficult, and found professional consultants to present fewer uncertainties. NGOs' tendency to work 'through their own networks,' sometimes leading to initiatives not prescribed in the project plan, was 'aggravating' even to the most sympathetic staff (Africa staff no. 3). Other staff also singled out 'professionalism' as a key virtue in NGOs they had made contact with (Policy staff no. 5; LAC staff no. 1), and a member of the NGO liaison unit summed up the Bank's goals as seeking a 'more businesslike' relation with NGOs (NGO-World Bank Committee Meetings, October 1994).

Prevailing views of participation in the Bank

This premium on professionalism is in keeping with the view I encountered of the basis for NGO participation in design. In general, NGOs were sought out to fill roles much as a consultant might be: their special expertise, not any claim to local knowledge or to represent local peoples' views, was the quality valued. Official guidance on 'involving NGOs in Bank-supported activities' points staff toward NGOs with 'particular professional expertise and managerial capabilities' in a sector or region, or NGOs in 'developed countries' with 'specialized experience... in managing foreign assistance...' (OD 14.70, 1989, pp. 1–2). If expertise is the sole grounds for participation, then NGO demands for a representative role make little sense. For example, NGOs in the country where one staffer had negotiated a social spending fund objected that they weren't involved in its design. 'I don't see why,' he complained. 'If we produce a project that is satisfactory to them, what's their problem?' (Asia staff no. 3).

This conception of NGOs' role in project design reflects a prevailing, narrow idea of 'participation' in the World Bank that bears little resemblance to that promoted by many NGOs and students of local organizations and social change. Participation is widely discussed outside the Bank as involving people in initiating and shaping plans that affect them (Oakley and Marsden, 1984; Esman and Uphoff, 1984). But at the Bank, participation means mobilizing people to carry out project plans, and projects need 'incentives to elicit participants' contribution to the project objectives' (OMS 2.12, 1978, p. 5). What is sought are not views, priorities and wishes of affected populations but their 'full commitment to the project' (OMS 2.20 1984, p. 10) when it has been sketched out. The Bank's participation learning process, in the end, continued this essentially instrumental view of participation, valuing and encouraging participation for its ability largely as a tool for expanding 'ownership' of Bank-financed activities.

Projects involving NGOs in Laos and in Nigeria illustrate this limitation. The Laos Agricultural Rehabilitation and Development Project (1978) calls for the Ministry of Agriculture to initiate water users groups to coordinate irrigation initiatives, and to train cooperatives (PCR, Report No. 7250, p. 12). 'Few, if any' such groups were formed, even though they were to be assigned 'full responsibility' for maintaining canals and coordinating water distribution. The formation of the groups appears to have been peripheral to the projects' design; it merits only a paragraph's discussion in the Project Completion Report, and no comment in the document's 'Lessons Learned' section.

The Nigeria Multi-State Agricultural Development (II) Project, (1989) involved a similar role for newly-created Water Users Associations and Village Cooperative Societies. The project's predecessor was criticized in the OED Rural Development study for failing to build local institutions and relying too heavily on Bank financing. According to the Bank's project summary, the second project 'will assist local governments in establishing village cooperative societies to raise funds for spares, operational maintenance, and eventual replacement of machinery and equipment for bore holes.' Group formation and contribution of 10 per cent of capital costs are prerequisites for drilling and construction in a community.

In these projects and others, the community organizations involved are newly created by local or national governments and assigned responsibilities for implementing and maintaining the project. In these projects as in most World Bank discussions, participation is not a process of joint planning and accountability but a measure to mobilize those whom the projects' planners aim to benefit. Participation is a measure to improve project performance (Cernea, 1987; Paul, 1988), 'sold' to staff in terms of economic efficiency (Strategic Planning and Review, 1989). In many instances it is employed for its value in promoting cost recovery in irrigation and other projects that involve user maintenance.

Planned participation: managing uncertainty and resistance

Such directed participation, in fact, is proposed as a tool to limit uncertainty and increase efficiency. Staff's guidance on project design calls participation only one option when a 'cooperation problem' arises: 'Measures can be built into the projects to reduce conflicts, strengthen and re-orient traditional local organizations, or adopt a technology that minimizes the need for cooperation' (OMS 2.12, 1978, p. 6).

Planned participation, initiated by project authorities to minimize uncertainty, is the norm: '"spontaneous" participation... occurs only rarely...."' (Yudelman, 1985, p. 16). One World Bank document (SPRIE, 1989, p. 1) now defines participation as including 'influence on development decisions...', but proactive community participation arises rarely, most often where organized pressure interrupts planning or implementation by demanding changes.

Interpreting and overcoming resistance to projects is another dimension of the Bank's control of lending operations. Projects such as Philippine slum clearance operations in Metro Manila, education policy changes in Bolivia, and numerous resettlement, energy development and other projects in environmentally sensitive areas (road construction in Brazil, resettlement in India and Indonesia) illustrate this tendency.

The conflictive origins of community organizations' roles in many projects illustrates the fact that 'participation' is not necessarily the cooperative grassroots action that aid agencies and project managers desire. Like other development agencies, the Bank assumes that 'participation' implies 'cooperation.' The record of NGO conflict with the World Bank shows that resistance is also a form of participation. As Scott (1985) and Scott and Kerkvliet (1986) show in studies of peasant resistance to other forms of social and economic change, often the 'weapons of the weak' – footdragging, non-cooperation, passive resistance – are the way poor people participate in planned development projects.

In the Malaysia Krian-Sungei Manik Integrated Development Project (1978), project managers resorted to talking with local organizations about the project's design after encountering resistance to initial project plans. The project called for draining local dikes as part of the estab-

Organizational Culture and Participation

lishment of new tertiary irrigation systems and introduction of new rice varieties. 'Farmers were reluctant to lower the water in the drains ... [which] were also used for fishing, etc. It took several years to get the farming community to agree to lowering drain water levels' (Project Completion Report, p. vii). This resistance – referred to as 'farmer resistance to change' and 'farmer non-acceptability of drainage' – eventually led to action to deal with these 'social problems' of implementation, including extension efforts to 'reach' 388 farmer groups. Farmers' cooperation was gained, and the project implemented, unchanged but delayed by four to five years. The Project Completion Report concludes that cooperation in such a project should be secured through 'close cooperation with local leaders and related agencies, especially the district office,' if implementation delays are to be avoided. Longer implementation periods should be allowed, and pilot and demonstration projects used to secure farmer acceptance of new practices (Project Completion Report, p. x).

Students of local organizations and the OED recognize that organizations imposed by project authorities are ineffective. Yet directed participation remains the norm for participation at the World Bank. The preference for directed community participation is shaped by factors in the organizational culture and by external political interests. Governments' fear of raising expectations is often cited as a reason for caution in involving local groups in early stages of the project cycle (OED, 1988; Paul, 1988; White, 1989; Strategic Planning and Review 1990, p. 6). Some staff acknowledge that Bank project managers' unwillingness to be accountable to affected people is an important reason as well (Policy staff no. 3; Ayres, 1983, p. 225); and the time required and the challenge implied to the all-sufficiency of planning expertise are also cited in interviews (Asia staff no. 3; Policy staff no. 3). Nagle's and Ghose's (1989, p. 3) interviews of staff and review of internal literature on participation led them to conclude that:

> there appears to be a reluctance on the part of Bank staff who have written on the subject to press the application of theory into Bank practice. It is as though such applications might be seen as implicitly critical of the way the Bank goes about its business. It would appear that even non-operational staff see something sacrosanct and immutable about both the procedures and time tables of the project cycle.

A Bank-wide Learning Process on Popular Participation

Until 1990, learning about popular participation in the World Bank was built primarily around the *ad hoc* experience of a few staff. In interviews NGOs and staff alike recognize that most project initiatives reflect individual commitments to participatory development strong enough to overcome organizational pressures and disincentives (Africa staff no. 1; Africa staff no. 2; de los Reyes, November 1989).

But a more deliberate 'learning process on participation' was launched in 1991, in part at the instigation of the NGO-World Bank Committee. The learning process was an effort by supporters of participatory practices to make them more central to the Bank's discourse and practice by interpreting and analyzing staff's experiences with managing participatory projects.

The learning process was a well-conceived and extensive effort to broaden support in the Bank through informal processes. It involved studies of 20 participatory Bank-financed projects; seminars and conferences with practitioners from within and outside the Bank; training and a 'best practices' sourcebook to promote participatory methods. The team directing the learning process recognized and opened for discussion several structural constraints to participation. They also saw the need to press their case vigorously in the Operations division. They recognized the limits in the Bank's institutional commitment and designed a process that relied on informal exchanges to advance their cause.

Believing that participatory development was best promoted in the Bank by demonstrating its economic value, the learning group set out to document this value. The result, in discussions with key managers, seems to be that management will be persuaded of the value of participatory methods on a sector-by-sector basis. The formation of water-users' groups in irrigation schemes, for example, seems to be widely accepted as a cost-effective implementation strategy. As other Bank-sponsored research is completed, operations management say they are prepared to acknowledge other sectors where giving affected people the right to shape Bank-sponsored projects is 'worth the effort' according to the Bank's and borrower's bottom line.

Stiefel and Wolfe, comparing the Bank's participation work to that of other international bodies, consider it 'ironical' that while other agencies efforts are often 'superficial, half-hearted and hypocritical,' the Bank 'seems to have embarked on a relatively systematic effort to come to grips with the interpretation of popular participation and to realize it in its field projects' (pp. 222–3). Their conclusion is a credit to the committed and vigorous efforts of the participation learning group within the Bank, and to the learning group's pragmatic approach to promoting participation within the agency. The Bank is helped, too, in such a comparison, by the high level of rhetoric from many of the UN bodies, and most observers' initial low expectations of the Bank in this field.

In appraising the learning process it is important to keep in view the substantial limitations and obstacles within the Bank. Nothing in the experience to date suggests that the process can overcome the obstacles its leaders recognize: staff's skewed skills mix; the disbursement imperative; government reticence and the sovereignty issue; and a dominant mindset that gives little consideration to socio-cultural issues. The informal promotion strategy is well-chosen given the limited possibilities for full-fledged institutional support. Like other initiatives on socio-cultural issues, the learning process has no funds from the Bank's budget, but is supported by voluntary payments from donors. Staff have no clear mandate from management; training, seminars, and other events and resources are used entirely at staff's discretion.

A change made in the learning group's final report by senior managers highlights a final barrier: the inability or unwillingness to side decisively with poor people. The Bank has historically steered clear of the partisanship that characterizes many NGOs. When poverty reduction is embraced as a priority, it is not in terms of relative poverty or income distribution but of absolute conditions and basic needs. So in the participation discussion, the Bank's management finally rejected a distinction between primary and secondary 'stakeholders' in Bank investments that sought to give precedence to participation by the poor. Over objections from NGO participants (see NGO Annex to World Bank 1994g (Annex VI, p. 5)) and some Bank staff, the learning group's report was tilted subtly away from the pro-poor mandate that some had sought to impart.

The learning group's report and policy recommendations, modified somewhat in a management review, have been accepted by the Bank's Board. Proponents within the Bank have sought NGO support for the most sweeping of the recommendations, a requirement that each loan agreement include a participation framework laying out opportunities for participation surrounding the project.

Implementing the learning group's approach to participation throughout the Bank will confront substantial obstacles. An internal memo notes that most Environmental Assessments – the activity for which staff are already instructed to ensure that local NGOs' and affected people's views are taken into account – have failed to incorporate 'any participation whatever' (James Adams memorandum to Managing Director Sven Sandstrom, 15 January 1993). But promoters in the Bank have devised steps to spread the practices. A small Participation Fund, for example, offers matching support within the Bank to regions or country offices that proposed specific new participatory activities in projects or in economic and sector research.

Assessing the World Bank Dialogue with NGOs

Just as project collaboration is structured to minimize disruption and protect the stability of the Bank's operations, so the dialogue with NGOs and other critics has generally been structured, and the input filtered, to minimize its impact on basic premises and assumptions. The management is most transparent in those fora that are sanctioned by the Bank, where the Bank has some control over agenda and participation. But it is also evident in the Bank's interpretation of NGO and popular issue campaigns.

Staff who manage the NGO consultations are often in a position to limit and define the criticism that will be accepted and heard. Bank staff on the NGO-World Bank Committee said privately in 1989, and many times since, that they had heard and learned enough from the NGOs on adjustment lending and the environment, and wished to move on to discuss participation and details of operational collaboration. More generally, it is now policy to be open to criticism from NGOs 'when it is constructive and valid' (Strategic Planning and Review, 1990, p. 11). Some 'single-issue environmental groups ... criticize the Bank in ways which often are not constructive' (EXTIE, 1990 Progress Report 20). Qualifying adjectives are a regular reminder that the Bank's participants will judge what subjects, information and criticism are appropriate.

Not only is the character of acceptable criticism defined in advance, the dialogue is often later interpreted to render it collegial and acceptable. After angry protests and confrontations in Berlin at the 1988 IMF/World Bank annual meetings, the Bank's *Annual Report* (1989, p. 95) blandly reports that 'unofficial conferences and NGO events are increasingly prominent during the annual meetings of the Bank and the IMF.... NGOs ... contribute to the Bank's thinking on important development issues in various ways.' The 1987 *Annual Report* (p. 62) similarly renders international conflict over environmental policy and adjustment in the most antiseptic terms: 'Consultations with NGOs ... have dealt extensively with the concerns of both environmental and poverty-oriented groups. Their views are increasingly taken into consideration in the formulation of appropriate development strategies.'

NGOs have none the less noted positive trends in the dialogue, particularly in substantive discussions of sectoral policies, and the improved access to decision-makers from the Bank's operational divisions. But even as the quality of the dialogue improves, NGOs face an organizational style that threatens to erode the influence they have gained. One concern is that as the dialogue has become more routine, with the routinization of exchanges, NGO input may be losing the sharp edge that captured the Bank's attention in the first place. Several Bank staff say that the dialogue with NGOs no longer needs to be adversarial, because the Bank is now sensitive to NGOs' concerns (Salmen and Eaves, 1989, pp. 43-4). Other staff also view NGOs as moving from an isolated, confrontative style toward negotiations and partnership with the Bank (Policy staff no. 3).

Similarly the Bank characterizes NGO advocacy on environmental issues and tribal people's rights as 'help[ing] to sensitize public opinion and development practitioners, including the Bank...' (World Bank, 1990d, p. 14). The successful NGO effort to 'direct the attention of the Bank and its member governments to the environmental and social costs of some large-scale projects' is described in the past tense, carrying the message that the complaints have been heard, taken into consideration, and that the issue is now in the Bank's hands.

A second danger lies in the gap between rhetoric and performance. Theory, policy and intellectual work on 'progressive' themes – women, environment, poverty, impact of adjustment on the poor, involuntary resettlement – are often substituted by World Bank representatives for changes in actual performance.

A 1989 policy paper (Strategic Planning and Review Department 1989) on participation dwells on the evolving history of World Bank *thinking* on the subject. Nagle and Ghose (1989, p. 5) note that Bank literature on participation 'has outdistanced both the policy development and the practice of encouraging participation in Bank projects.' NGO-World Bank Committee co-chair Alexander Shakow emphasized *new articulations* of development goals by President Conable in the 1989 Committee meetings, and discussed the changing, improved, responsive *interpretation* of questions. World Bank staff objected strenuously to the NGOs' Position Paper because it didn't reflect the Bank's *'changing interpretation* of these questions' (NGO-World Bank Committee Meeting, 1 November 1989; emphases added).

Likewise, the legal principle of 'no net losers' for involuntary resettlement in World Bank-funded schemes is touted to academic and NGO audiences as evidence of progressive social science at work in the World Bank (Cernea, 1989; Golan, NGO-World Bank Committee Meeting, 1989). Legal and social principles were carefully worked through in developing a policy for treatment and compensation of displaced populations (Escudero, 1988). But Rich (1990, pp. 313–14) draws on internal reviews and local sources in Zaire, Rwanda, Indonesia, Kenya and India to show that the policy is largely ignored in the field.

John Clark (1988, p. 2), then of OXFAM-UK, argues that special publications on poverty are outside the mainstream of the Bank's operations and research. Poverty is discussed in special documents 'while the central issues remain export promotion, debt service management, control of public spending, reducing parastatals, market liberalization, price de-control....' 'Which,' he asks, 'is the real World Bank? The World Bank which writes special small circulation reports on poverty alleviation? Or the Bank which views poverty as just one of oh-so-many issues to be remembered (on the last page) by those who are responsible for managing the economic affairs of our planet?'

CONCLUSION

The World Bank's organizational culture selects the information that reaches its decision-makers, creating a fictional world in which its analytic, technical and financial resources can be applied impartially and effectively. The information bias isolates the Bank from important input as it protects it from perspectives that challenge its assumptions and myths. Individuals within the Bank experiment and learn, critics speak and receive responses, but a variety of organizational defense mechanisms protect the basic assumptions that guide its operations.

These characteristics shape the Bank's interactions with NGOs. 'Participation' by NGOs and affected people is generally limited to mobilizing communities to carry out their parts of a project. 'Beneficiary groups' are formed to improve project implementation or cost-recovery: this recognizes the need for social organization, but limits its role to consent and mobilization.

Criticism and protest by NGOs and their allies can change World Bank-funded projects. A campaign of protest has also stimulated the creation of an environmental unit, the hiring of regional environmental staff, and a new set of Environmental Impact Assessment procedures that include consultation with local NGOs.

But the dynamics of learning – and of not learning – still present formidable obstacles to reformers within and outside the institution. An organizational culture and information selection mechanism tend to reinforce and perpetuate a lending mandate and organizational myths that define limited roles for NGOs.

8 Conclusions

The *National Journal* speculated in 1988 that the World Bank might 'never be the same' after entering into policy dialogues with US-based environmental and development NGOs (1988, p. 3250). Throughout the 1980s and early 1990s the Bank has, indeed, been the target of pressures from NGOs and others on areas as diverse as human rights, the environment, project performance, debt management and structural adjustment.

But in 1994, at the fiftieth anniversary of the Bank's creation, the variety of changes that are in process in the Bank stop short of any basic change in its operations. Initiatives within the Bank have created more room for innovation and variance by staff in areas such as popular participation and microfinance. And new commitments in environmental policy and a partial opening in information disclosure have marginally increased the ability of groups affected by the Bank's loans to demand a measure of accountability.

But neither its main lending programs nor the organizational factors that have lent stability in the past have been altered. The Bank's influence, through conditionality and its dominant role in donor coordination, has grown faster than the ability of member governments or citizens to demand accountability. This chapter sums up the evidence of change and resistance to change, touches on the significance for some broader theoretical discussions, reviews policy implications for the World Bank and for NGOs, and proposes a program of further monitoring and research.

PROJECTS: THE TERMS OF ENGAGEMENT

NGOs are involved in an increasing number of World Bank-financed projects, and engaged in discussions with the Bank in a larger number of fora than was the case a decade ago. The growing number of project contacts began with the initiative of individual staff members interested in NGOs and the work of the staff unit that promotes NGO collaboration. It has benefited from encouragement by some managers, and increasing interest by some international NGOs in securing contracts from the Bank. While some staff members consider the Bank's

'NGO work' a passing fad, there is no doubt that the number of 'NGO projects' has grown substantially.

But as to the nature of the project interaction – the 'terms of engagement' (Hellinger, 1987) – the record is not as favorable. For most projects, NGO influence is limited to implementing a component of a project designed and negotiated by World Bank staff and government officials. This arrangement, which dominates project collaboration, reflects appreciation by some staff for NGOs' efficiency as service deliverers, but little desire to cultivate NGOs as organizers and agents of accountability.

The implementing role has sometimes grown into more dynamic and potentially influential NGO participation. Implementing NGOs can monitor project impact and help communicate wishes of affected people to government, Bank staff and a wider audience. But this initiative is absent from most NGO-implemented projects, reflecting the caution and narrow mission of many NGOs as well as the reluctance of most Bank staff to enter into such dialogue.

The reported growth in NGO contributions to designing Bank-financed projects since 1988 diminishes under a close review even only of project documents. Much of the reported role in design involved not input to an entire project or even a component of the investment, but NGO design of their own projects, to be submitted for support to a fund financed under the project.

Second, a substantial amount of NGO 'design' work is for projects to provide temporary relief from the adverse effects of Bank-sponsored adjustment plans. NGOs participate not in shaping the adjustment conditions, perhaps by facilitating consultations with organized groups of poor people, but in contributing to plans for social safety net programs. Participation in the design of government programs to be financed by World Bank investments remains an exception to the norm, in which NGOs implement projects and mobilize people's 'participation' in them.

Cooperating groups of international, national and grassroots organizations appear to have been most able and disposed to engage Bank staff and government officials in discussions of sectoral policies, project design and implementation. Whether collaborative or conflictive in tone, these cases, prominent especially in environmental and urban housing and services projects, illustrate the potential for NGO influence and the concerted effort required by NGOs to play this role.

But the much larger number of projects, in which NGOs deliver Bank-financed services for the state, raises the likelihood that the engagement is changing NGOs more than it is the Bank. In the process,

NGOs, the Bank and other donors are allowing the NGOs' potential significance for effective democratization to be compromised.

PROJECTS AND POLICY: ASSESSING THE IMPACT OF THE ENGAGEMENT

The World Bank is a large and complex organization, and assessing the extent and nature of change in policy and practice can be difficult. No approach can remove the ambiguity entirely, but four factors derived from organizational theory are useful indicators of the nature of change in the Bank. Significant changes in policy and practice would likely mean changes in:

1. aspects of the standard operating procedures, including the project cycle, staffing, training and incentives;
2. the organizational myths of sovereignty and apolitical development, and of development impact as measured by economic rate of return;
3. the organizational culture, especially sources of information and its processing within the organization; and
4. patterns of resistance and support from key actors in the environment.

Reviewed against these indicators, the World Bank's record with NGOs points toward the importance and resilience of the structure, procedures and organizational culture of the Bank, the dominance of narrow national, financial, corporate and professional interests, and toward the tendency of these factors to resist change.

Training and experience dispose most Bank staff to see economic, political and social issues through the eyes of elite planners and economists. These inclinations are strongly reinforced by organizational practices and career incentives that discourage spending extra time building relationships with NGOs. The creation of a special unit to handle relations with NGOs offers a convenient and frequently used contact point, but it also puts the liaison in the hands of staff skilled in representing the Bank to outsiders, and in rendering outside input compatible with prevailing thinking and practice.

There are initiatives within the Bank that could be seeds of change: post-Wapenhans concerns with borrower 'ownership' of programs; new, consultative approaches in the Southern Africa department; a group promoting participatory methodologies; and even a proposal that questions the basic framework of the Bank's project cycle.

But these initiatives face a formidable and durable set of organizational interests and mandates. A strong organizational culture sifts and selects information with remarkable consistency. Discourse and innovation are shaped, especially in written work produced in the Bank, in ways that are consonant with the Bank's own understanding of its mission. New mandates are appended to an approach to development finance that rests on the tenets of neo-orthodox economic theory, the myths of apolitical development and of borrower sovereignty, and that squares with the interests of major industrialized countries and international banks.

Has the liaison with NGOs effected any change in these elements of the core technology, myths and organizational culture? Most evidence of NGO impact is not on these systemic factors, but on individual projects. Some urban sector projects have been affected by project experiences involving NGOs; irrigation projects now tend to involve local grassroots groups in cost recovery and maintenance of irrigation systems; the Aga Khan Foundation has had fruitful exchanges in some South Asia operations; and environmental advocates have modified several individual projects, created an environmental impact assessment procedure and initiated a Bank role in national environmental policy planning. These are important accomplishments.

But the evidence of more systematic change is slim. In policy areas where NGOs have been involved – environment, popular participation and adjustment – external pressure is reinterpreted, managed, and responded to in ways that protect or reinforce established assumptions and operations.

Environmental Policy

The most promising products of NGO advocacy are the system of Environmental Impact Assessments (EIA) for projects judged likely to have an adverse environmental impact; mandated National Environmental Action Plans; and an expanded environmental staff in Bank headquarters.

But the promise of these changes is as yet far from fulfilled. EIA procedures, for example, encourage regular participation of concerned NGOs. How the EIAs will work, and how the Bank will manage the conflict between its environmental mandates, growth-based model and the prevailing drive to disburse capital is a matter for close monitoring. The early record, reviewed in an internal 1993 memo, shows participation to be nonexistent in African EIAs, and not much stronger in the other regions. The requirement for EIA, further, extends only to certain projects and not at all to policy-based lending. Excluding projects unlikely to have direct environmental impact is sensible, but setting aside SAPs is tantamount to scrutinizing individual schemes while allowing whole economic plans (including export agriculture, mining, energy development, timber production) to grow without formal regard for resource use or environmental impact.

In sectoral policy areas – water, energy, agriculture – the Bank has sought to involve NGOs in discussions of draft policy papers. While noting certain limitations in the process and content of these consultations, NGO participants recognize the value of the discussions and the candor of participants. But Bank policy with respect to project-related forced resettlement is an example of a regularly observed pattern in social and environmental fields: policy is carefully crafted but not enforced. When governments balk at meeting resettlement standards in full, the Bank has been extremely reluctant or unable to win compliance. Driven by the need to move money and faced with declining influence with some major borrowers, the Bank invokes borrower sovereignty and stops short of using its leverage to protect those ousted by the project.

At its best, World Bank policy should have the exemplary effect claimed by its recent review, changing expectations for all government policy and performance in resettlement associated with major infrastructure works. But given governments' reluctance to bear the financial and political costs of accommodating minority needs, the Bank needs to play a more active role. If the Bank were serious about leading a global change in standards for infrastructure development, it would (1) promote its perspective through training and supervision as vigorously as it has in macro-economic policy; and (2) take seriously the NGO proposals that it shift its priority from monumental infrastructure projects to less centralized, more efficient energy-generation schemes.

The Bank's role in the Global Environment Fund embodies another organizational trait, the capacity to convert pressure for reform into support for new resources by thrusting itself into a leading role in the GEF. NGOs suddenly found the Bank – the target of their critique – in charge of global resources for global environmental protection. As it had three decades before, in the creation of IDA, the Bank managed to neutralize a troublesome new demand (for a concessional lending facility in the IDA case) by absorbing it into its own operations.

The Bank has taken more steps in environmental policy and practice than in any other area in response to NGO concerns and pressure.

But those working for policy change within the Bank are limited by its export- and growth-oriented development model. And it is unprepared to propose and support another paradigm for development, lacking the will and the mandate to devise a new development path and to commit the resources needed to compensate borrowers for the sacrifices the industrial countries want them to make.

This final point was re-emphasized in a highly critical statement by Herman Daly, the Bank's leading environmental economist until he resigned after six years in the Bank's environment department. Daly attacks the assumption of the Bank's basic model that countries' interests are served by inserting them into international production patterns. Without international bodies capable of regulating increasingly internationalized capital, he argues, the Bank's borrowers would be better served by policies that reduce or slow capital's internationalization (Daly, 1994). He charges that the Bank's inability to influence policy in the North renders it 'nearly useless' for dealing with the pressing global issues of consumption, resource use and trade.

Popular Participation

The involvement of NGOs in Bank-funded projects and its learning process on participation reflect the interest of a growing number of individual staff in the possibilities for more participatory operations. Project staff involved with NGOs still characterize their work as mainly individual initiative, requiring the will to bend project design procedures and ignore existing career incentives. Even staff most involved in project collaboration value NGOs mainly as efficient service deliverers, not for any more dynamic, formative role in collaboration.

Discussion and policy papers on participation in World Bank-financed projects deal mostly with techniques for mobilizing and informing local populations, to gain their acceptance and participation in an already planned project activity. The use of water users' associations and other farmer groups to manage local irrigation networks has generally meant that project managers or a government authority encourages the formation of these groups. This process of directed participation through newly-created organizations has little prospect of producing lasting social organization or vehicles for accountability and representation.

The participation learning process has included discussions that correctly diagnose some of these limitations, but lacked the authority to change them. The opening created by the learning process and by pressure on the Bank's 'non-performing' portfolio gives some reason for hope.

Probably the most positive general conclusion to be drawn to date is that the increased interest in NGOs among Bank officials and in the agency's policy statements may help to counterbalance the disincentives that otherwise discourage interested staff from making contact and building working relationships with NGOs.

But the Bank's new focus on 'portfolio management' and on improving financial performance also threatens to make popular participation only an adjunct to the management goal of deepening borrowers' 'ownership' of investments. Participation at the Bank, as at most donor agencies, has more to do with enlisting project stakeholders' support than with building on their input.

Adjustment

Dialogue on participation has been promoted vigorously by some in the Bank but constrained by a variety of limiting factors. On adjustment issues, NGOs have made fewer inroads. The Bank has successfully reduced the varied NGO positions on adjustment to their common element – that adjustment policies are in some way harming poor people – and responded by financing compensatory measures to soften the short-term impact of adjustment. This has in turn focused most Bank-NGO discussions on the adequacy of compensatory measures and safety nets in improving the 'social dimensions' of adjustment.

The Bank's NGO and poverty specialists express interest in 'pro-poor' adjustment and in using conditionality to improve the operating environment for NGOs. But these interests have yet to produce any significant variation from the Bank's program of liberalization and deregulation. And while the Bank's NGO specialists affirm the need to liberalize the operating environment for the NGO sector as much as for private for-profit actors, an effective initiative has yet to materialize. The Bank's modifications of its adjustment package have been measures to improve the implementation record or to cushion short-term impact, not to broaden the options or change the reform agenda. Nor have any but a few NGOs insisted on more fundamental changes, stranding the handful that do call for a new approach without broad support.

The Bank's most recent self-assessment on adjustment makes it clear that its course is set, and that where investment response or other hoped-for results have been slow in coming, what is needed is greater rigor and effort in attracting and reassuring potential external investors. While the Bank remains willing to discuss NGOs' views, it is clear by now that continued dialogue about adjustment plans will not sway the Bank. The mixed record in environmental policy and popular participation and the inflexibility of adjustment policy have frustrated many NGO activists. But the limited impact is not only a function of the Bank's organizational defenses, development myth and ideology. It also reflects the absence of a widespread, concerted effort by NGOs to adopt the representative, innovating and demonstration roles needed to expand their influence.

NGOs AND THE WORLD BANK

Although this study has focused on the World Bank, relations between the Bank and NGOs have important implications for NGOs as well. New patterns of cooperation among Northern and Southern NGOs, and the roles of Southern NGOs in their own societies are being shaped in the interaction with the Bank. For Northern-based NGOs, the effectiveness of networks that include international, national and community-based organizations in gaining influence in Bank-financed projects confirms the potential for Northern NGOs to operate as partners, supporters and advocates for NGOs based in the South. As NGOs based in the industrialized countries face the options and challenges for their identity and their roles, the record of the partnership and advocacy role in these interactions with the World Bank provides some evidence of the expanded impact NGOs can have.

Similarly, international NGOs that have devoted staff and given priority to influencing the Bank through collaboration and example have seen some effect. But such influence requires more than chance collaboration, and few NGOs have committed themselves to a deliberate advocacy and demonstration role. NGO protest and strategies of critical collaboration produce evidence of change only over time. NGOs, like other organizations, prefer to focus on issues and elements of their work environment they can control. For international NGOs, further impact on the World Bank will require commitments of energy and resources to objectives less tangible and immediate than relief or community development projects.

Southern NGOs face different but related choices. Decisions about how to relate to government or intergovernmental bodies such as the Bank affect NGOs' political posture in the immediate term, and the cumulative effect of many such decisions will help define the role of NGOs in civil society. Delivering goods or services for government and Bank-designed programs sets up a tension between constituencies – donors and community-level partners – that is a constant challenge. Many NGOs are seizing the resource of official funding without a strategy and commitment to managing this tension without abandoning their fundamental identification with poor communities.

The tension for NGOs confronts the Bank and other donors in two ways as well. First, if they wish to nurture active NGO movements that support accountability in public and civic institutions, they need to be deliberate in facilitating this connection and accountability to communities and people's organizations. This may mean active facilitation as Alan Fowler argues, encouraging in the process discussions and organizing that is critical of government and Bank policy and practice. The Bank's engagement with NGOs has shown a contrary tendency, encouraging a focus on operational cooperation even in those NGOs most interested in policy debate.

Second, while the Bank emphasizes that its operational engagement is increasingly with local and nationally based NGOs in the borrowing countries, it is probably true that working with such NGOs through appropriate intermediaries is less likely to compromise their relations to their constituencies. The project record to date suggests that NGO networks, rather than community-based organizations alone, are likely to be associated with active, critical NGO involvement in a Bank-financed project.

An Anti-NGO Backlash?

No one should assume that the Bank's enthusiasm for NGOs and its willingness to debate and accommodate them will continue indefinitely. NGOs and other critics hope that each new concession will increase their leverage or the momentum for change at the Bank. But there is limited tolerance in key circles for NGO criticism and the highly political and public nature of their critique.

Resentment of the Bank's concessions to NGOs has simmered among some in management and the board. As criticism reaches the media more effectively, signs of a potential backlash are appearing. The Bank's senior management overturned months of work on a new strategy paper for cooperation with NGOs in August 1994, opting for a less sweeping, 'business as usual' approach.

Public criticism of the Bank in its 1993 forum on Overcoming World Hunger also irked some in the Bank who felt the Bank's spokespeople did too little to defend its record. NGO criticism and demonstrations

Conclusions

at the Bank's fiftieth anniversary annual meetings in Madrid heightened the irritation within the Bank. As the criticism broadens and NGOs outside the environmental movement adopt strategies that have won influence for environmentalists, resistance in the Bank will likely grow. The evidence of backsliding on NGO-related issues includes the rejection in August 1994 of staff's NGO strategy paper; the demise of the small, two-year old fund for innovative social and humanitarian initiatives; discussions among senior management of the option of a decisive retreat from rhetorical commitments on poverty and participation, which some feel have given external critics too much leverage over the institution. As James Wolfensohn assumes the presidency of the Bank (in June 1995), his early signals on these issues will help to determine the opportunities for change in the near future.

Will the resistance produce a sharp scaling-back of engagement with development NGOs? While this is possible, what appears more likely is a greater emphasis on the Bank's division between cooperative and 'constructive' NGOs and those whose critique of its policies is more fundamental. Links between such networks, especially environmental networks and most major operational international NGOs, are already tenuous. If the Bank succeeds in strengthening its links to operational groups by providing even very small facilities for grant funding, it will have little difficulty broadening the split. The implications for a strong international voluntary sector would be substantial, and NGOs need to resist such a split. Engagement with external donors provides a legitimacy and protection that strengthens the position of NGOs in many countries. If NGOs allow the donors, led by the Bank, to divide them, it will likely accelerate the trend toward service-delivery NGOs in the South, and weaken the message of the non-governmental movement in the North.

SOME IMPLICATIONS: CIVIL SOCIETY AND NGOs; SUSTAINABLE DEVELOPMENT AND WORLD ORDERS; FUTURE MULTILATERALISM

The Bank's global scale and its economic policy-making role have won it a major role in discussions of future global economic orders. Its engagement with NGOs is also a consideration in current debates over NGOs, civil society and democratization.

Global Civil Society

As production becomes increasingly internationalized and international actors such as the Bank assume larger roles in states' policy-making and administration, a global level of civil society may become increasingly significant. Questions about how such networks function, set agendas and govern themselves are being worked out in *ad hoc* ways, often in the midst of struggles with the Bank and other donors over particular projects and policies. Links among interest groups, social movements, international NGOs and their constituencies in the industrialized countries may become a vehicle for deeper ties of solidarity and mutual interest.

At the national level, the Bank plays a variety of roles in shaping NGO-government relations in the diverse political environments of its borrowing countries. Governments' accountability to international creditors including the Bank, especially on debt and adjustment issues, has often limited state accountability to active groups in civil society. States can, and often do use the international financial institutions as scapegoats, redirecting public resentment toward the Bank and IMF. In areas of social and environmental policy, however, NGOs have often found the Bank and other donors to be a useful ally or lever. Where the Bank is more susceptible to critique (on resettlement, indigenous people's rights, global environmental issues) than is an individual government, NGOs have brought international norms to bear through the Bank's leverage.

The Bank has accepted and played both of these roles. But its institutional focus on project and policy lending means that its appreciation of NGOs will continue to emphasize the instrumental – service delivery – rather than their implicit importance in society. This focus has the salutary effect that the Bank has seldom sought to mobilize NGO opinion to support its policy initiatives with governments. Recent appeals for NGO attention to public expenditure reform may signal a change in this posture. But as the Bank's engagement with national NGOs remains operationally focused, it falls to other actors – international NGO movements and interested donors – to support NGOs in strengthening and maintaining their links and accountability to excluded groups in society. With major projects and social fund money available to NGOs, international NGOs and other donors have an important role to play in encouraging and supporting NGOs' links to popular and community organizations, and links among Southern NGOs and networks.

This building and shaping of international networks may be the most significant outcome of the Bank's relations with NGOs. Observers and participants in the international environmental movement have emphasized the emergence of networks around shared interests or commitments. Equally broad networks exist among development NGOs who relate to the Bank and other donors, principally as sources of program funds. Internationally, these two networks have found relatively little common ground on economic and development policy issues. Their diverse relations to donor funding tend to keep them divided.

NGOs, the Bank and Alternate Economic Futures

After more than a decade of dominance by orthodox adjustment packages and debt management arrangements, some theorists and activists continue to hope for greater openness to alternative strategies and more varied forms of engagement with the global economy. What are their prospects?

There is little in the World Bank's current posture to inspire hope. Despite institutional second thoughts about the East Asia miracle, and discomfort about the record of adjustment in Africa, no paradigm shift appears near. If space is to be made for any alternative economic future – based on regional cooperation or on a renewed emphasis on self-reliance (as suggested by Shaw, 1994) – it will require some loosening of the Bretton Woods institutions' still strong hold on standards and arrangements in development finance. The NGO challenge to the Bank and the IMF could play a role by slowly eroding their credibility and authority on adjustment, debt and the environment. It is even possible that concerted NGO efforts to produce and support alternative economic adjustment packages might compel the Bank to support economic programs that vary somewhat from the present orthodoxy. But it would likely require a significant revolt among the Bank's major shareholders, more decisive than the Japanese dissent to date, to expand the options significantly.

Future Economic Multilateralism

The Bretton Woods organizations' hold on the development finance regime is essentially unchallenged. Although debtor countries continue to have net negative capital flows to the IBRD and the IMF, the G-7 and the institutions themselves have been content with a patchwork of minor debt and finance arrangements. As yet, no significant institutional alternatives have emerged from the fiftieth anniversary discussions.

And despite proposals for a process to consider such alternatives (Helleiner, 1994), no international movement toward a serious debate is in sight.

The Bank, despite its praise for the virtues of market competition, maintains a virtual monopoly as the only player in the marketplace of development strategy with significant finance to back and support its program. Either major bilateral funding in support of divergent strategies, or an institutional change in the Bank's control of both project and policy design, and finance, might provide the Bank and its clients the benefits of a competing service provider. A separate facility to assist governments in preparation of projects independent of Bank staff – without financing capacity – would force the Bank to consider genuinely independent proposals for financing (Turid Sato, personal communication 1994). Neither appears likely.

Still, global political changes in the late 1980s and early 1990s remind us how quickly long-standing features of the global political economy can change. Even if the prospects for major change appear slim, it is incumbent on NGOs to craft policy agendas that encourage reform efforts within the Bank, strengthen Southern networks' ability to influence Bank and government policies, and intensify the pressure on the institution and its major shareholders to justify arrangements that serve the majority in the borrowing countries so poorly. The final section of this study outlines some elements of such an agenda.

STRATEGIC ADVOCACY: AN NGO POLICY AGENDA FOR THE 1990s

NGOs have tended to gain victories on targeted issues within the Bank, modifying or blocking individual projects, influencing a sectoral policy paper or Operational Directive, or provoking a new round of declarations on poverty alleviation as a policy priority. But even as they chalk up victories on these issues, the larger policy direction of the Bank – managing debt repayment and adjustment and controlling funds for global environmental problems, for example – remains beyond their influence. NGOs need a more strategic approach to the Bank, and an agenda that reflects both policy priorities and organizational realities.

The breadth and difficulty of issues, the power of the interests involved, and the organizational complexity of the Bank itself require strategies that identify key issues, recognize organizational roadblocks to change, and identify tangible and verifiable changes to be sought in

World Bank practice. The following is a contribution to such agenda-making. Some of the proposals are already part of the advocacy agendas of some NGOs, notably the '50 Years Is Enough' campaign. Others are more modest proposals of the kind that could surface if more radical initiatives force the Bank toward major reforms. The agenda is by no means exhaustive.

Three Policy Issues for the 1990s

1. *Debt and structural adjustment.* The issues most central to the Bank's global role have been most difficult for NGOs to address. NGOs have helped persuade major creditor countries to adopt more flexible terms in negotiations with debtors in the Paris Club, but more decisive action to relieve the debt burden is needed in this setting and in the World Bank. The IDA Fund for relief of commercial debt of IDA borrowers should be employed quickly to expand its use. But with much of the debt once owed to commercial creditors now converted to debt owed to MDBs, the burden of this debt itself must be addressed, at least for the lowest income, severely indebted countries.

NGOs should articulate a debt relief strategy where relief is based on need and ability to pay, rather than arbitrary percentages and other considerations. The Bank and others have acknowledged that, for the poorest countries, even the most generous debt relief terms under discussion by the G-7 do not lift the debt burden sufficiently to really improve development prospects (World Bank, *World Debt Tables 1992–93* vol. 1, pp. 8–9). The MDBs and creditor governments should be pressed to adopt a new principle: reduce debts sufficiently to shrink service payments to a level of export earnings (perhaps 20 per cent) that permits a country to invest again in its own development. Assent to this principle from the Bank – even if not accompanied immediately by steps to apply it to debt owed to the Bank itself – could help stimulate agreement among the G-7 countries.

Debt relief is a strategic linchpin in the constellation of issues on which NGOs seek to influence the Bank. The debt burden underlies many governments' weak position in negotiating adjustment agreements with the Bank. The debt and finance crisis also makes concessional IDA funds so vital to the lowest-income borrowers that governments and NGOs are constrained from threatening IDA funding, even when this is their most effective source of leverage.

NGO advocacy on adjustment, beyond calling for safety net programs, has been almost entirely ineffective. Southern NGOs and interest groups in borrowing countries have managed to weaken governments' resolves or limit the implementation of adjustment agreements. Northern NGOs seem to have made little headway with the Bank or their governments by documenting the ills of adjustment. Discussions of global adjustment are too general to reach and motivate citizen support in the North. Without mass political support, further NGO input at this global level will not sway the Bank's economists from their models and plans. It is time for alternative strategies.

First, Northern NGOs and NGO networks should focus their critique of adjustment on countries where there is significant resistance and alternatives to orthodox adjustment plans. Major campaigns focused on, for example, Mexico, India, the Philippines, Zimbabwe and Bangladesh could give new energy to the critique of adjustment. It would increase credibility and specificity, strengthen the local basis for global NGO action, and facilitate local political action in support of alternatives. In other cases, NGOs should acknowledge that many governments have accepted liberalization strategies. Where this is the case, the Bank should be urged to focus not on imposing further conditions but on financing the institutions and measures needed to implement the strategy effectively. NGOs could essentially call for 'no new conditionality,' making the reasonable claim that governments not persuaded by the first 15 years of technical advice, policy dialogue and financial pressure are not going to buy the Bank's solution, and that those who have adopted it deserve assistance in implementing it, not further arm-twisting.

A third option, perhaps compatible in some cases with either of the others, is to acknowledge the need for macro-economic adjustment – balanced current accounts and good economic management – and help stimulate development and discussion of concrete, locally-based plans in the national political context.

It is time to recognize that the NGO critique of the World Bank role in adjustment will not carry this issue with donor governments or the Bank. Where strong resistance to anti-egalitarian strategies exists, NGOs should support it. Where it does not, or where a dialogue is called for with donors and the Bank, a strategy that focuses on debt relief and limits on further conditionality is worth trying.

2. *Popular participation.* Both in World Bank-funded activities and as a goal of its policy dialogue with borrowers, participation of broad segments of the population should be a major theme in World Bank practice, and a top strategic priority for NGOs.

Broad, early popular participation in economic and sectoral planning and in project identification, design and implementation could boost the quality and impact of a range of Bank-financed and related activities. The Bank has committed itself to encouraging participation in Poverty Targeted Investments, National Environmental Action Plans, Poverty Assessments, and other planning and policy making processes. The successful promotion of participatory methodologies in the Bank would influence the process and product in each of these, as well as in many Bank-financed projects.

No other single measure would penetrate the Bank's standard operations and its information system as thoroughly as the expanded use of participatory methods. NGOs should capitalize on Bank management's commitments in principle to participation, and work with supporters in the Bank to document its value to Bank investments and to protect it as much as possible from dilution in practice. A concerted effort to promote popular input in Bank-financed activities, coupled with expanded access to Bank documents under a new information policy, is the best tool the NGOs have to change the fundamental operations of the Bank.

Expanded public participation in decisions on matters of policy has implications far beyond the World Bank. The Bank's stated support for NGOs has probably already expanded the space for nongovernmental bodies' participation in national policy deliberations and implementation in some borrowing countries. An earnest effort from the Bank to enlarge that effect, including persistent pressure in policy dialogue with governments, could help level the political and economic playing fields and boost the vitality and effectiveness of public deliberation and action.

But the Bank remains cautious, with senior officials saying that pressure on human rights, administrative and legal issues related to the operating environment for NGOs will not extend beyond the conditions relevant to implementing specific Bank investments (meetings with Canadian human rights advocates, June 1993).

Globally and at Bank headquarters, advocacy on popular participation is complex. There are many fronts on which progress can be made or stymied, and subtle gradations of popular involvement in an agency's decisions and action. NGOs should press for increased participation on as many fronts as possible – NEAPs, poverty assessments, and project loans included – as well for stronger management support for popular participation in overall programming. Policy pressure at headquarters and through the Board needs to be matched by initiatives in the borrowing countries to comment on project plans, discuss sectoral or regional strategies, protest at objectionable projects and jointly evaluate NGO experiences.

Most of the evidence of participation in Bank activities will be widely dispersed and difficult to aggregate. But NGOs can watch for and encourage certain changes at headquarters that would be indicators of organizational progress in promoting participation. More flexible limits and allocation of staff time to project development and implementation would open up room for participatory methods and reduce the incentives to push money. Shifting significant numbers of staff from headquarters to permanent missions would expand the opportunity for contact with local realities. Expanded, accelerated and mandatory training in social science skills related to participatory development would provide important support. And a more flexible approach to the project cycle, downgrading the importance of the definitive pre-appraisal and regularizing the process of feedback and revision during implementation would open opportunities for planning that reflects the dynamics of social change and responds to emerging problems and opportunities.

3. *Reconsidering IDA as institution.* The debate over IDA-10 ended with many NGOs concluding that, in the absence of an alternative channel for funds, they must give IDA at least conditioned support. The fact that neither donors nor borrowers have another viable channel for concessional funding on IDA's scale allows the Bank its pattern of sluggish action or noncompliance in response to official and unofficial demands for change.

This is why the proposal, promoted by the '50 Years is Enough' campaign, to separate the concessional lending function from the World Bank, should be seriously studied. There is no reason why concessional lending funds such as IDA's need to be administered by a bank. Since public tax monies, not financial market proceeds, are being lent, conventional banking standards are not essential. And since IDA concessional loans should fit into the poorest countries' development strategies, it would make more sense for an institution governed by development ministers and directors of national aid agencies, rather than finance ministers, to oversee its operation. In the short term, international consideration of a proposal to remove the multilateral concessional lending function from the Bank would at least give the Bank a strong incentive to take poverty-related demands more seriously. If it failed to do so, the international community could choose to create an institution that might win more widespread and enthusiastic support.

NGO Institutions and Modes of Action

To increase impact and marshall the kind of influence needed to advance their agendas in the coming decade, NGOs need institutions for action that emphasize three priorities: a more integrated agenda and campaign; closer communication among the principal activist networks; and expanded South-South networking and monitoring, and consultations with the World Bank in the borrowing countries.

1. *Integrating NGO agendas*, especially environmental and development agendas, is a priority. NGOs made some progress in the 1980s toward this integration. But the NGO agenda, especially in the North, remains bifurcated, and the differences in priorities, resources and networks are readily exploited by the Bank. Many environmental organizations have taken their agenda well beyond conservation issues, tying the human effects of resource degradation closely to more traditional concerns for wildlife and habitat preservation. Sectoral concerns, however, often dominate environmental agendas, and the Bank has been able to stave off many of its environmental critics with minor concessions on energy, forestry, and water policies.

Still, environmental NGOs, with greater financial resources, a history of advocacy and legal work in the industrialized countries, and a broader constituency among middle class North Americans and Europeans, have had far greater effect on the Bank than poverty-focused NGOs. To take the next step and begin to influence the core policies and practices of the Bank, including adjustment and debt management, an integrated agenda and campaign will be required.

A joint and integrated effort would also require much greater commitment of resources by Northern development NGOs. With fewer staff and resources committed to World Bank work, development NGOs generally cannot match the pace and intensity of environmental NGO advocacy. Nor have most given much attention or support to policy changes promoted by the environmental community on energy and forestry, among other sectors, that have enormous human impact. To implement an agenda that embraces debt, sustainable development, participation and adjustment along with key resource use issues would require a greater commitment to advocacy by the Northern development NGOs, and closer integration of advocacy and program activities.

2. *Greater coordination among NGO advocacy networks* could help to stimulate this broader commitment, and increase the impact of existing

efforts. The most important step would be increased planning and coordination among the major nodes of NGO strategizing and information: the cluster of Washington-based environmental NGOs; the Asian NGO coalition ANGOC; the NGO Working Group on the World Bank; the European coalition EURODAD, NGOs such as OXFAM-UK, Community Aid Abroad (Australia), the Third World Network (Malaysia); the new Bank network based in Montevideo, Uruguay; and the US-based development NGOs through InterAction.

Some have called for a global NGO secretariat to coordinate work on the World Bank, or on structural adjustment (Woodward, 1992). The time may come when NGOs conclude that such a body is necessary, but experience suggests that they should concentrate first on thickening, expanding and connecting present networks of communication and action, and on energizing and democratizing present coordinating institutions. The establishment of advocacy offices in Washington by NGO networks based outside the US – now including the Federation of African Voluntary Development Agencies (FAVDO) and the international Oxfam network – should help in this process.

The NGO Working Group on the World Bank could vastly expand its contribution if its NGO participants actively coordinated and facilitated NGO advocacy and monitoring of the Bank in their home countries and regions. This and other imperatives suggest that the Working Group's organization be re-thought. Rather than a NGO forum for sanctioned discussions with the Bank, the Working Group should re-establish itself as a gathering point for NGOs active on key policy issues. Rather than a self-selecting body with a membership list, the Working Group should become a coordinating forum for all organizations seeking cooperative NGO involvement on structural adjustment, debt and popular participation issues.

3. *Expanded South-South regional consultation, coordination and monitoring* would confront the Bank with more frequent and widespread articulation of NGO concerns. The current expansion of monitoring and accountability efforts, especially those with substantial Southern initiative, are an encouraging trend that calls for international cooperation and support. Major Southern networks including the Asian NGO Coalition for Agrarian Reform and Rural Development (ANGOC), PRIA in India, the Center for the Study of Agrarian Change (CECCAM) in Mexico and a Latin American/Caribbean network serviced by Instituto del Tercer Mundo in Uruguay, have attracted international support. As other international groups (Bread for the World Institute and the NGO

Working Group on the World Bank among them) adopt monitoring as a priority, they should work to support and expand existing Southern initiatives.

No amount of effort will produce universal agreement among NGOs, even those already active in advocacy with the Bank, to a full policy agenda. But if a united front could be formed behind some concrete objectives on environmental policy, debt reduction, adjustment, poverty lending and popular participation, a powerful bloc of NGO opinion would be created, a basis for additional work on specialized issues, campaigns, and collaborative efforts.

Unanswered Questions: the Need for Monitoring

It is standard in academic studies to end with a list of questions for further research. But this call for monitoring and further study is integral to the call for action by NGOs and scholars to hold the Bank accountable. Monitoring the nature of World Bank investments, the character of its interaction with NGOs, changes in its internal operations as well as in its policy dialogue with borrowing governments, is vital to effective advocacy. It has been the weakest link in most NGO relations with the Bank.

The World Bank's liaison with NGOs has the potential to open important international financial policies to popular input. But the obstacles are formidable and the effort required by NGOs would be great. Several critical policy questions for the Bank and for NGOs require careful consideration and monitoring. Five such areas are highlighted here as priorities for further monitoring.

1. *Monitoring the actual outcome of proposed project involvement.* Virtually all of the World Bank's claims about NGO involvement in investments are based on projects as documented at the time of appraisal and Board approval. No review of actual implementation of these projects has been undertaken either at the Bank or outside, and a careful survey of a sample would be instructive in two ways. First, it would clarify and evaluate the Bank's actual performance in a field from which it now gains considerable public relations benefits. Even the very limited survey carried out for this study revealed important issues and questions about the actual nature and extent of collaboration.

Second, documenting the varied patterns of collaboration and their results could serve Bank staff who are open to broader contact with the populations affected by Bank policies and projects. Documenting not only 'best practice' but also pitfalls and issues in contacting and building relations with NGOs could help promote further contact and raise the qualitative issues that have plagued some project collaboration.

2. *Assessing the value and effects of NGO participation in compensatory social service programs under structural adjustment.* There is little evidence now collected as to how NGOs became involved in providing social services to soften the impact of adjustment programs on the poor. The immediate needs of people affected by unemployment, food price increases and reduced social services present compelling reasons for NGO interventions.

NGOs that may oppose new adjustment policies are forced to balance the immediate needs against the need to press for alternative policies. Choosing to participate in compensatory programs may give an NGO greater standing with government and the World Bank. But it may also weaken the NGO's ability to articulate popular needs and serve as an agent of accountability. A review of the World Bank-State-NGO interactions in some of the new cases of adjustment-related NGO programs would afford insight into the costs and advantages of such cooperation with compensatory programs.

3. *Observing the effects of new environmental review procedures on the design of Bank-financed projects.* Do the environmental impact assessments carry enough authority within the Bank to block or significantly slow investment plans when environmental danger signs arise? What role will NGOs assume in the dialogue in this assessment process? Environmental NGOs will need to assess the new EIAs in order to decide on the next steps in their relationship with the Bank.

4. *Monitoring the Bank's work with governments to improve the operating environment for NGOs.* Some staff and observers of the NGO dialogue regard this potential role as the most important aspect of the World Bank's relationship with NGOs. The Bank routinely employs persuasion and financial leverage to support major economic policy changes geared to create an 'enabling environment' for the for-profit private sector. Will the Bank use its influence to support the unleashing of the 'other' private sector in countries where government policies restrict its operation? Government policies, from registration and licensing requirements to active suppression of independent organization by NGOs, limit NGO program and action in many countries.

5. *Documenting World Bank performance in implementing IDA-replenishment agreements.* The agreements on policy and finance negotiated among donor countries stipulate policy directions, emphases and changes. But the Bank's board has generally not assessed implementation of these in any but the most cursory way, noting some progress on each initiative and calling for further action in the next replenishment. NGOs have two options, potentially complimentary. They can monitor the Bank's implementation of the agreements, and lobby their governments to hold the Bank more closely accountable throughout the replenishment, and in negotiating and financing IDA-11 and future replenishments.

But in addition, NGOs should agree to clear standards of their own, against which the next replenishment (IDA-11) will be judged and upon which their position on future replenishments will be decided. The Bank sought out NGO support for IDA-10 vigorously. If broad agreement could be reached on what would constitute satisfactory implementation of IDA-10 and successive replenishments, and if performance could be monitored more closely, NGOs could increase their leverage over the Bank considerably.

Appendix 1 Key to Interviews Cited in Text

World Bank staff and consultant interviews are cited in the text by reference to the region in which operations staff work, or by reference to the division for staff in Finance, Policy, Research and External Affairs Divisions. Citations in the text include a number (e.g. Asia staff no. 1), corresponding to the number used below. Numbers do *not* refer to the numerical system by which the Bank describes countries within each region.

Staff members' remarks in the staff training seminar 'Involving NGOs in Bank-Supported Activities' are also cited in the text. These citations reflect comments and questions of staff members, and were not made in the context of a formal interview. The comments are identified in the text by reference to the division in which they work, and the date 6 October 1989. Many of those whose comments are cited are not among the list of staff interviewed.

Interviews of Bank staff and consultants were conducted in Washington, DC, unless otherwise noted.

Finance staff member, interview 21 May 1990.
Africa region staff no. 1, interview 2 May 1990.
Africa region staff no. 2, interview 4 May 1990.
Africa region staff no. 3, interview 8 May 1990.
Asia region staff no. 1, interview 25 September 1989, telephone; 11 October 1989 interview.
Asia region staff no. 2, interview 25 September 1989, telephone.
Asia region staff no. 3, interview 2 May 1990.
Asia region staff no. 4, interview 4 May 1990.
Asia region staff no. 5, interview 10 May 1990.
Latin America/Caribbean (LAC) staff no. 1, interview 1 May 1990.
Latin America/Caribbean (LAC) staff no. 2, interview 11 October 1990, Madison, Wisconsin.
Policy, Research and External Affairs consultant (staff no. 1), interview 22 September 1988.
Policy, Research and External Affairs staff no. 2, interview 22 September 1988; 27 July 1989; 1 October 1989; 2 May 1990.
Policy, Research and External Affairs staff no. 3, interview 22 October 1988 (by telephone); 11 September 1989; 16 May 1990.
Policy, Research and External Affairs staff no. 4, interview 2 May 1990.
Policy, Research and External Affairs staff no. 5, interview 10 May 1990.
Policy, Research and External Affairs staff no. 6, interview 16 May 1990.
Policy, Research and External Affairs staff no. 7, Private Sector specialist, interview 17 May 1990.
Policy, Research and External Affairs staff no. 8, interview 11 July 1990.
Policy, Research and External Affairs staff no. 9, interview 16 September 1990.

Appendix 2 Methodological Note

I interviewed 30 World Bank staff during 1989 and 1990, including both staff who had already shown interest in NGOs by attending an internal training session on working with NGOs, and other informants chosen irrespective of their views on NGOs. Some 40 NGO informants were interviewed during 1989 and 1990. These interviews have been supplemented by dozens of meetings and conversations during 1992 and 1993.

Documents for most of the 304 projects were reviewed only in one- to three-page summaries produced by the Bank's International Economic Relations Department, the unit responsible for liaison with NGOs. Staff Appraisal Reports, the documents prepared for Board approval before a loan is made, were reviewed in a few cases. More detailed documentation, including Project Completion Reports, was obtained for 22 projects where disbursement has been completed. The data collected on the universe of 304 projects was analyzed and relationships tested with simple bivariate statistical tests.

Because projects involving NGOs since 1989 are more numerous, and because of the World Bank's claims that the new projects are distinguished by their more frequent solicitation of NGO and grassroots group participation in project design, I have also surveyed summary information on 156 projects approved in fiscal 1991 and 1992, and reviewed less complete information on 1993 projects.

In addition to project documents, I reviewed documents and files from the last 15 years of discussions, correspondence and meetings with NGOs. My own involvement with World Bank policy dates from debates in the US Congress and Administration over poverty targeting in the early 1980s, and now continues in research and advocacy work relating to debt management, structural adjustment and poverty and popular participation in World Bank lending. This engagement with Bank policy has exposed me to a collection of sources, documentary and personal, formal and off the record, that underlie much of this research.

My own work with development and environmental NGOs was supplemented by interviews and a mailed questionnaire to NGO leaders involved in recent dialogues with the World Bank. I attended meetings of the NGO-World Bank Committee in 1989 as observer and as 1992, 1993 and 1994 as a participant, and took part in numerous NGO gatherings on structural adjustment, popular participation and the Bank. Seventeen present and past NGO participants in the NGO-World Bank Committee were interviewed or responded to a letter and questionnaire.

NGO perspectives on World Bank operations in the Philippines were gathered during six weeks of field work in that country, November and December of 1989. The Philippines was chosen as the field study country because of the active NGO sector, its government's relatively tolerant and cooperative policy toward many NGO operations, and the substantial record of project collaboration in the Philippines cited by the World Bank.

Notes

Introduction and Overview

1. Organizational analysis of the World Bank has sometimes attributed Bank behavior to the perversity of bureaucracy or to its sheer size and scope (Crane and Finkle, 1981; Kardam, 1989). Organizational approaches have rarely been integrated with political economy to show that the World Bank's structural and operational features are consonant with and reinforce the interests that dominate it. Important exceptions, Gran (1986) and Hellinger (1988), are discussed in later chapters.

'Accountable to Whom?' And Other Issues for NGOs

1. Some of the US-based and other Northern NGOs have been persistent and vocal critics of the Bank's structural adjustment policies, most notably the Development Group for Alternative Policies and Oxfam UK/Ireland. Emerging proposals for multilateral debt reduction in the Non-Aligned Movement (NAM), now chaired by the government of Indonesia, have led to consultations between NAM representatives and some US-based NGOs. There is the prospect, even in the next two years, for more cooperative efforts on World Bank- and IMF-held debt, by a governmental and non-governmental coalition.

World Bank-NGO Project Cooperation: Less than Meets the Eye?

1. Data from 1991, 1992 and 1993 projects are not sufficiently detailed to determine which involve newly-created groups.
2. The World Bank makes no claim that NGOs involved in project collaboration necessarily represent the interests of the poor. But in light of the general association of NGOs and poverty alleviation issues, the distinction is worth noting. The issue is particularly relevant where NGOs are consulted on the design of adjustment conditionality, where the Bank's attentiveness to the interests of poor producers and consumers is an issue.
3. EMENA has been reorganized with the Bank's expanded program in Eastern and Central Europe. The former regional breakdown is retained for this review.

Moving Money: Organizational Aspects of a Development Model

1. Hurni (1980), Van de Laar (1983), Hellinger (1988), Rich (1990), Ayres (1983), and McKitterick (1986) have made similar arguments.
2. The Bank's 1994 review of resettlement policy and performance (World Bank 1994h) acknowledges that no Bank-financed project has fully met its own standards for treatment of resettled populations. It defends continued

financing of projects with resettlement components by arguing that projects with Bank financing have a less destructive overall record than other resettlement schemes.
3. Similar arguments have been made, in less detail and less convincingly, for the perceived failure of the Bank to make population planning and 'women in development' concerns integral parts of its lending program. See Crane and Finkle (1981) and Kardam (1989).
4. The experience of the Asian Miracle countries has since been reviewed in detail by a Bank study. Its findings are discussed in Chapter 6.
5. The same concerns are recognized in Preston's memo accompanying the Wapenhans Report. Noting the tension between new lending and 'effective implementation,' Preston hints that change may be needed at least at the level of country programs, and calls for 'understanding' from staff, borrowers and the international financial community (Preston, memorandum to Executive Directors).

Organizational Culture and Participation in Development

1. Economist Michael Lipton documents similarly selective use of information in his analysis of 'pricist' doctrine in the 1987 WDR. While praising the flexibility and openness of some Bank studies, Lipton finds dogmatism most evident on topics that are most central to the Bank's conditionality. Lipton shows that conclusions in the 1987 WDR rest on highly selective use of the World Bank's own research evidence. The selection is the basis for a one-dimensional plea for 'governments to get smaller, let markets work, and thus set prices right' (Lipton, 1987, pp. 197–208).
2. Argyris calls this 'double loop' learning.
3. First class air travel privileges have subsequently been downgraded to business class for most Bank staff.
4. This discussion of individual motivation in organizations draws on the management literature on motivation, particularly Hersey and Blanchard (1988) and Vroom and Yetton (1973).
5. An overhaul of the project cycle such as that being promoted by the director of the Operations Evaluation Division (see Chapter 5) is the kind of fundamental change that could alter this dynamic. Without such a change, the current emphasis on project impact and supervision are unlikely to break through the Bank's durable organizational culture.

Bibliography

Abugre, Charles (1992) 'The Global Environment Facility: perpetuating unsustainable economic models.' *Third World Economics.* 1 (15 April): pp. 14–20.

Adams, James (1992) World Bank Office Memorandum to Sven Sandstrom. 'Participatory Development: Interim Report of the Learning Group: Implementation Status of Recommendations.' Draft, 15 January 1992.

'Africa – A flicker of light.' *The Economist* 5 March 1994, pp. 21–4.

Agarwala, Ramgopal (1983) 'Price Distortions and Growth in Developing Countries.' World Bank Staff Working Paper 575. Washington, DC: World Bank.

Agency for International Development (1986) *Development Effectiveness of Private Voluntary Organizations (PVOs).* Report to the Appropriations Committee, U.S. House of Representatives, February.

Alderman, Harold (1990) *Nutritional Status in Ghana and its Determinants.* Working Paper No. 3, Social Dimensions of Adjustment in Sub-Saharan Africa. Washington, DC: The World Bank.

Alexander, Nancy (1992) 'Testimony for the House Select Committee on Hunger on The World Bank and Poverty by Nancy Alexander, Bread for the World, June 4' Typescript.

ANGOC (Asian NGO Coalition) (1988) 'Democratizing Asian Development: A Commitment to Leadership.' ANGOC Monograph Series No. 7, ANGOC, Manila, Philippines.

Annis, Sheldon (1987) 'Can Small-Scale Development be a Large-scale Policy? The Case of Latin America.' *World Development.* 15 (Supplement), pp. 129–34.

Antrobus, Peggy (1987) 'Funding for NGOs: Issues and Options.' *World Development.* 15 (Supplement), pp. 95–102.

Argyris, Chris (1982) *The Applicability of Organizational Sociology.* Cambridge: Cambridge University Press.

Argyris, Chris (1987) 'How Learning and Reasoning Processes Affect Organizational Change.' Pp. 47–86 in *Change in Organizations* edited by Paul S. Goodman and associates. San Francisco: Jossey-Bass.

Arruda, Marcos (1993) 'NGOs and the World Bank: Possibilities and Limits of Collaboration.' Paper based on an oral presentation to the Seminar 'World Bank and NGOs: Operational and Policy Approaches for Collaboration,' Washington DC, 29–30 June.

'Articles of Agreement of the International Bank for Reconstruction and Development (as amended February 16, 1989).' Washington, DC, March 1989.

Ascher, Robert (1983) 'New Development Approaches and the Adaptability of International Agencies: The Case of the World Bank.' *International Organization* 37, pp. 205–29.

Aufderheide, Pat, and Bruce Rich (1988) 'Environmental Reform and the

Bibliography

Multilateral Banks.' *World Policy Review* 5, pp. 301–21.
Ayres, Robert (1983) *Banking on the Poor.* Cambridge, MA: MIT.
Bacha, Edman L., and Richard E. Feinberg (1986) 'The World Bank and Structural Adjustment in Latin America.' *World Development* 14, pp. 333–46.
Balassa, Bela (1984) 'Adjustment Policies in Developing Countries, 1979–83.' World Staff Working Paper No. 675.
Bamberger, Michael (1986) 'The Role of Community Participation in Development Planning and Project Management,' EDI Policy Seminar Report No. 13, Washington, DC: World Bank.
Bangladesh Rural Advancement Committee (1986) 'Unraveling Networks of Corruption.' Pp. 135–55 in *Community Management: Asian Experience and Perspectives,* edited by David C. Korten. West Hartford, CT: Kumarian.
Bangura, Yusuf (1987) 'IMF/World Bank Conditionality and Nigeria's structural adjustment program.' In *The IMF and the World Bank in Africa,* edited by Kjell Havnevik. Uppsala: Scandinavian Institute for African Studies.
Bank Check – Views from the Environment and Development Community (1990) Washington, DC: Bank Check.
Bank Information Center, ed. (1990) *Funding Ecological and Social Destruction: The World Bank and the International Monetary Fund.* Washington, DC: Bank Information Center.
Bassett, Thomas J. (1988) 'Development Theory and Reality: The World Bank in Northern Ivory Coast.' *Review of African Political Economy* 41, pp. 45–59.
Baum, Warren (1978) 'The World Bank Project Cycle.' *Finance and Development* 15, pp. 10–17.
Bebbington, Anthony and John Farrington (1993) 'Governments, NGOs and Agricultural Development: Perspectives on Changing Inter-Organisational Relationships.' *The Journal of Development Studies* 29(2), pp. 199–219.
Beckmann, David (1986) 'The World Bank and Poverty in the 1980s.' *Finance and Development.* September, pp. 26–9.
Bello, Walden, David Kinley and Elaine Elinson (1982) *Development Debacle: The World Bank in the Philippines.* San Francisco: Institute for Food and Development Policy.
Bello, Walden with Shea Cunningham and Bill Rau (1994) *Dark Victory: The United States, Structural Adjustment and Global Poverty.* London: Pluto.
Berg, Elliot and Don Sherk (1994) 'The World Bank and its Environmentalist Critics.' Background Paper in Bretton Woods Commission, *Bretton Woods: Looking to the Future.* Washington, DC: Bretton Woods Commission.
Bhatnagar, Bhuvan and Aubrey C. Williams, eds (1992) *Participatory Development and the World Bank: Potential Directions for Change.* World Bank Discussion Paper 183. Washington, DC, World Bank.
Bienefeld, Manfred (1994) 'The New World Order: echoes of a new imperialism.' *Third World Quarterly* 15(1), pp. 31–48.
Bonné, B. (1989) 'Development Assistance for Policies'. MA Thesis, Roskilde University Centre.
Bowden, Peter (1990) 'NGOs in Asia: issues in development.' *Public Administration and Development* 10, pp. 141–52.
Bradford, Colin I., Jr (1986) 'East Asian Models: Myths and Lessons.' in *Development Strategies Reconsidered,* edited by John P. Lewis and Valeriana

Kallab. Washington, DC: Overseas Development Council, pp. 115–28.
Bratton, Michael (1989) 'The Politics of Government – NGO Relations in Africa,' *World Development* 17, pp. 569–87.
Bratton, Michael (1989a) 'Non-Governmental Organizations in Africa: Can They Influence Public Policy?' *Development and Change* 21, pp. 87–118.
Bratton, Michael (1989b) 'Beyond the State: Civil Society and Associational Life in Africa.' *World Politics.* 41 April, pp. 407–30.
Bratton, Michael and Nicolas van de Walle (1992) 'Toward Governance in Africa: Popular Demands and State Responses' in *Governance and Politics in Africa*, edited by Goren Hyden and Michael Bratton. Boulder, CO: Lynne Rienner, pp. 27–56.
Brett, E.A (1993) 'Voluntary Agencies as Development Organizations: Theorizing the Problem of Efficiency and Accountability.' *Development and Change* 244, pp. 269–303.
Broad, Robin (1988) *Unequal Alliance: The World Bank, The IMF and the Philippines.* Berkeley: University of California Press.
Broad, Robin and John Cavanagh (1988) 'No More NICs.' *Foreign Policy,* Fall, pp. 81–103.
Brodhead, Tim (1989) 'Strings and Things: Does Positive Conditionality Exist? Some Considerations for World Bank Lending.' Unpublished, prepared for the November 1989 meeting of the NGO Working Group on the World Bank.
Brown, L. David and David C. Korten (1989) 'Understanding Voluntary Organizations: Guidelines for Donors.' Working Papers, Public Sector Management and Private Sector Development. Washington, DC: Country Economics Department of The World Bank. WPS 258.
Bryant, C. and L.G. White (1982) *Managing Development in the Third World.* Boulder, CO: Westview Press.
Burki, Shahid Javed (1980) 'Sectoral Priorities for meeting basic needs,' Pp. 13–17 in *Poverty and Basic Needs.* Washington, DC: World Bank.
Cahn, Jonathan (1993) 'Challenging the New Imperial Authority: The World Bank and the Democratization of Development.' *Harvard Human Rights Journal*, 6 (Spring), pp. 159–93.
Callaghy, Thomas M. (1993) 'Political Passions and Economic Interests: Economic Reform and Political Structure in Africa.' In Thomas M. Callaghy and John Ravenhill, eds, *Hemmed In: Responses to Africa's Economic Decline.* New York: Columbia.
Carlsson, Jerker, Gunnar Köhlin and Anders Ekbom (1993) *The Political Economy of Evaluation: International Aid Agencies and the Effectiveness of Aid.* New York: St Martin's.
Carroll, Thomas (1992) *Intermediary NGOs: The Supporting Link in Grassroots Development.* West Hartford, Conn.: Kumarian.
Cavanagh, John, Daphne Wysham and Marcos Arruda, eds (1994) *Beyond Bretton Woods: Alternatives to the Global Economic Order.* Boulder: Pluto Press.
Cernea, Michael M. (1987) 'Farmer Organizations and Institution Building for Sustainable Development.' *Regional Development Dialogue*, 8(2), Summer, pp. 1–19.
Cernea, Michael M. (1988) *Nongovernmental Organizations and Local Development.* World Bank Discussion Papers no. 40. Washington, DC: World Bank.

Chambers, Robert (1987) 'Poverty, Environment and the World Bank: The Opportunity for a New Professionalism.' Prepared for Strategic Planning and Review Department, World Bank.

Charlton, Robert (1993) 'External Debt, Economic Success and Economic Failure: State Autonomy, Africa and the NICs' in Stephen P. Riley, ed., *The Politics of Global Debt*. New York: St Martin's.

Clark, John (1986) 'NGO Perspectives on Debt and Adjustment. Paper for NGO-World Bank Meeting, November, 1986.' October, 1986, Unpublished typewritten manuscript.

Clark, John, et al. (1987) 'An NGO Reaction to the World Bank Paper "Protecting the Poor During Periods of Adjustment."' Unpublished typewritten manuscript, 20 February.

Clark, John (1991) *Democratizing Development: The Role of Voluntary Organizations*. West Hartford, Conn: Kumarian Press.

Cohn, Theodore (1973) *Influence of the Less Developed Countries in the World Bank Group*. Ph.D. Diss., University of Michigan.

Colchester, Marcus (1986) 'Banking on Disaster: International Support for Transmigration.' *Ecologist* 16 (2/3), pp. 61–70.

Cole, Sam (1987) 'World Economy Forecasts and the International Agencies.' *International Studies Quarterly* 31, pp. 367–85.

'Cooperation Between the World Bank and NGOs; Progress Report.' Memorandum from Vice President and Secretary to Executive Directors and Alternates. SecM90–290, 8 March 1990.

Corbridge, Stuart (1993) 'Discipline and Punish: The New Right and the Policing of the International Debt Crisis,' in *The Politics of Global Debt*, Stephen P. Riley, ed., New York: St Martin's, 1993, pp. 25–50.

Cornia, Giovanni Andrea, Richard Jolly, Frances Stewart, eds. (1987) *Adjustment with a Human Face: Protecting the Vulnerable and Promoting Growth*. Oxford: Clarendon Press.

Cornia, Giovanni Andrea, Rolf van der Hoeven and Thandika Mkandawire, eds (1992) *Africa's Recovery in the 1990s: From Stagnation and Adjustment to Human Development*. Florence, Italy: UNICEF International Child Development Centre.

Country Economics Department, The World Bank (1988) *Adjustment Lending: An Evaluation of Ten Years of Experience*. Washington, DC: World Bank.

Country Economics Department, The World Bank (1992) *Adjustment Lending and Mobilization of Private and Public Resources for Growth*. Policy and Research Series, No. 22. Washington, DC: World Bank.

Cox, Robert W., and Harold K. Jacobson (1981) 'The Decision-Making Approach to the Study of International Organization.' in *The Concept of International Organization*, edited by Georges Abi-Saab. Paris: UNESCO.

Cox, Robert W. (1987) *Production, Power and World Order: Social Forces in the Making of History*. New York: Columbia.

Cox, Robert W. (1992) 'Multilateralism and World Order.' *Review of International Studies*. 18, April 1992.

Crane, Barbara and Jason L. Finkle (1981) 'Organizational Impediments of Development Assistance: The World Bank's Population Program.' *World Politics* 33, pp. 516–38.

Cruz, Wilfrido and Robert Repetto (1992) *The Environmental Effects of*

Stabilization and Structural Adjustment Programs: The Philippines Case. Washington, DC: World Resources Institute.

Cumings, Bruce (1984) 'The origins and development of the North East Asian Political Economy: Industrial Sectors, Product Cycles, and Political Consequences.' *International Organization* 38, pp. 237–94.

Cypher, James M. (1988) 'The Crisis and the Restructuring of Capitalism in the Periphery' Pp. 43–80 in *Research in Political Economy*, edited by Paul Zarembka, vol 2. Greenwich, Connecticut: JAI Press.

Cypher, James M. (1989a) 'The Debt Crisis as 'Opportunity': Strategy to Revive U.S. Hegemony.' *Latin American Perspectives* 16(1), Winter 1989, pp. 52–78.

Cypher, James M. (1989b) 'Strings Attached: World Bank tightens control of Third World economies.' *Dollars and Sense*, December 1989, pp. 9–11, 19.

Daly, Herman E. (1994) 'Farewell Lecture to the World Bank,' in *Beyond Bretton Woods*, edited by John Cavanagh, Daphne Wysham and Marcos Arruda. London: Pluto Press.

Danaher, Kevin, ed. (1994) *50 Years is Enough: The Case Against the World Bank and the International Monetary Fund.* Boston: South End Press.

DeGraaf, Martin (1987) 'Context, Constraint or Control, Zimbabwean NGOs and their Environment.' *Development Policy Review* 5, pp. 277–301.

De Lusignan, Guy (1986). 'The Bank's Economic Development Institute'. *Finance and Development* 23 (2), pp. 28–31.

Deal, Terrence E. and Allen A. Kennedy (1982) *Corporate Cultures: The Rites and Rituals of Corporate Life.* Reading, MA: Addison-Wesley.

Demery, Lionel and Tony Addison (1987) *The Alleviation of Poverty under Structural Adjustment.* Washington, DC: World Bank.

Denning, Stephen (1994) 'Programme Aid Beyond Structural Adjustment.' Presented to Workshop on New Forms of Programme Aid. Harare, Zimbabwe. 31 January – 1 February.

Development Committee (1987) *Environment, Growth and Development.* Washington, DC, Joint Ministerial Committee of the Boards of Governors of the World Bank and the International Monetary Fund on the Transfer of Real Resources to Developing Countries, Publication 14.

Development Committee (1989) *The Impact of the Industrial Policies of Developed Countries on Developing Countries.* Washington, DC: Joint Ministerial Committee of the Boards of Governors of the World Bank and the International Monetary Fund on the Transfer of Real Resources to Developing Countries, Publication 20.

Development Committee (1990) *Problems and Issues in Structural Adjustment.* Washington, DC: Joint Ministerial Committee of the Boards of Governors of the World Bank and the International Monetary Fund on the Transfer of Real Resources to Developing Countries, Publication 23.

Diamond, Larry (1989) 'Beyond Authoritarianism and Totalitarianism: Strategies for Democratization.' *Washington Quarterly*, Winter, pp. 141–61.

Dichter, Thomas W. (1988) 'The Changing World of Northern NGOs: Problems, Paradoxes, and Possibilities,' pp. 177–88 in *Strengthening the Poor: What Have We Learned?* US-Third World Policy Perspectives No. 10, Overseas Development Council, edited by John P. Lewis. New Brunswick: Transaction.

DiMaggio, Paul J., and Walter W. Powell (1983) 'The Iron Cage Revisited: Institutional Isomorphism and Collective Rationality in Organizational Fields,' *American Sociological Review* 48, pp. 147–60.
Donnelly-Roark, Paula (1991) 'Grassroots Participation: Defining New Realities and Operationalizing New Strategies.' UNDP Discussion Paper. New York: UNDP.
'Draft Proposal for Establishing a Consultative Group to Assist the Poorest of the Poor (CGAPP) – A Micro-finance Program.' Typescript. 26 September 1994.
Durning, Alan B. (1989) *Action at the Grassroots*: *Foreign Policy*, Winter 1989–90, pp. 66–82.
Early Warning. Vol 1, No.1, December 1992.
Earwaker, Frank (1989) World Bank Office Memorandum, 'Macro-economic Projections and the Appraisal of Adjustment Loans.' 21 September.
Eaton, Jonathan and Mark Gersovitz (1981) 'Poor Country Borrowing in Private Financial Markets and the Repudiation Issue.' *Princeton Studies in International Finance*, no. 47, June.
Edwards, Michael and David Hulme (1992) 'Scaling up NGO Impact on Development: learning from experience.' *Development in Practice* 2 (2): pp. 77–91.
'Effective Implementation: Key to Development Impact.' Report of the World Bank's Portfolio Management Task Force (1992) Washington, DC: World Bank.
Escudero, Carlos R. (1988) *Involuntary Resettlement in Bank – Assisted Projects: An Introduction to Legal Issues.* Washington, DC: World Bank.
Esman, Milton J., and Norman T. Uphoff (1984) *Local Organizations: Intermediaries in Rural Development.* Ithaca: Cornell.
Esquel Group Foundation (1993) 'Civil Society, State and Market: An Emerging Partnership for Equitable Development.' Presented to the Social Forum Convened by the Inter American Development Bank and the United Nations Development Programme. Washington, DC, pp. 10–13, February.
Fatouros, A.A. (1977) 'The World Bank', Pp. 2–79 in *The Impact of International Organizations on Legal and Institutional Change in the Developing Countries.* New York: International Legal Center.
Feeney, Patricia (1994) 'Planofloro: Has the World Bank Learnt its Lesson?' Typescript, Oxfam UK/Ireland.
Freedom from Debt Coalition (Philippines) (1994) 'Unity Statement'.
French, Hilary F. (1994) 'Rebuilding the World Bank.' *State of the World*, Lester R. Brown and others. New York: Norton.
French, J.R.P. and B. Raven (1959) 'The Bases of Social Power,' in *Studies in Social Power* edited by D. Cartwright. Ann Arbor: University of Michigan, Institute for Social Research.
Fried, Edward R. and Henry D. Owen, eds (1982) *The Future of the World Bank.* Conference at the Brookings Institution, 7 January 1982) Washington, DC: Brookings.
Friends of the Earth (1992) *Who Pays the Piper? The Operations of Multilateral Development Banks in Central and Eastern Europe.* Washington, DC: Friends of the Earth.
Garilao, Ernesto D. (1987) 'Indigenous NGOs as Strategic Institutions: Managing the Relationship with Government and Resource Agencies.' *World Development* 15 (Supplement), pp. 113–20.

George, Susan and Fabrizio Sabelli (1994) *Faith and Credit: The World Bank's Secular Empire.* Boulder: Westview.

Gerster, Richard (1993) 'Accountability of Executive Directors in the Bretton Woods Institutions.' *Journal of World Trade.* 27, December, pp. 87–116.

Gibbon, Peter (1992) 'The World Bank and African Poverty, 1973–1991.' *Journal of Modern African Studies* 30(2), pp. 193–220.

Gillies, David (1992) 'Human Rights, Democracy, and 'Good Governance': Stretching the World Bank's Policy Frontiers.' Paper prepared for the President, International Centre for Human Rights and Democratic Development, Montreal.

Glewwe, Paul (1988) 'The Poor in Latin America During Adjustment: A Case Study of Peru.' Washington, DC: World Bank.

Goldsworthy, David (1988) 'Thinking Politically about Development.' *Development and Change* 19, pp. 505–30.

Gow, David D. 1979) *Local Organizations and Rural Development: A Comparative Reappraisal.* Washington, DC: Development Alternatives, 2 vols.

Gran, Guy (1986) 'Beyond African Famines: Whose Knowledge Matters?' *Alternatives* 11, pp. 275–96.

Griesgraber, Jo Marie, ed. (1994) *Rethinking Bretton Woods: Towards Equitable, Sustainable and Participatory Development.* Conference Report and Recommendations, 'Rethinking Bretton Woods,' June 12–17, 1994. Washington, DC: Center of Concern.

Guest, D.E. (1984) 'Social Psychology and Organizational Change,' in *Social Psychology and Organizational Behaviour,* ed. Gruneberg and Wall. Chichester: John Wiley and Sons.

Hagan, Ernestina N. (1992) 'NGO's Women and the Social Dimensions of Adjustment.' Resource Paper Presented at the Roundtable Workshop on NGOs and Structural Adjustment, Accra Ghana, 23–25 March.

Hall, Anthony (1987) 'Social Analysis in Official Foreign Aid.' *Human Organization* 46, pp. 368–72.

Hamilton, Clive (1983) 'Capitalist Industrialisation in East Asia's Four Little Tigers.' *Journal of Contemporary Asia* 13, pp. 35–73.

Hayter, Teresa and Catharine Watson (1985) *Aid: Rhetoric and Reality.* London: Pluto Press.

Healey, John and Mark Robinson (1992) *Democracy, Governance and Economic Policy: Sub-Saharan Africa in Comparative Review.* London: Overseas Development Institute.

Helleiner, Gerald (1994) 'Agendas for the Bretton Woods Institutions.' Notes for Presentation at the Conference 'Fifty Years after Bretton Woods: The Future of the IMF and the World Bank,' 29–30 September, Madrid, Spain. Typescript.

Hellinger, Douglas (1987) 'NGOs and the Large Aid Donors: Changing the Terms of Engagement.' *World Development* 15 (Supplement), pp. 135–43.

Hellinger, Douglas (1988) 'The World Bank's Diminishing Credibility.' Typescript, August.

Hellinger, Stephen and Doug Hellinger (1985) 'Mainlining Major Donor Support for Indigenous NGOs: Guidelines for Constructive Collaboration.' Washington, DC: The Development Group for Alternative Policies.

Hellinger, Stephen, Douglas Hellinger and Fred M. O'Regan (1988) *Aid for Just Development.* Boulder: Lynne Rienner.

Heredia, Carlos A. and Mary E. Purcell (1994) *The Polarization of Mexican Society: A Grassroots View of World Bank Economic Adjustment Policies*. Washington, DC: The Development Group for Alternative Policies.

Hersey, Paul and Kenneth Blanchard (1988) *Management of Organizational Behavior*. Englewood Cliffs, NJ: Prentice-Hall, Fifth edition.

Hodges, Tony (1988) 'Ghana's Strategy for Adjustment with Growth.' *Africa Recovery* 2(3), pp. 16–21, 27.

Holdcroft, Lane E. (1978) 'The Rise and Fall of Community Development in Developing Countries, 1950–65: A Critical Analysis and an Annotated Bibliography.' Washington, DC: USAID.

Holden, Constance (1987) 'The Greening of the World Bank.' *Science* 240, pp. 1610.

Holloway, Richard, ed. (1989) *Doing Development: Government, NGOs and the Rural Poor in Asia*. London: Earthscan.

Howard, John B. (1977) 'General Observations,' pp. 1–12 in *The Impact of International Organizations on Legal and Institutional Change in the Developing Countries*. New York: International Legar Center.

Hulme, David (1989) 'Learning and Not Learning From Experience in Rural Project Planning.' *Public Administration and Development* 9, pp. 1–16.

Hurni, Bettina S. (1980) *The Lending Policy of the World Bank in the 1970s: Analysis and Evaluation*. Boulder: Westview.

Hyden, Goran (1983) *No Shortcuts to Progress: African Development Management in Perspective*. Berkeley: University of California Press.

Irwin, Michael (1990) 'Let Them Eat Honey-Roasted Peanuts – Memos of the Month.' *Washington Monthly*, June, pp. 34–7.

Jacobson, Harold K., William M. Reisinger and Todd Mathers (1986) 'National Entanglements in International Governmental Organizations.' *American Political Science Review* 80, pp. 141–59.

Jazairy, Idriss, Mohiudiin Alamgir and Theresa Panuccio (1992) *The State of World Rural Poverty*. New York: NYU Press (for the International Fund for Agricultural Development).

Jolly, Richard (1985) 'Adjustment with a Human Face.' The Barbara Ward Lecture, 18th Society for International Development Conference, Rome, 1–4 July.

Kahler, Miles (1989) 'International Financial Institutions and the Politics of Adjustment.' Pp. 139–59 in *Fragile Coalitions: The Politics of Economic Adjustment*, edited by Joan M. Nelson. Washington, DC: Overseas Development Council.

Kakabadse, Yolanda N. with Sarah Burns (1994) 'Movers and Shapers: NGOs in International Affairs.' Washington, DC: World Resources Institute. May.

Kanbur, S.M. Ravi (1987) 'Measurement and Alleviation of Poverty with an Application to the Effects of Macro-economic Adjustment.' IMF Staff Papers, vol. 34, Washington, DC: The International Monetary Fund.

Kardam, Nuket (1989) 'Women and Development Agencies.' Pp. 133–54, *The Women and International Development Annual*, edited by Rita S. Gallin. Boulder: Westview.

Kardam, Nüket (1993) 'Development Approaches and the Role of Policy Advocacy: The Case of the World Bank.' *World Development* 21(11), pp. 1773–86.

Khagram, Sanjeev (1993) 'Visions, Coalitions and the State: India's Narmade Valley Projects and Paths of Democratic Development in the Third World.' typescript, Stanford University. 15 August.

Kolko, Gabriel (1975) 'The US Effort to Mobilize World Bank Aid to Saigon.' *Journal of Contemporary Asia* 5(1), pp. 42–52.

Korten, David C. (1980) 'Community Organization and Rural Development: A Learning Process Approach,' *Public Administration Review*, 40, pp. 480–511.

Korten, David C. (1986) 'Unraveling Networks of Corruption: Bangladesh Rural Advancement Committee,' in David C. Korten, ed., *Community Management: Asian Experience and Perspectives*. West Hartford, Conn.: Kumarian Press, pp. 135–55.

Korten, David C. (1987) 'Third Generation NGO Strategies: A Key to Peoplecentered Development.' *World Development* 15 (Supplement), pp. 145–59.

Korten, David C. (1989) 'Social Science in the Service of Social Transformation' in *A Decade of Process Documentation Research*, edited by Cynthia C. Veneracion. Manila: Institute of Philippine Culture, pp. 5–20.

Korten, Frances F. and Robert Y. Siy, Jr., eds (1988) *Transforming a Bureaucracy The Experience of the Philippine National Irrigation Administration*. West Hartford: Kumarian.

Kothari, Smitu (1993) 'Challenging Economic Hegemony: In Search of Sustainability and Justice.' Paper prepared for the conference on 'Sustainable Development with Equity in the 1990s: Policies and Alternatives,' University of Wisconsin, Madison, 13–16 May.

Krasner, Stephen D. (1981) 'Transforming International Regimes: What the Third World Wants and Why.' *International Studies Quarterly* 25, pp. 119–48.

Krasner, Stephen D. (1982) 'Regimes and the Limits of Realism: Regimes as Autonomous Variables.' *International Organization* 36, pp. 499–515.

Krueger, Anne O. (1985) 'Importance of General Policies to Promote Economic Growth.' *World Economy* 8:2, pp. 93–108.

Kydd, J. and A. Hewitt (1986) 'The Effectiveness of Structural Adjustment Lending: Initial Evidence from Malawi.' *World Development* 14, pp. 347–65.

Lafay, Jean-Dominique and Jacques Lecaillon (1993) *The Political Dimension of Economic Adjustment*. Paris: OECD.

Lawyers Committee for Human Rights (1993) *The World Bank: Governance and Human Rights*. New York: Lawyers Committee.

Lecomte, Bernard J. (1986) *Project Aid: Limitations and Alternatives*. Paris: OECD.

Lee, Ducksoo (1989) Memo to Moeen A. Qureshi, the World Bank.

Leff, Nathaniel F. (1985) 'The Use of Policy-Science Tools in Public-Sector Decision Making: Social Benefit-Cost Analysis in the World Bank.' *Kyklos* 38, pp. 60–76.

Leff, Nathaniel F. (1988) 'Disjunction between Policy Research and Practice: social benefit-cost analysis and investment policy at the World Bank.' *Studies in Comparative International Development*, Winter, pp. 77–87.

Lehman, Howard P. (1993) *Indebted Development: Strategic Bargaining and Economic Adjustment in the Third World*. New York: St Martin's.

LePrestre, Philippe (1982) *The Ecology of the World Bank*. Ph.D. dissertation, Indiana University.

LePrestre, Philippe (1986) 'A problematique for international organizations.' *International Social Science Journal* 38, pp. 127–38.
LePrestre, Philippe (1989) *The World Bank and the Environmental Challenge*. Selinsgrove: Susquehanna University Press and London: Associated University Presses.
LePrestre, Philippe (1993) 'Environmental Learning at the World Bank.' Prepared for presentation at the 34th Annual Convention of the International Studies Association, Acapulco, March, pp. 23–27.
Lessard, Donald (1986) *International Financing for Developing Countries: The Unfulfilled Promise*. World Bank Staff Working Papers No. 783, Series on International Capital and Economic Development, No. 2. Washington, DC: World Bank.
Levinson, Jerome (1992) 'Multilateral Financing Institutions: What Form of Accountability?' *The American University Journal of International Law and Policy*. 89(1), pp. 39–64.
Levitt, B. and J.G. March (1988) 'Organizational Learning.' *Annual Review of Sociology* 14, pp. 319–40.
Libby, Ronald T. (1975a) 'International Development Association: A Legal Fiction Designed to Secure an LDC Constituency.' *International Organization* 29, pp. 1065–72.
Libby, Ronald T. (1975b) 'The Ideology of the World Bank.' Ph.D. dissertation, University of Washington.
Lipton, Michael (1987) 'Limits of Price Policy for Agriculture: Which Way for the World Bank?' *Development Policy Review* 5, pp. 197–215.
Lipton, Michael (1988) *The Poor and the Poorest*. World Bank Discussion Papers No. 25. Washington, DC: World Bank.
Lister, Frederick (1984) *Decision-Making Strategies for International Organizations: The IMF Model*. Denver: University of Denver School of International Studies Monograph Series in World Affairs.
Loxley, John (1986) *Debt and Disorder: External Financing for Development*. Boulder: Westview and Ottawa: North-South Institute.
Macdonald, Laura (1992) 'Turning to the NGOs: Competing Conceptions of Civil Society in Latin America.' Presented to the 1992 Annual Meeting of the Latin American Studies Association, Los Angeles, 24–27 September.
McAfee, Kathy (1991) *Storm Signals: Structural Adjustment and Development Alternatives in the Caribbean*. London: Zed.
McCormack, Gavan (1978) 'The South Korean Economy: GNP Versus the People.' pp. 91–111 in *Korea North and South: The Deepening Crisis*, edited by Gavan McCormack and Mark Selden, New York: Monthly Review.
McKitterick, Nathaniel M. 1986) 'The World Bank and the McNamara Legacy.' *The National Interest*, Summer 1986, pp. 45–52.
McNamara, Robert (1973) 'Address to the Board of Governors' (Nairobi, Kenya: 24 September).
'Managing Quality' 1994. Southern Africa Department. World Bank.
March, James G. and J.P. Olsen (1975) 'The Uncertainty of the Past: organizational learning under ambiguity.' *European Journal of Political Research* 3, pp. 147–71.
Martens, Jens (1992) 'NGOs in the UN System: The Participation of Non-Governmental Organizations in Environment and Development Institutions

of the United Nations.' Bonn: Projektstelle UNCED, DNR/BUND.
Mason, Edward S. and Robert E. Asher (1973) *The World Bank Since Bretton Woods*. Washington, DC: Brookings Institution.
Mayatech Corporation (1991) *Gender and Adjustment*. Prepared for Office of Women in Development, Bureau for Program and Policy Coordination, USAID.
Meyer, John W. (1984) 'Organizations as Ideological Systems.' Pp. 187–205 in *Leadership and Organizational Culture*, edited by Thomas Sergiovanni and John Corbally. Chicago: University of Illinois.
Meyer, John W. (1986) 'Myths of Socialization and of Personality,' Pp. 187–205 in *Reconstructing Individualism*, edited by T.C. Heller, M. Sosna and E.E. Welbery. Stanford, CA: Stanford.
Meyer, John W., and W. Richard Scott (1983) *Organizational Environments: Ritual and Rationality*. Beverly Hills, CA: Sage.
Meyer, John W. and Brian Rowan (1983) 'Institutionalized Organizations: Formal Structure as Myth and Ceremony,' in Meyer and Scott, eds pp. 21–44.
Mihevc, John (1993) 'The Fundamentalist Theology of the World Bank.' Paper delivered to the Canadian Association of African Studies Conference, 14 May 1993.
Mistry, Percy (1991) 'World or Wonderland Bank?' *Banker* 141, October, pp. 39–40, 45–8.
Morgan, Mary (1990) 'Stretching the Development Dollar: The Potential for Scaling-Up,' *Grassroots Development* 14, pp. 1, 2–11.
Moser, Caroline (1987) 'Approaches to Community Participation in Urban Development Programs in Third World Countries,' in EDI, Readings in Community Participation, Vol II. Washington, DC: World Bank.
Mosley, Paul (1985) 'The Politics of Economic Liberalization: USAID and the World Bank in Kenya, 1980–1984.' *African Affairs* 85, pp. 107–19.
Mosley, Paul (1987) 'Conditionality as Bargaining Process: Structural Adjustment Lending, 1980–1986.' *Essays in International Finance*, No. 168, October. Princeton: Princeton University Department of Economics, International Finance Section.
Mosley, Paul and John Toye (1988) 'The Design of Structural Adjustment Programmes.' *Development Policy Review* 6, pp. 395–413.
Mosley, Paul, Jane Harrigan and John Toye (1991) *Aid and Power: The World Bank and Policy-based Lending*. Vol. 1. London: Routledge.
Moulton, Anthony D. (1978) 'On Concealed Dimensions of Third World Involvement in International Economic Organizations.' *International Organization* 32, pp. 1019–35.
NGO Working Group on the World Bank (1989) 'Non-Governmental Development Organisations Guidelines for Possible Collaboration with the World Bank.' Draft for the NGO Working Group on the World Bank, 30 October 1989 in Bangkok.
Nagle, William J., and Sanjoy Ghose (1989) 'Beneficiary Participation in some World Bank Supported Projects.' Prepared for the International Economic Relations Division of the Strategic Planning and Review Department, The World Bank.
Nelson, Joan (1984) 'The Politics of Stabilization,' in *Adjustment Crisis in*

Bibliography 213

the Third World, edited by Richard E. Feinberg and Valeriana Kallab. New Brunswick: Transaction.

Nelson, Joan (1989a) 'The Politics of Long-Haul Economic Reform.' Pp. 3–26 in *Fragile Coalitions: The Politics of Economic Adjustment*, edited by Joan Nelson. Washington, DC: Overseas Development Council.

Nelson, Joan (1989b) 'The Politics of Pro-Poor Adjustment.' Pp. 95–114 in *Fragile Coalitions: The Politics of Economic Adjustment*, edited by Joan M. Nelson. Washington, DC: Overseas Development Council.

Nerfin, Marc (1986) 'Neither Prince nor Merchant: Citizen.' *IFDA Dossier*, pp. 171–95.

Ness, Gayl D., and Steven R. Brechin (1988) 'Bridging the Gap: international organizations as organizations,' *International Organization* 42, 2, Spring, pp. 245–73.

Nicholas, Peter (1988) *The World Bank's Lending for Adjustment: An Interim Report*. World Bank Discussion Papers, 34. Washington, DC: World Bank.

Nyang'oro, Julius E. (1994) 'Reform Politics and the Democratization Process in Africa.' *African Studies Review* 37, 1, pp. 133–49.

Nzomo, Maria (1992) 'Beyond Structural Adjustment Programs: Democracy, Gender, Equity, and Development in Africa, with Special Reference to Kenya.' in *Beyond Structural Adjustment in Africa*, edited by Timothy M. Shaw and Julius Nyang'oro. New York: Praeger.

Oakley, Peter and David Marsden (1984) *Approaches to Participation in Rural Development*. Geneva: ILO.

O'Donnell, Guillermo (1981) 'Reflections on the Patterns of Change in the Bureaucratic-Authoritarian State. *Latin America Research Review* pp. 3–38.

Operations Evaluation Department (1988) *Rural Development: World Bank Experience 1965–86*. Washington, DC: World Bank.

Operations Evaluation Department (1990) *Evaluation Results for 1988: Issues in World Bank Lending Over Two Decades*. Washington, DC: World Bank.

Organisation for Economic Co-operation and Development (1988) *Voluntary Aid for Development: The role of Non-Governmental Organisations*. Paris: OECD.

Osieke, Ebere (1984) 'Majority Systems in the ILO and the IMF.' *International and Comparative Law Quarterly* 33, pp. 381–408.

Overseas Development Institute (1986) 'Adjusting to Recession: Will the Poor Recover?' ODI Briefing Paper.

Overseas Development Institute (1988) 'Development Efforts of NGOs.' *Development* 1988, 4, pp. 41–46.

Padrón, Mario (1987) 'Non-governmental Development Organizations: From Development Aid to Development Cooperation.' *World Development* 15, Supplement, pp. 69–77.

Pastor, Manuel, Jr. (1989) 'Latin America, the Debt Crisis, and the I.M.F.' *Latin American Perspectives* 16, pp. 79–110.

Patkar, Medha (1989) Statement concerning a Critique of the World Bank Financed Sardar Sarovar Dam, before the Subcommittee on Natural Resources, Agricultural Research and Environment, Committee on Science, Space and Technology. US House of Representatives. 24 October.

Paul, Samuel (1987) 'Community Participation in World Bank Projects.' *Finance and Development*, December, pp. 20–3.

Paul, Samuel (1988) 'Governments and Grassroots Organizations: From Co-Existence to Collaboration' pp. 61–71 in *Strengthening the Poor: What Have We Learned?* U.S.-Third World Policy Perspectives No. 10, Overseas Development Council, edited by John P. Lewis. New Brunswick, NJ: Transaction Books.

Paul, Samuel and Arturo Israel, eds (1991) *Nongovernmental Organizations and the World Bank: Cooperation for Development.* Washington, DC: World Bank.

Payer, Cheryl (1982) *The World Bank: A Critical Analysis.* New York: Monthly Review.

Pease, Stanley (1984) *The Hobbled Giant: Essays on the World Bank.* Boulder: Westview.

Perrow, Charles (1986) *Complex Organizations A Critical Essay*, Third Edition. New York: Random House.

Peter, T.J., and R.H. Waterman (1984) *In Search of Excellence: Lessons from America's Best Run Companies.* New York: Warner Books.

Pfeffer, Jeffrey and Gerald R. Salancik (1978) *The External Control of Organizations – A Resource Dependence Perspective.* New York: Harper and Row.

Piddington, Kenneth (1988) Internal Memorandum, World Bank.

Pion-Berlin, David (1983) 'Political Repression and Economic Doctrines.' *Comparative Political Studies* 16, pp. 37–63.

'Portfolio Management: Next Steps' (1993) Memorandum to the Executive Directors, April 5. World Bank.

Powell, Walter W. ed. (1987) *The Nonprofit Sector: A Research Handbook.* New Haven: Yale University Press.

Pratt, R. Cranford (1983) 'The Global Impact of the World Bank.' Pp. 55–66 in *Banking on Poverty*, edited by Jill Torrie. Toronto: Between the Lines.

Preston, P.W. (1985) 'The Ethico-Political Notion of Development: a memorandum on commitments' in P.W. Preston, *New Trends in Development Theory.* London: Routledge.

Project Policy Department of the World Bank (1985) 'Bank/NGO Cooperation: A Successful Case of Cooperation Between the Government of Liberia, CARE International, and the World Bank.' 6 June.

Qureshi, Moeen (1988) 'The World Bank and NGOs: New Approaches.' Speech to Society for Economic Development Conference. 'Learning from the Grassroots,' Washington, DC, 22 April.

Rahnema, Majid (1985) 'NGOs: Sifting the Wheat from the Chaff.' *Development: Seeds of Change* 3, pp. 68–71.

Raison, Timothy (1986) 'Challenges to the International Donor Community.' in *Recovery in the Developing World, The London Symposium on the World Bank's Role.* Washington, DC: World Bank, pp. 3–11.

Rau, Bill (1991) *From Feast to Famine: Official Cures and Grassroots Remedies to Africa's Food Crisis.* London: Zed.

Raven, B.H. and W. Kruglanski (1975) 'Conflict and Power,' in *The Structure of Conflict*, edited by P.G. Swingle. New York: Academic Press, pp. 179–219.

Reid, Walter V., James N. Barnes and Brent Blackwelder (1989) *Bankrolling Successes: A Portfolio of Sustainable Development Projects.* Washington,

DC: Environmental Policy Institute and National Wildlife Federation.
Ribe, Helena, Soniya Carvalho, Robert Liebenthal, Peter Nicholas and Elaine Zuckerman (1990) *How Adjustment Programs Can Help the Poor: The World Bank's Experience.* World Bank Discussion Papers No. 71. Washington, DC: World Bank.
Rich, Bruce (1985) 'The Multilateral Development Banks, Environmental Policy, and the United States.' *Ecology Law Quarterly.* 12, pp. 681–784.
Rich, Bruce (1989) 'Funding Deforestation: Conservation at the World Bank.' *The Nation*, 23 January, 1, pp. 88–91.
Rich, Bruce (1990) 'The Emperor's New Clothes: The World Bank and Environmental Reform.' *World Policy Journal*, Spring, pp. 305–29.
Rich, Bruce (1994) *Mortgaging the Earth: The World Bank, Environmental Impoverishment, and the Crisis of Development.* Boston: Beacon.
Riker, James V. (1993) 'State-NGO Relations and the Politics of Sustainable Development in Indonesia: An Examination of Political Space.' Prepared for presentation at the 1993 Annual Meeting of the American Political Science Association, Washington, DC, 2–5 September.
Ruttan, Vernon W. (1984) 'Integrated Rural Development Programmes: A Historical Perspective.' *World Development* 12(4), pp. 393–401.
Salamon, Lester M. (1994) 'The Rise of the Nonprofit Sector.' *Foreign Affairs* 73(4), pp. 109–22.
Salamon, Lester M. and Helmut K. Anheier (1994) *The Emerging Sector: An Overview.* Baltimore: Institute for Policy Studies, The Johns Hopkins University.
Salmen, Lawrence F. (1987) *Listen to the People.* Oxford: Oxford University Press, for the World Bank.
Salmen, Lawrence F. (1992) *Beneficiary Assessment: An Approach Described.* Working Paper No. 1, Poverty and Social Policy Division, Technical Department, Africa Region, World Bank.
Salmen, Lawrence F. and A. Paige Eaves (1989) 'World Bank Work with Non-governmental Organizations.' World Bank PRE Working Paper 305.
Sanford, Jonathan E. (1984) 'Status of the Poverty Alleviation Focus of the International Development Association'. Washington, DC: Congressional Research Service.
Sardar Sarovar. The Report of the Independent Review. Bradford Morse, Chairman, Thomas R. Berger, Deputy Chairman. Ottawa: Resource Futures International.
Schechter, Michael G. (1987) 'Leadership in International Organizations: systemic, organization and personality factors.' *Review of International Studies* 13, pp. 197–220.
Schein, Edgar H. (1985) *Organizational Culture and Leadership – A Dynamic View.* San Francisco: Jossey-Bass.
Schein, Edgar H. (1987) 'Individuals and Careers,' in *Handbook of Organizational Behavior*, edited by Jay Lorsch. Englewood Cliffs, NJ: Prentice-Hall.
Schoultz, Lars (1982) 'Politics, Economics and US Participation in Multilateral Development Banks.' *International Organization.*
Schwartzman, Stephan (1989) 'Deforestation and Popular Resistance in Acre: From Local Movement to Global Network.' Paper Presented to Symposium,

The Social Causes of Environmental Destruction in Latin America, 88th Annual Meeting of the American Anthropological Association, Washington, DC, 15–19 November.
Scott, James C. (1985) *Weapons of the Weak – Everyday Forms of Peasant Resistance.* New Haven: Yale Press.
Scott, James C. and Benedict J. Tria Kerkvliet (1986) *Everyday Forms of Peasant Resistance.*
Scott, Richard (1985) *Organizations: Rational, Natural and Open Systems.* Englewood Cliff, NJ: Prentice Hall.
Self, Peter (1975) *Econocrats and the Policy Process: The Politics and Philosophy of Cost-Benefit Analysis.* Boulder, CO: Westview.
Serageldin, Ismail (1989) *Poverty, Adjustment and Growth in Africa.* Washington, DC: World Bank.
Serrano, Isagani (1989) 'The Philippine Rural Reconstruction Movement and the Challenges of Development Cooperation.' *Rural Reconstruction Forum* 1, 1, pp. 11–14.
Shaw, Timothy (1993) 'Third World Political Economy and Foreign Policy in the post-Cold War era: Towards a Revisionist Framework with Lessons from Africa.' *Journal of Asian and African Affairs.* 5, Fall, pp. 1–20.
Shields, Elisabeth (1993) 'EDI Expands Its Horizons: A New Role Working with NGOs.' *Bank's World* 12/7–8, pp. 8–10
Shihata, Ibrahim F.I. (1992) 'Human Rights, Development, and International Financial Institutions.' *The American University Journal of International Law and Policy.* 8(1), pp. 27–38.
Sikkink, Kathryn (1993) 'Human rights, principled issue-networks, and sovereignty in Latin America.' *International Organization.* 47(3), pp. 411–41.
Singer, Hans W. (1989) 'The World Bank: Human Face or Facelift? Some Comments in the Light of the World Bank's Annual Report.' *World Development* 17, pp. 1313–16.
Singer, Hans W. (1990) '"Reading between the Lines": A Comment on the World Bank Annual Report 1989.' *Development Policy Review* 8, pp. 203–6.
Smith, Brian H. (1990) *More than Altruism: The Politics of Private Foreign Aid.* Princeton: Princeton University Press.
Squire, Lyn and Herman van der Tak (1975) *Economic Analysis of Projects.* Baltimore: Johns Hopkins, for the World Bank.
Stiefel, Matthias and Marshall Wolfe (1994). *A Voice for the Excluded: Popular Participation in Development.* London: Zed.
Stokes, Bruce (1986) 'Liberals and Conservatives Struggling over the World Bank's Proper Role.' *National Journal*, 8 February, pp. 334–7.
Stokes, Bruce (1988) 'Storming the Bank.' *National Journal* 31 December, pp. 3250–53.
Stokes, Bruce (1993) 'Reinventing the Bank.' *National Journal* September 18, pp. 2232–36.
Strategic Planning and Review Department, The World Bank (1989) *Strengthening Popular Participation in Development: World Bank Experience.* Typescript.
Strategic Planning and Review Department, The World Bank (1990) *The World Bank and Nongovernmental Organizations (NGOs): A Review of Operational Experience.* Typescript, 25 January.

Straw, Barry M. (1982) 'Counterforces to Change,' in *Change in Organizations*, edited by Paul S. Goodman and Associates. San Francisco: Jossey-Bass.

Streeten, Paul (1987) 'A Basic-Needs Approach to Economic Development,' in *Directions in Economic Development*, edited by K. Jameson and C. Wilber. Notre Dame: Notre Dame Press.

Stremlau, Carolyn (1987) 'NGO Coordinating Bodies in Africa, Asia and Latin America. *World Development* 15 (Supplement), pp. 213–25.

Stryker, Richard E. (1979) 'The World Bank and Agricultural Development: Food Production and Rural Poverty.' *World Development* 7, pp. 325–36.

Subramanian, Asok (1985) 'Community Participation in Development Projects.' Public Sector Management Unit, Projects Policy Department, The World Bank. Washington, DC: World Bank.

Swedberg, Richard (1986) 'The Doctrine of Economic Neutrality of the IMF and the World Bank.' *Journal of Peace Research* 23(4), pp. 377–90.

Tandon, Rajesh (1991) 'Civil Society, The State and Roles of NGOs.' IDR Reports 8(3). Boston: Institute for Development Research, August.

Tendler, Judith (1975). *Inside Foreign Aid*. Baltimore: Johns Hopkins.

Tendler, Judith (1982). *Turning Private Voluntary Organizations into Development Agencies: Questions for Evaluation*. Washington, DC: Agency for International Development.

Thenuis, Sjef (1988) 'The Aid Relationship: A New Sound from Donors.' *Development* 4, pp. 26–30.

Thomas, Karen (1980) *Communication and Decision-Making in International Organizations: A Cross-Cultural Perspective on Organizational Behavior in the World Bank*. Ph.D. dissertation, Berkeley.

Thompson, James D. (1967) *Organizations in Action*. New York: McGraw-Hill.

Thompson, Michael and Aaron Wildavsky (1986) 'A Cultural Theory of Information Bias in Organizations.' *Journal of Management Studies* 23, pp. 273–86.

Treakle, Kay (1994) 'Report on the NGO Strategy Meeting on the Multilateral Development Banks, Guadalajara, Mexico, April 8–13.' Typescript, 30 May.

UNICEF (1986) *The State of the World's Children 1986*. Oxford: Oxford University Press (for UNICEF).

UNICEF (1989) *State of the World's Children 1989*. Oxford: Oxford University Press (for UNICEF).

UNICEF (1992) *State of the World's Children 1992*. Oxford: Oxford University Press (for UNICEF).

US Agency for International Development (1986) *Development Effectiveness of Private Voluntary Organizations (PVOs)*. Report to the House Appropriations Committee, February.

US Department of the Treasury (1982) *United States Participation in the Multilateral Development Banks in the 1980s*. Washington, DC: Department of the Treasury.

US News and World Report (1989) 'Bankrolling debacles?' 25 September, 43–7.

Udall, Lori (1989) Statement concerning the Environmental and Social Impacts

of the World Bank Financed Sardar Sarovar Dam in India, before the Subcommittee on Natural Resources, Agricultural Research and Environment, Committee on Science, Space and Technology, US House of Representatives. October 24.
United Nations Economic and Social Council (1994) *General Review of Arrangements for Consultations with Non-Governmental Organizations*. Report of the Secretary General (26 May).
Van der Heijden, Hendrik (1987) 'The Reconciliation of NGO Autonomy, Program Integrity and Operational Effectiveness with Accountability to Donors.' *World Development* 15 (Supplement), pp. 103–12.
Van de Laar, Aart (1980) *The World Bank and the Poor*. Boston: Martinus Nijhoff.
Vansant, Jerry (1989) 'Opportunities and Risks for Private Voluntary Organizations as Agents of LDC Policy Change.' *World Development* 17, pp. 1723–31.
Van Wicklin, Warren A. III (1990) 'Private Voluntary Organizations as Agents of Alternative Development Strategies: Existing Constraints and Future Possibilities.' Paper Presented at the International Studies Association Meetings, 10–14 April, Washington, DC.
Vroom, Victor and Philip Yetton (1973) *Leadership and Decision Making*. Pittsburgh: University of Pittsburgh Press.
Wapenhans, Willi A. (1994) 'Efficiency and Effectiveness: Is the World Bank Group Well Prepared for the Task Ahead?' In *Bretton Woods: Looking to the Future*, Commission Report of the Bretton Woods Commission, C289–C304.
Wasserstrom, Robert (1985) *Grassroots Development in Latin America and the Caribbean, Oral Histories of Social Change*. New York: Praeger.
Watson, Catharine (1985) 'Working in the World Bank'. Pp. 268–75 in *Aid: Rhetoric and Reality*, by Teresa Hayter and Catharine Watson, London: Pluto.
White, Howard (1989) 'Community Participation in Development: Problems and Prospects.' Discussion Paper, Strategic Planning and Review Department, World Bank.
Woodward, David (1992) *Debt, Adjustment and Poverty in Developing Countries*. London: Save the Children Federation/Pinter Publishers.
World Bank (annual). *Annual Report*. Washington, DC: The World Bank.
World Bank (annual). *World Development Report*. Oxford: Oxford University Press (for the World Bank).
World Bank (monthly) *Monthly Operation Summary of Bank and IDA Proposed Projects*. SecM90–546, 1 May.
World Bank (1978) Operational Manual Statement 2.12. Project Generation and Design.
World Bank (1981) *Accelerated Development in Sub-Saharan Africa: An Agenda for Action*. Washington, DC: World Bank.
World Bank (1981–90) Internal reports of the World Bank-NGO Committee, unpublished.
World Bank (1982) *Focus on Poverty: A Report of a Task Force of the World Bank*. Washington, DC: World Bank.
World Bank (1983a) *Focus on Poverty*. Washington, DC: World Bank.

Bibliography

World Bank (1983b) *Learning by Doing: World Bank Lending for Urban Development, 1972-1982*. Washington, DC: World Bank.
World Bank (1988a) 'Adjustment Lending.' Report to the Executive Directors, 1 August. Unpublished.
World Bank (1988b) 'Operational Collaboration with Nongovernmental Organizations.' Operational Policy Memorandum, Draft, 15 January.
World Bank (1988c) *Targeted Programs for the Poor during Structural Adjustment*. A Summary of a Symposium on Poverty and Adjustment April. Washington, DC: World Bank.
World Bank (1988d) *The World Bank's Support for the Alleviation of Poverty*. Washington, DC: World Bank.
World Bank (1989a) *Striking a Balance: The Environmental Challenge of Development*. Washington, DC: World Bank.
World Bank (1989b) *Sub-Saharan Africa: From Crisis to Sustainable Growth A Long-term Perspective Study*. Washington, DC: World Bank.
World Bank (1989c) Operational Manual Statement 14.70. 'Involving Non-Governmental Organizations in Bank-Supported Activities.'
World Bank (1990a) *The World Bank Annual Report 1990*. Washington, DC: World Bank.
World Bank (1990b) *Making Adjustment Work for the Poor: A Framework for Policy Reform in Africa*. Washington, DC: World Bank.
World Bank (1990c) *The World Bank and the Environment. First Annual Report Fiscal 1990*. Washington, DC: World Bank.
World Bank (1990d) *How the World Bank Works with Nongovernmental Organizations*. Washington, DC: World Bank.
World Bank (1992a) *Governance and Development*. Washington, DC: World Bank.
World Bank (1992b) *The World Bank and the Environment*. Fiscal. Washington, DC: World Bank.
World Bank (1993) *Implementing the World Bank's Strategy to Reduce Poverty*. Washington, DC: World Bank.
World Bank (1994a) *Governance: The World Bank's Experience*. Washington, DC: World Bank.
World Bank (1994b) *The World Bank Policy on Disclosure of Information*. Washington, DC: World Bank. March.
World Bank (1994c) 'The World Bank: A Global Partnership for Development.' Washington, DC: World Bank.
World Bank (1994d) 'Poverty Reduction and the World Bank: Progress in Fiscal 1993.' Washington, DC: World Bank.
World Bank (1994e) *Adjustment in Africa. Reforms, Results and the Road Ahead*. New York: Oxford (for the World Bank).
World Bank (1994f) 'The World Bank: A Global Partnership for Development.' Pamphlet.
World Bank (1994g) 'The World Bank and Participation.' Operations Policy Department. September.
World Bank (1994h) 'Resettlement Review.' Environment Department.
World Bank (1994i) *Progress Report on the Implementation of Portfolio Management: Next Steps A Program of Actions*. Washington, DC: World Bank Operations Policy Department (September).

World Bank (n.d.) *Guide to International Business Opportunities*. Washington, DC: World Bank.
World Bank (n.d.) 'World Bank and IDA, Questions and Answers'.
World Bank-NGO Consultation India – Short Report (1990).
World Wide Fund for Nature (1993) *The Southern Green Fund: Views from the South on the Global Environment Facility*. Gland, Switzerland: WWF-International.
Wyss, Hans (1987) World Bank Office Memorandum: 'Reorganization and NGOs.' 27 April.
Yudelman, Montague (1985) *The World Bank and Agricultural Development – An Insider's View*. WRI Paper No. 1, Washington DC, World Resources Institute.
Zuckerman, Elaine (1989) *Adjustment Programs and Social Welfare*. World Bank Discussion Paper 44, Washington, DC: World Bank.

Index

Abugre, Charles, 18
accountability, 186
 World Bank, 29, 125, 129, 167, 176
accountability (of NGOs), 7, 36, 66, 130, 141, 181, 184, 196
 aid donors, 47–51
 analytic approaches, 39–44
 approaches to World Bank, 51–5
 civil society and democratization, 45–7
 definition/description, 37–9
 World Bank–NGO dialogue, 56–65
Adams, James, 58, 59, 172
Addison, Tony, 134
adjustment
 compensatory social programs, 68, 74, 76, 79, 134–6, 182, 196
 competition and, 26–30
 defending, 136–41
 impact of engagement, 182–3
 loans, *see* structural adjustment lending
 monitoring NGO participation, 196
 plans, 68, 73, 180
 poverty and politics, 18–31
 social costs, 23, 134–5, 182
 unequal, 136–8
 see also structural adjustment
advocacy NGOs, 132–3, 193–4
Africa, 25–6, 45, 47, 50–1, 53, 58, 194
 apolitical development, 131, 134
 project cooperation, 83–4, 85–6
African Development Foundation, 47
Aga Khan Foundation, 39, 53, 179
Agarwala, Ramgopal, 147
agenda (development–environment NGO division), 53–5
Agricultural Credit IV Project (Honduras), 131

Agricultural Rehabilitation and Development Project (Laos), 167
agriculture, 15–16, 19, 24, 47, 77, 131, 167, 168–9
aid
 bilateral, 17, 34, 113, 118, 121–2, 188
 coordination, 9, 17–18, 29, 121–2
 disbursement imperative, 9, 88–93, 102–11
 multilateral, 62, 121, 192
 NGO organization/operation, 47–51
 transfer of capital, 9, 87–111
alternative economic strategies, 187
analytic approaches/categories, 39–44
Annis, Sheldon, 133
annual country allocation exercises, 90, 100
anti-poverty lending, 34, 61, 88, 96, 99–100, 102
 rural, 15–16, 19, 97, 103
Antrobus, Peggy, 49
apolitical development, 9, 31–2, 112, 178, 179
 sovereignty myth, 122–36
 sovereignty myth (defending adjustment and managing information), 136–41
 World Bank and, 113–18
 World Bank's influence, 118–22
appraisal process, 116–18
'approval culure', 92, 143
APRODEV, 55
Aquino government, 107
Argentina, 92, 131
Argyris, Chris, 151
Articles of Agreement, 15
Ascher, Robert, 123, 158
Asher, Robert, 14–16, 88, 94, 156, 161

221

Asia, 53, 58, 59, 83–4
Asian NGO coalition (ANGOC), 194
'Miracle' economies, 101, 146–9, 187
NICs, 26–7
Society for Participatory Research in Asia (PRIA), 40, 45, 46, 194
Asian Development Bank, 2, 152–3
Asian NGO Coalition (ANGOC), 194
Association Française des Volontaires de Progrès, 135
Audobon Society, 55
Aufderheide, Pat, 55
Australia, 194
austerity policies, 29, 45
Ayres, Robert, 16, 18–19, 30, 88, 90, 96–100, 102, 115, 119, 123–4, 156, 157, 169

Bacha, Edman L., 101
Baker Plan, 92, 101
balance of payments problems, 100
Balassa, Bela, 119
Bamberger, Michael, 91
Bangladesh
BWDB Systems Rehabilitation project, 77
Rural Advancement Committee, 37, 51, 130
Bangura, Yusuf, 22
Bank Check, 59
Bank Information Center, 59, 61, 110
banks, 17, 21, 31, 35, 101
multilateral development, 30, 89, 189
Basic Needs theory, 97
Bassett, Thomas, 22
Batchelder, Alan, 126
Baum, Warren, 95, 144
Bebbington, Anthony, 38, 45–6, 50
Beckman, David, 140
Bello, Walden, 18, 30, 31
'beneficiary groups', 146, 174
Berg, Elliot, 63, 126
Bern Declaration, 55

Bienefeld, Manfred, 147–8
bilateral donors, 17, 34, 113, 118, 121–2, 188
Black, Eugene, 112
blueprint (NGOs style), 43–4
blueprint (pre-appraisal process), 116, 117
Bolivia, 134–5
Bonné, B., 17
borrower–credit relationship, 119–29
'boundary-spanning units', 94
Bradford, Colin, 147
Brady Plan, 92
Bratton, Michael, 28, 51
Brazil, 92, 133
Bread for the World Institute, 54, 194
Brechin, Steven R., 92
Brett, E.A., 49
Bretton Woods system
Agreements, 13, 35, 159
institutions, 26, 60, 129, 187
Broad, Robin, 26, 123, 127, 128
Brodhead, Tim, 40, 130, 137
broker (NGO style), 43–4
Brookings Institution, 92
Brown, David, 36, 41, 42, 47, 48, 130
Bryant, C., 99
bureaucratic organizations, 151
Burns, Sarah, 60, 63

Cahn, Jonathan, 129
Cairo Businessmen's Associations, 79
Callaghy, Thomas M., 29
Camdessus (IMF Managing Director), 59
Canadian Council for International Cooperation (CCIC), 40
Canadian International Development Agency (CIDA), 47
capital
accumulation, 6, 115
disbursement imperative, 9, 88–93, 102–11
transfer of, 9, 87–111
CARE, 37, 47, 50, 53, 54
Carlsson, Jerker, 116

Index

Carroll, Thomas, 38, 39
Carvalho, Soniya, 25, 134
Catholic Relief Services, 47, 50, 76
Cavanagh, John, 26
Center for the Study of Agrarian Change (CECCAM), 194
Cernea, Michael, 37, 89, 145, 150, 168, 174
'certifying' NGOs, 162–3
Chambers, Robert, 158
Chambers of Commerce (Turkey and Sri Lanka), 79
change
  organizational culture and learning, 156–62
  social, 167, 192
China, 92
Choksi, Armeane, 33
Christian Aid, 54
Church World Service, 54
CIDSE, 55
civil rights, 112, 114
civil society, 3, 7, 39–41, 44, 50
  democratization and, 45–7, 185
  global, 186–7
  NGOs and, 185–8
Clark, John, 18, 20, 45, 137, 174
co-financing projects, 17, 121, 153
Coalition of Swiss Development Organizations, 54
CODAIK, 131
Cold War, 30, 31, 118
Cole, Sam, 17, 27, 148
collaboration, 4–5, 8–9, 36, 165, 195–6
  NGO roles, 71–4
  NGO voices, 51–5
  World Bank–NGO cooperation, 67–86
commercial banks, 17, 21, 31, 35, 101
community-based organizations, 43, 70, 77, 80–2, 85, 168, 184
Community Aid Abroad, 194
community development initiatives, 48
comparative advantage, 6, 28, 142
Compensatory Feeding Program (of CRS), 76
compensatory projects, 68, 74, 76, 78
  NGOs in, 134–6, 182, 196
compensatory services, 23
competing new initiatives, 33–4
competition, adjustment and, 26–30
Conable, Barber, 5, 59, 137, 173
Conakry Urban Development Supplemental Finance Project, 136
conditionality, 6, 23, 29, 182, 190
  politics of, 126–9
confidentiality, 139, 141
constituencies (development–environment division), 53–5
consultation, regional, 194–5
Consultative Group to Assist the Poorest of the Poor (CGAPP), 34
Consultative Group on International Agricultural Research (CGIAR), 15
consultative groups, 15, 33–4, 121, 123, 125
context/data (projects), 68–9
'contractor' projects, 73, 74
control (in organizational culture), 160–74
cooperation, *see* project cooperation (World Bank–NGO)
Cooperative League of the USA (CLUSA), 47
coordination, 17–18, 193–5
coping strategies, 154
Corbridge, Stuart, 149
'core poverty program', 20
core technologies, 71, 85, 93–7, 100, 102, 151, 165, 179
Cornia, Giovanni Andrea, 21, 22
cost–benefit analysis, 102, 116–17, 151, 164
Costa Rica, 24
country allocation exercise, 90, 100
country dialogues, 54–5
Country Economics Department, 20–1, 22, 23, 24, 27, 127
Country Program paper, 100
Cox, Robert, 129
Crane, Barbara, 92

credit unions, 53
creditworthiness, 121, 128
'Critical Look at World Bank and IMF Policies, A' (NGO publication), 59
Cruz, Wilfrido, 22
cultural limits on organizational learning, 150–6
culture, *see* organizational culture
currency valuation, 20
Cypher, James, 16, 101, 126, 127, 134

Daly, Herman, 181
Danaher, Kevin, 18
data/context (projects), 68–9
Davao Medical School Foundation/ Institute for Primary Health Care, 162–3
De Lusignan, Guy, 17, 120
Deal, Terrence, 143
debt, 9
 crisis, 13, 92, 100, 101
 for-equity swaps, 27
 relief, 64–5
 servicing, 21, 28, 52, 92–3, 101
 structural adjustment and, 189–90
debt management, 5, 31, 92, 102, 125, 149, 174, 187, 193
 adjustment lending, 20–30
decision-making, 11
definition of NGOs, 37–9
DeGraaf, Martin, 43, 130
Demery, Lionel, 134
democratic pluralism, 41
democratization, civil society and, 45–7, 185
demonstration effect of NGOs, 48
Denning, Stephen, 29, 123
design (of projects), 77–9, 85, 91, 144, 146, 163–4, 166–7, 177
development
 apolitical, *see main entry*
 contrasting visions of, 5–7
 –environment division, 53–5
 myth, 9, 112–13, 116–18, 138, 141, 145, 149, 159, 165, 178–9
 participation in, 9, 142–75
 sustainable, *see main entry*

development banks, 30, 89, 189
Development Committee, 22, 23, 100, 101, 103, 128, 137
Development Group for Alternative Policies, 53
development model, 9, 87
 disbursement imperative, 88–93
 NGOs and staff time, 102–11
 uncertainty reduction, 93–102
'deviant memories', 152
Dichter, Thomas, 39, 49
Dimaggio, Paul, 116
disbursement imperative, 9
 performance measurement, 88–93
 staff time and, 102–11
disbursement mandate (in India), 154–6
disclosure, 139, 141, 176
dissent, self-suppression of, 156–7
division of labor, 144, 145
 international, 26, 28, 35, 40–1, 142
Donnelly-Roark, Paula, 48
donors, 21, 50–1
 bilateral agencies, 17, 34, 113, 118, 121–2, 188
 coordination, 9, 17–18, 29, 121–2
 multilateral agencies, 62, 121, 192
Durning, Alan, 36, 37, 38, 83

Early Warning (1992), 33
'Earth Increment', 32, 61
'Earthworks Maintenance Groups', 77
Earwaker, Frank, 149, 164
East Asian 'Miracle' economies, 101, 146–9, 187
Eastern Region Agricultural Development Project (Yemen), 77
Eaton, Jonathan, 27
Eaves, Paige, 44, 47, 70, 72, 75, 130, 173
Economic Development Institute (EDI), 17, 106–7, 115, 120, 128
economic integration, 15–16

Index

economic multilateralism, 185–8
economic orthodoxy, apolitical image and, 113–15
economic strategies/futures, 187
economic sustainability, 2, 32–3, 36, 40, 87–8, 118, 185–8
Ecuadorian Association of Municipalities, 79
Education Sector Adjustment Credit (Guinea), 131
Edwards, Michael, 48, 50
Ekbom, Anders, 116
Elinson, Elaine, 18, 30, 31
EMENA region, 83–4, 104
Emergency Social Funds, 76, 134, 135
environment
 –development division, 53–5
 Global Environmental Facility, 32, 110–11
 National Environmental Action Plans, 179, 191
 pressure on World Bank, 31–5
Environmental Defense Fund, 55, 61–2, 90, 110, 133, 155
Environmental Impact Assessment, 32, 64, 165, 171, 174, 179–80, 196
environmental NGOs, 42–3, 55–6, 109–12, 154–5, 193, 194, 196
environmental policy, 179–81
environmental protection, 1–2, 5
environmental review procedures, 107, 196
environmentally sustainable development, 2, 51, 52
Escudero, Carlos, 174
Esman, Milton, 39, 47, 48, 49, 167
Esquel Group Foundation, 3, 39
EURODAD, 194
Europe
 EMENA region, 83–4, 104
 NGOs, 54–5, 61
Executive Directors, 32, 55, 109, 122–3, 125, 127, 139, 140, 155
 Board of, 14, 30–1
expertise, 160–2
export-oriented adjustment, 5, 26, 28, 101, 137–8

export credit financing, 121
export promotion, 21, 137, 174
External Affairs (EXTIE), 68, 172

Farrington, John, 38, 45–6, 50
Fatouros, A.A., 88, 120–1, 123, 124, 158
Federation of African Voluntary Development Agencies, 194
Feeney, Patricia, 54
Fei, J., 148
Feinberg, Richard, 101
feminization of poverty, 154
'50 Years in Enough' campaign, 189, 192
finance of World Bank, 13–18
Finance and Development journal, 3, 17
'finessing' (disbursements), 90, 103–8
Finkle, Jason, 92
'first-level' issues, 108–10
First Housing Sector Project (in Argentina), 131
fiscal policy, 20, 29
five-year plans, 90, 100
Focus on Poverty, 97
food crisis (1972–4), 15–16
Ford Motors, 100
Fowler, Alan, 45, 50
Freedom from Debt Coalition, 52
Fried, Edward, 92
Friends Committee on National Legislation, 54
Friends of the Earth, 55
functional roles (NGOs), 44
Fund for Innovative Approaches to Social and Human Development, 33
Fundación del Centavo (FDC), 49
future economic multilateralism, 187–8

G-7 countries, 187, 189
Garilao, Ernesto, 49
'generations' of NGOs, 42–3
George, Susan, 18, 149
Gersovitz, Mark, 27
Gerster, Richard, 14

Ghana, 134, 135
Ghose, Sanjoy, 91, 169, 173
Gibbon, Peter, 17, 92, 121–2
Gillies, David, 112
Glewwe, Paul, 22
global civil society, 186–7
Global Environment Facility, 32, 110–11, 180
Global Hunger Conference (1993), 34, 35, 54, 184
global integration, lending for, 15–16
Golan, Amnon, 174
Goldsworthy, David, 114
governance
  adjustment and, 28–30
  role of World Bank, 113, 122–3, 129
Governance and Development, 29
governments, World Bank work with, 196
Governors, 14, 122–3
Gow, David, 43–4
Gran, Guy, 98, 158, 159
Green Revolution, 5, 110, 119
Griesgraber, Jo Marie, 137
growth, 19
  redistribution with, 96–7, 98
  'with equity', 88
Guatemala, 49
Guide to International Business Opportunities (World Bank), 140
Guinea, 131, 135, 136

Hagan, Ernestina, 22
Hamilton, Clive, 28, 101
Harrigan, Jane, 28, 127, 128, 148
Healey, John, 29
Health Development III Project, Philippines, 69, 106, 107
Health Services Project (Guinea), 136
Helleiner, Gerald, 188
Hellinger, Douglas, 30, 40, 50–1, 53, 90, 124, 130, 133, 156, 177
Hellinger, Stephen, 40, 90
Heredia, Carlos, 22
Herfkens, Evelyn, 65

hierarchical organizational culture, 144, 145, 150, 152
Hodd, Michael, 120
Hodges, Tony, 22
Holdcroft, Lane, 38
Holden, Constance, 5
Honduras, 131
Howard, John 120
Hulme, David, 48, 50, 152–3
human face campaign, 21–4, 136
human rights, 31–5, 42, 51, 52, 191
Hurni, Bettina, 124, 125, 160, 161
'hybrid loans', 101

IDA-10 agreement, 32, 33, 60–3, 110, 133, 192, 197
IDA-11 agreement, 197
IMF, 28, 30, 32, 52–3, 55, 59–60, 120, 122, 127, 172, 186–7
  Development Committee, 22–3, 100–1, 103, 128, 137
  Extended Financing Facility, 128
  Finance and Development, 3, 17
  stabilization policy, 27, 134, 147
implementation, 20, 31–5, 72, 126–9
import-substitution strategies, 101
incentives, 90–2, 118
income
  distribution, poverty and, 21–2
  redistribution with growth, 96–8
independence, NGO accountability and, 49, 50
India, 52–3, 111, 163
  infrastructure lending, 154–6
  Sardar Sarovar project, 9, 33, 58, 61–2, 133, 154–6
  Singrauli energy project, 133, 154–5
  World Bank–NGO Consultation Committee, 58
Indonesia, 51, 57–8
infant industry protection, 148
information
  bias, 9, 98, 143–9, 174
  disclosure, 139, 141, 176
  managing, 136–41
  on organizational learning, 152–6
  privileged, 138–41

promotion strategy, 171
system, 100, 191
infrastructure, 26, 52, 180
lending (India), 154–6
rural, 15, 19, 103
innovative lending, 103–4
Institute for Development Research, 54
institutional self-deception, 154–6
Instituto del Tercer Mundo, 58–9, 194
insularity, intellectual, 156, 159–60
integrating NGO agendas, 193
integration, global, 15–16
intellectual influence, 119–21
intellectual insularity, 156, 159–60
Inter-American Development Bank, 2
Inter-American Foundation, 47
InterAction, 194
'Interaction with NGOs on the Bank's Project Cycle', 59
interest-based NGOs, 42–3, 70, 82–3
International Bank for Reconstruction and Development, 13–15, 28, 48, 89, 92, 111, 154, 187
International Council of Voluntary Agencies, 49
International Development Association, 3, 13–15, 48, 65, 100, 111, 113, 134–6, 139, 154–5, 180, 189
IDA–10, 32, 33, 60–3, 110, 133, 192, 197
IDA–11, 197
international division of labour, 26, 28, 35, 40–1, 142
International Economic Relations Unit of the Operations Division, 67–8, 170, 173, 199
International Finance Corporation, 14–15
International Fund for Agricultural Development (IFAD), 47
International Monetary Fund, see IMF
International NGO Forum on Indonesia, 51

International NGOs, 70, 81–2
International Rivers Network, 55, 61
internationalized advocacy campaigns, 132–3
interviews (cited in text), 198
investment, 6, 7, 26–8, 95, 96
infrastructural, 15, 19, 103
sustainability, 32–3, 87–8
irrigation systems, 77, 108, 168, 169, 170, 179, 181
Irwin, Michael, 161
Israel, Arturo, 3, 144
'issue networks', 42

job creation, 135
Jolly, Richard, 21

Kakabadse, Yolande, 60, 63
Kardam, Nüket, 165
Kennedy, Allan A., 143
Kenya, 37
Kerkvliet, Benedict J. Tria, 168
Keynes, J.M., 120
Kinley, David, 18, 30, 31
Köhlin, Gunnar, 116
Kolko, Gabriel, 30
Korten, D.C., 36, 41–2, 47–8, 99, 130
Krian-Sungei Manik Integrated Development Project, 168–9
Krueger, Anne, 147
Kwango-Kwilu project, 131

Labor Act (Zimbabwe), 24
LAC region, 57–8, 83–4, 85
Lacaillon, Jacques, 28
Lafay, Jean Dominique, 28
land-settlement schemes, 153
land distribution, 49
Laos, 167
Latin America, 45, 57, 58, 83–4, 85
learning/learning process, organizational, 56, 108, 153–4, 160, 170–2, 181
LeComte, Bernard, 50
Lee, Ducksoo, 130
Lehman, Howard, 28

Index

lending/loans
  anti-poverty lending, 34, 61, 88, 96–7, 99–100, 102–3
  disbursement imperative, 9, 88–93, 102–11
  financing debt servicing, 92–3
  for global integration, 15–16
  IBRD loans, 13–15
  new-style, 97–100
  policy-based, 9, 13, 21, 86, 101, 126
  poverty lending, 18–20, 96–102
  sectoral adjustment, 20, 26, 79, 101, 127
  transfer of capital, 9, 87–111
  see also structural adjustment lending
LePrestre, Philippe, 94, 110, 121, 123–4, 152
leverage, sovereignty and, 136–8
Levinson, Jerome, 29, 112, 114
Levitt, Barbara, 150–2
Libby, Ronald, 111, 115, 120, 124, 162
Liebenthal, Robert, 25, 134
Lipton, Michael, 119
Lister, Frederick, 14
Livestock Rehabilitation Project (Guinea), 136
loans, see lending/loans; structural adjustment lending
low income countries, 25–6
Loxley, John, 28, 92
Lutheran World Relief, 54

McCormack, Gavan, 28
Macdonald, Laura, 38, 45, 50
McKitterick, Nathaniel, 90, 100, 104, 109, 123, 125
McNamara, Robert, 3, 5, 18–20, 90, 96–7, 100, 109
macro-economic performance, 25–6
major NGO roles, 72–3
Malaysia, 152–3, 168–9
'Managing Quality' (1994), 29
managing uncertainty, 93–4, 168–9
March, James, 150–2
market failure, 41
Marsden, David, 77, 167

Mason, Edward, 14–16, 88, 94, 156, 161
Mayatech Corporation, 22
MDB Information Center, 110, 155
means of production (protection of), 93–102
mediation (World Bank role), 124–5
Meier, G., 106
methodological note, 199
Meyer, John, 118
micro-enterprise lending, 34
micro-finance facility, 33
Mihevc, John, 149
Minear, Larry, 50
minor NGO roles, 73–4
Mkandawire, Thandika, 22
monetary policy, 20, 29
money (in development model), 9
  disbursement imperative, 88–93
  disbursement and staff time, 102–11
  uncertainty reduction, 93–102
monitoring, 54, 194–7
Monthly Operational Statements, 139
Morocco, 76
Moser, Caroline, 91, 154
Mosley, Paul, 28, 126, 127, 128, 148
Mshana, Rogate, 76
Multi-State Agricultural Development (II) Project (Nigeria), 167
multilateral aid/donors, 62, 121, 192
multilateral development banks, 30, 89, 189
Multilateral Investment Guarantee Agency (MIGA), 3, 14
multilateralism, 185–8

Nagle, William, 91, 169, 173
National Council of Women (Kenya), 37
National Environmental Action Plans, 179, 191
National Journal, 3, 65, 176
national NGOs, 70, 81–2

Index

National Rural Electrification Council of America, 47, 84
National Wildlife Federation, 37, 55
Natural Resources Defense Council, 55
Nelson, Joan, 29, 127, 134
neoclassical economics, 157–8, 160
neoliberalism, 115, 148, 149
Nerfin, Marc, 37, 41
Ness, Gayl, 92
networks, 45, 185–90 *passim*
  advocacy networks, 193–4
  issue networks, 42
  pyramidal, 39–41
  South–South networking, 194–5
New Directions campaign (1970s), 19
'new professionalism', 158
newly industrialized countries, 26–7, 28, 138
NGO–World Bank Committee, 56–9, 61, 114, 132, 137–40, 156, 163, 166, 170, 172–4, 199
NGO–World Bank project cooperation, 8, 67, 86
  data/context, 68–9
  NGO participants/roles, 69–74, 80–5
  NGO participation (over time), 74–9
NGO–World Bank projects
  exercising control in, 165–9
  impact of engagement, 178–83
  terms of engagement, 176–8
NGO Position Paper on the World Bank, 137
NGO Working Group on the World Bank, 18, 54, 58, 62, 135, 194–5
NGOs
  accountability of, *see main entry*
  analytic approaches/categories, 39–44
  advocacy campaigns, 132–3, 193–4
  approaches to donor agencies, 47–51
  backlash/backsliding, 184–5
  'certifying', 162–3
  civil society and, 45–7, 185–8
  community-based organizations, 70, 80
  compensatory projects, 134–6
  contrasting visions of development, 5–7
  definition/description, 37–9
  development/environmental split, 53–5
  environmental, *see main entry*
  functional roles, 44
  generations of, 42–3
  interest-based, 42–3, 70, 82–3
  international, 70, 81–2
  national, 70, 81–2
  Northern-based, 38, 40, 52, 54, 62–5, 82, 140, 183, 185, 190
  organizational culture and, 162–74
  policy agenda (for 1990s), 188–97
  policy change and uncertainty, 163–5
  political role subordinated to service delivery, 130–2
  projects (terms of engagement), 176–8
  role in design, 77–9
  role in project collaboration, 71–4
  Southern-based, 38, 40, 52, 62–3, 65, 81–2, 183, 185, 186, 189
  sovereignty and, 129–33, 138–41
  sub-projects, 78
  voices (and World Bank), 51–5
  Washington-based, 53, 59, 62–5, 194
  World Bank and, 1–5, 183–5
  World Bank dialogue, 56–65, 172–4
Nicholas, Peter, 21, 23, 25, 134
Nigeria, 167
non-project lending, 21
Northern-based NGOs, 38, 40, 52, 54, 62–5, 82, 140, 183, 185, 190
NOVIB, 40, 54
Nzoma, Maria, 154

Oakley, Peter, 77, 167
O'Donnell, Guillermo, 28
OECD, 37, 38, 47, 121

OMS, 124, 130, 165, 167, 168
Operational Directives, 37, 39, 81, 139, 163, 188
Operational Manual Statement, 124, 130, 165, 167, 168
operations (World Bank), 13–18
Operations Evaluation Department (OED), 32, 77, 91, 95–9, 103, 105, 117–18, 146, 167, 169
OPRIE, 67, 68, 170, 173
O'Regan, Fred, 40, 90
organization, old-style, 97–100
Organization for Rehabilitation through Training (ORT), 47, 84–5
organizational control, 160–2
organizational culture, 9, 11, 175, 178–9
  approaches/definitions, 142–5
  information bias, 145–9
  learning and change, 156–62
  organizational learning, 150–6
  quality, control and uncertainty, 162–74
organizational learning, 11
  culture and change, 156–62
  information/limits on, 152–6
  information bias, 145–9
  limits on, 150–6
  nature, of 150–2
organizational mandate, 88–90
organizational myths, 116, 118
organizational theory (general), 9, 10–12, 87
Osieke, Ebere, 14
outcome monitoring, 195–6
Overseas Development Institute, 39, 137
Owen, Henry, 92
'ownership' of investments, 182
'ownership' of projects, 167, 178
OXFAM, 37
OXFAM–America, 40
OXFAM–UK, 20, 40, 54, 174, 194

Padrón, Mario, 39–40
Page, John, 147
Pakistan, 53
Paris Club, 189

participation, 56, 107–8, 181–2
  in development, 9, 142–75
  learning process, 113, 170–2
  policy issues (for 1990s), 190–2
  in World Bank, 166–9
Participation Fund, 33, 34, 172
Participatory Development Learning Group, 114
Pastor, Robert, 27
Patkar, Medha, 133
Paul, Samuel, 3, 168, 169
Payer, Cheryl, 30
Pearson Commission Report (1969), 89
Pentagon, 100
People's Forum, 60
performance measurement (disbursement imperative), 88–93
Peters, T.J., 143
Pfeffer, Jeffrey, 93
Philippine Business for Social Progress, 162
Philippines, 52, 69, 106, 123, 162
Piddington, Kenneth, 107
Pion-Berlin, David, 28
planned participation, 168–9
Planofloro project (Brazil), 54
pluralism, 42, 45
policy, 4–5, 119
  agenda (NGOs in 1990s), 188–97
  -based lending, 9, 13, 21, 86, 101, 126
  change, learning without, 153–4
  change, uncertainty and, 163–5
  dialogue, 54–5
  projects and (impact assessed), 178–83
Policy Analysis and Review Unit, 149
political economy perspective, 10
political rights, 112, 114
politics
  adjustment and poverty, 18–31
  conditionality/implementation, 126–9
  NGOs role subordinated to service delivery, 130–2
Polonoroeste project (Brazil), 54

popular participation, *see* participation
portfolio management, 182
postwar industrialization, 148
poverty, 1-2, 5, 87, 171, 174
　adjustment and politics, 18-31
　anti-poverty lending, 34, 61, 88, 96, 99-100, 102-3
　feminization of, 154
　human-face campaign, 21-4, 136
　income distribution and, 21-2
　taskforce, 96, 98, 103
Poverty Assessments, 191
poverty lending, 18-20
　case of, 96-102
Poverty Targeted Investments, 191
Powell, Walter W., 116
power/power relations, 30-1, 112, 113
Pratt, R. Cranford, 30, 31
Preston, Lewis, 5, 17, 32-3, 35, 62, 159, 185
private good/self-interest, 44
privateness (NGO accountability), 49
privileged information, 138-41
procedural limits on organizational learning, 150-6
process-broker, 44
process-oriented NGOs, 43-4
production, means of (protection of), 93-102
professional development NGOs, 70, 82-3
professionalism, 166
Program of Action to Mitigate the Social Costs of Adjustment (Ghana), 135
Project Completion Reports, 68, 104, 131, 155, 167, 169, 199
project cooperation (World Bank-NGO), 8, 67, 86
　data/context, 68-9
　NGO participants/roles, 69-74, 80-5
　NGO participation over time, 74-9
　project cycle, 59, 71-2, 91, 95, 98-100, 108, 144, 146, 163-4, 169, 178, 192

Project Implementation Reviews, 146
Project Information Document, 139
Project Performance Reviews, 146
projects
　aid, 101, 102
　appraisal, 164, 165
　collaboration, *see* collaboration
　design, 77-9, 85, 91, 144, 146, 163-4, 166-7, 177
　identification, 124
　outcome (monitoring), 195-6
　planning, 116-17, 118, 153
　proposals, 94-5
　regional distribution, 83-5
　scale, 47-8
　slippage, 102
　terms of engagement, 176-83
projects (NGO-World Bank)
　exercising control in, 165-9
　impact of engagement, 178-83
　terms of engagement, 176-8
Protecting the Poor during Periods of Adjustment (1987), 22, 23
public goods, 41, 44
public relations (World Bank), 34-5
Purcell, Mary E., 22
pyramidal networks, 39-41

quality, 29, 95
　expertise and, 160-2
　organizational culture, 162-74
Qureshi, Moeen, 67, 81, 130, 131

Rahmena, Majid, 39
Raison, Timothy, 137
Ranis, Gustav, 148
rational-technical organizations, 151
Rau, Bill, 18
Reagan administration, 101
redistribution with growth, 96-7, 98
regional consultation, 194-5
regional distribution of projects, 83-5
Regional Workshop on Cooperation for Education and Training in Eastern and Southern Africa, 58
Religious Task Force on Central America, 55

Repetto, Robert, 22
resistance, 168–9, 178
RESULTS, 54
Ribe, Helena, 25, 134
Rich, Bruce, 18, 51, 55, 63, 90, 93, 110, 174
Riker, James, 51
Robinson, Mark, 29
Rondônian project, 54
routines, organizational, 150, 151
rubber production schemes (Malaysia), 152–3
rural anti-poverty lending, 15–16, 19, 97, 103
rural development, 19, 38, 97–8, 105, 117, 167
information bias, 9, 145–9
Rural Development unit, 98
rural infrastructure, 15, 19, 103
Rural Reconstruction Movements, 37
Rural Support Programme (Pakistan), 53
Ruttan, Vernon, 38

Sabelli, Fabrizio, 18, 149
Salamon, Lester, 37
Salancik, Gerald, 93
Salmen, Lawrence, 44, 47, 70, 72, 75, 130, 164–5, 173
Sandstrom, Sven, 172
Sanford, Jonathan, 16, 96, 103
Sardar Sarovar project, 9, 33, 58, 61, 62, 133, 154, 155–6
Sarvodaya Shramadana movement, 37
Sassower, 115
Sato, Turid, 188
Save the Children Federation, 37
scale (NGO projects), 47–8
Schechter, Michael, 98, 99
Schein, Edgar, 143
Schmidt, Mary, 39
Schoultz, Lars, 30
Schwartzman, Stephan, 110, 133
Scott, James, 168
Scott, Richard, 94
search behaviour, 144
second-level issues, 108–10

Sectoral Adjustment loans (SECALs), 20, 26, 79, 101, 127
selectivity, 156–60
self-assessment, 94, 102, 148, 155, 182
self-help, 7, 37, 46, 48
self-suppression of dissent, 156–7
Serageldin, Ismail, 33, 135
service delivery, 130–2
'settler capital', 153
Shakow, Alexander, 56, 173
shared interests/values, 41–2
Shaw, Robert, 39, 53, 187
Sherk, Don, 63
Sikkink, Kathryn, 41
Singer, Hans, 7, 23, 88, 103
Singrauli Thermal Energy Project, 133, 154, 155
social change, 115, 167, 192
social costs of adjustment, 1, 23, 134–5, 182
Social Development Action Project (Chad), 135
Social Dimensions of Adjustment (SDA), 21, 22, 106, 134–5, 182
'social diversity', 41
'social energy', 41
Social Investment Funds, 76, 135
Social Policy Division (in Ministry of Planning, Guinea), 135
social services, 23, 46, 76, 97, 196
socialization of staff, 156, 157–9, 165
Society for Participatory Research in Asia (PRIA), 40, 45, 46, 194
Socio-Economic Development Project (Guinea), 135
sociological issues, rural development and, 146
soft loans, 60
Solidarios, 37
South-South regional consultation, 194–5
Southern-based NGOs, 38, 40, 52, 62–3, 65, 81–2, 183, 185, 186, 189
Southern Cone of South America Meeting, 58

Index

sovereignty, 151
 appearance of, 122–6
 leverage and, 136–8
 NGOs AND, 129–33
 privileged information and, 138–41
sovereignty myth, 9, 31, 112–13, 178–9
 adjustment lending, 126–9
 compensatory projects, 134–6
 defending adjustment, 136–41
 formal procedures and reality, 122–6
 NGOs (role), 129–33
 policy-based lending, 126
 World Bank (role), 129
specialization, 144, 145
Staff Appraisal Reports, 68, 199
staff time, disbursement and, 102–11
Staff Working Papers, 17
standard-setting (development), 116–18
State of the World's Children, 22
Stern, Ernest, 61, 130
Stiefel, Matthias, 38, 45, 46, 63, 108, 170
Stokes, Bruce, 3, 55, 103, 140
strategic advocacy (NGO policy agenda), 188–97
Strategic Planning and Review, 68, 75, 107, 109, 114, 130, 132, 144–5, 168, 169, 172, 173
Streeten, Paul, 119
structural adjustment, 71, 196
 debt and, 189–90
 East Asian Miracle, 101, 146–9
 information bias, 145–9
 plans, 68, 73, 180
 social costs, 1, 23, 134–5, 182
structural adjustment lending, 35, 61
 apolitical development, 126–9, 135
 debt management and, 20–30
 development model, 87, 100–2
 evaluation of, 147–9
 NGO project links, 69, 74–6
 policy-based, 9, 13, 21, 86, 101, 126

politics of conditionality and implementation, 126–9
structural contingency theory, 93–4
structural limits on organizational learning, 150–6
'Structure Maintenance Groups', 77
structure of World Bank, 13–18
Stryker, Richard, 96, 119
styles (development–environment division), 53–5
sub-projects, 78, 136
success (standard setting), 116–18
sustainable development, 117, 193
 economically, 2, 36, 40, 88, 118, 185–8
 environmentally, 2, 51, 52
 global economic orders, 185–8
 investments, 32–3, 87–8
Swedberg, Richard, 112
systemic learning, 151, 152

Tandon, Rajesh, 40, 46
Tanzania, 76
tariff reduction, 20
task environment, 93, 94
Task Managers, 79, 106, 149
taskforce on poverty, 96, 98, 103
technical assistance, 131, 162
technical expertise, 160–2
technocrats/technocracy, 113, 118, 128–9, 151
technology, *see* core technologies
technostructure (of World Bank), 125
Tendler, Judith, 39, 48, 89, 90, 95
terms of engagement (projects), 176–8
Terms of Reference (NGO-World Bank Committee), 57
Thatcher government, 101
Theunis, Sjef, 40
third-generation strategy, 43
Third World debt, 9
Third World Network (Malaysia), 194
Thomas, Karen, 31, 104, 113, 156–7, 163
Thompson, James, 71, 93, 94
Thompson, Michael, 98, 144, 145

time/money crunch, 104–7
Toye, John, 28, 127, 128, 148
training, 9, 17, 31, 58, 106–7, 128, 178, 192
transparency, 29, 52
Treakle, Kay, 59
Tropical Forest Action Plan, 32
Turkey, 79

Udall, Lori, 133
uncertainty
  management of, 93–4, 168–9
  organizational culture and, 162–74
  policy change and, 163–5
  reduction, 93–102
unemployment, 21, 134, 135
unequal adjustment, 136–8
United Nations, 19, 31, 35, 111, 161, 171
  Conference on Environment and Development (UNCED), 60
  Educational, Scientific and Cultural Organization (UNESCO), 40
  International Children's Fund (UNICEF), 21–2, 23, 107
Uphoff, Norman, 39, 47, 48, 49, 167
Urban Sector Meetings, 58
Uruguay, 58–9, 194
US–Nicaragua Friendship Network, 55
US News and World Report, 3
USA, 31, 54, 58
  -based Bank Information Center, 59, 61, 110
  Treasury Department, 30, 60–1, 90
  Washington-based NGOs, 53, 59, 62–5, 194
USAID, 36, 39, 47, 49, 76, 147, 163

values-based NGOs, 42–3
Van de Laar, Aart, 27, 90, 91, 95–6, 161
van de Walle, Nicholas, 28
van der Heijden, Hendrik, 49
van der Hoeven, Rolf, 22
Vergin, Hans, 156
vertical integration, 94
village cooperative societies, 167
voluntarism, 41, 166
Volunteers in Technical Assistance, 135
voting powers, 14, 101, 122–3

Wapenhans, Willi, 33, 162
Wapenhans Report, 33, 91–2, 105, 108–9, 123, 143, 159
Washington-based NGOs, 53, 59, 62–5, 194
Wasserstrom, Robert, 36
Water Users Associations, 167
Waterman, R.H., 143
Watson, Catharine, 90
welfare schemes, adjustment-related, 79
White, Howard, 121, 169
White, L.G., 99
Wildavsky, Aaron, 98, 144, 145
Wirth, 59
Witness for Peace, 55
Wolfe, Marshall, 38, 45–6, 63, 108, 170
Wolfensohn, James, vii
women, 165
  impact of adjustment, 23, 153–4
Woodward, David, 18, 194
World Bank
  Annual Reports, 1, 3, 8, 14–15, 17, 20, 48, 88–9, 99, 101, 103, 120–1, 132, 144, 172
  apolitical development and, 9, 112–41
  contrasting visions of development, 5–7
  core technologies and uncertainty, 94–6
  Development Committee, 22–3, 100–1, 103, 128, 137
  as governance institution, 129
  image, 34–5
  influence, 118–22
  lending (global integration), 15–16
  monitoring (need for), 195–7
  –NGO dialogue, 56–65, 172–4

Index

NGO Working Group, 18, 54, 58, 62, 135, 194–5
NGOs and, 1–5, 183–5
Operational Directives, 37, 39, 81, 139, 163, 188
Operations Division, 67–8, 170, 173
Operations Evaluation Department, 32, 77, 91, 95–9, 103, 105, 117–18, 146, 167, 169
participation in, 166–72
poverty and politics, 18–31
pressure on, 31–5
Progress Report, 81
Project Summaries, 80, 82, 83, 135–6
response to human face campaign, 21–4, 136
structure, finance and operations, 13–18
studying (organizational theory), 10–12
World Debt Tables, 17, 189
World Development Report, 5, 15, 19, 103, 116, 119, 147
World Bank–NGO project

cooperation, 8, 67, 86
data/context, 68–9
NGO participants/roles, 69–74, 80–5
NGO participation (over time), 74–9
World Bank-NGO projects
exercising control, 165–9
impact of engagement, 178–83
terms of engagement, 176–8
World Bank Economic Review, 17
World Bank News, 3
World Bank Research Observer, 17
World Debt Tables, 17, 189
World Development Report, 5, 15, 19, 103, 116, 119, 147
World Hunger Conference, 34, 35, 54, 184
World Vision International, 54
Worldwatch, 37
Wyss, Hans, 131

Yudelman, Montague, 126, 144, 160, 168

Zuckerman, Elaine, 23, 25, 134, 160